EDUCATION IN CONTEMPORARY JAPAN
Inequality and Diversity

Rather than presenting 'Lessons for the West', this book offers a balanced introduction to and examination of contemporary Japanese education that considers criticisms of Japanese schooling practices made by the participants themselves. While the postwar system of schooling has provided valuable ingredients for economic success, Kaori Okano and Motonori Tsuchiya argue that these have been accompanied by unfavourable developments.

Education in Contemporary Japan examines the main developments of modern schooling in Japan, from the beginning of the Meiji era up to the present, and includes analysis of the most recent reforms. By drawing extensively on detailed ethnographic studies and interviews with students and teachers, Okano and Tsuchiya show the diversity of school experiences, and develop a new picture of the role that schooling plays for individuals and the wider society. This insightful and provocative study of the issues of social inequality and the scope for autonomy within the Japanese education system will be essential reading for students and educators alike.

KAORI OKANO is a senior lecturer in the Department of Asian Studies at La Trobe University. She is the author of *Transition from School to Work in Japan* (1993), and has also published widely in such journals as *Sociology of Education, Anthropology and Education Quarterly* and the *International Journal of Qualitative Studies in Education*.

MOTONORI TSUCHIYA is Dean of the Faculty of Human Development at Kobe University. He is a leading scholar of teacher education, education systems and education administration and has published widely in Japanese.

CONTEMPORARY JAPANESE SOCIETY

Editor:
Yoshio Sugimoto, La Trobe University

Advisory Editors:
Harumi Befu, Kyoto Bunkyo University
Roger Goodman, Oxford University
Michio Muramatsu, Kyoto University
Wolfgang Seifert, Universität Heidelberg
Chizuko Ueno, University of Tokyo

This series will provide a comprehensive portrayal of contemporary Japan through analysis of key aspects of Japanese society and culture, ranging from work and gender politics to science and technology. The series endeavours to link the relative strengths of Japanese and English-speaking scholars through collaborative authorship. Each title will be a balanced investigation of the area under consideration, including a synthesis of competing views.

The series will appeal to a wide range of readers from undergraduate beginners in Japanese studies to professional scholars. It will enable readers to grasp the diversity of Japanese society as well as the variety of theories and approaches available to study it.

Yoshio Sugimoto *An Introduction to Japanese Society*
    0 521 41692 2 hardback   0 521 42704 5 paperback

D. P. Martinez (ed.) *The Worlds of Japanese Popular Culture*
    0 521 63128 9 hardback   0 521 63729 5 paperback

EDUCATION IN CONTEMPORARY JAPAN

Inequality and Diversity

KAORI OKANO

and

MOTONORI TSUCHIYA

CAMBRIDGE
UNIVERSITY PRESS

PUBLISHED BY THE PRESS SYNDICATE OF THE UNIVERSITY OF CAMBRIDGE
The Pitt Building, Trumpington Street, Cambridge, United Kingdom

CAMBRIDGE UNIVERSITY PRESS
The Edinburgh Building, Cambridge CB2 2RU, UK   http://www.cup.cam.ac.uk
40 West 20th Street, New York, NY 10011–4211, USA   http://www.cup.org
10 Stamford Road, Oakleigh, Melbourne 3166, Australia

First published 1999

Printed in Singapore by Kin Keong Printing Co.

Typeset in New Baskerville 10/12 pt

A catalogue record for this book is available from the British Library

National Library of Australia Cataloguing in Publication data

Okano, Kaori.
Education in contemporary Japan: inequality and diversity.

Bibliography.
Includes index.
ISBN 0 521 62252 2.
ISBN 0 521 62686 2 (pbk).

1. Schools – Japan. 2. Schools – Japan – History – 20th
century. 3. Teachers – Japan. 4. Education – Social
aspects – Japan. 5. Education – Japan – History – 20th
century. 6. Education – Japan – Case studies. I. Tsuchiya,
Motonori, 1942– . II. Title. (Series: Contemporary
Japanese society).

370.952

ISBN 0 521 62252 2 hardback
ISBN 0 521 62686 2 paperback

Contents

Figures

Tables

Case Studies

Preface

The practice of schooling in any society exhibits a complex dynamism. In industrialised societies, schools accept children as young as five or six years of age, from diverse family backgrounds, for at least nine years of their most formative period. Modern schools involve almost all children (at least officially), and teach a set of knowledge that is deemed 'appropriate' to age-graded groups of children through the compulsory school years, and, later, more specialised knowledge to selected groups of students at secondary schools and beyond. Prior to the advent of modern schooling, only a small proportion of children received private formal lessons appropriate to their positions in the society, while others were educated informally at home. The introduction of modern schools therefore led to a profound reorganisation of social life, both at the individual level and for the society as a whole. The system of modern schooling continues to play a dynamic role in society and amongst individuals. This book examines the practice of such schooling in contemporary Japan, and explores the diversity in its relationships with individuals, social groups and the society as a whole, which often results in social inequality.

We hope that this book will make a small contribution to the existing knowledge of Japanese schooling in several ways. First, it will make concrete, and humanise, statistical aggregates that show nationwide tendencies, drawing on ethnographic studies and the accounts of the major participants (students and teachers). In so doing, our analysis will move between the policies and institutional *systems* and the interactive *process* of schooling in diverse settings. Second, the book will illuminate diversity and inequality in the schooling processes as experienced by the participants, who are positioned in diverse social locations, and explore the complex relationships between the process of schooling and other ongoing social processes. Third, the book will offer a balanced depiction

of Japanese schooling by discussing its negative aspects and Japanese
people's criticism of their own education system, as well as its positive
features. We hope that this book will also encourage further research
into Japanese schooling.

Many of those studies of Japan's modern schooling that are available in
the English language are concerned with the roles that schools have
played in the society's modernisation and economic development. We
have been informed that schooling during the Meiji modernisation and
in the post-war period was particularly effective in moving the society in
the directions set by the state: to create an imperial state and a modern
society in the former era, and to transform the imperial state imbued
with nationalism and militarism into a democratic society in the latter. It
is claimed that schools effectively socialised and acculturated the young
for the adult society, raised the population's literacy and numeracy,
transmitted modern skills and knowledge, and conducted meritocratic
selection of the nation's young talent. The popular focus on schooling's
role in modernisation and economic development derives, at least partly,
from the West's preoccupation with understanding the unprecedented
'success' of Japan's modernisation.

Some of the Japanese public also share this popular interpretation of
schooling. The Japanese people tend to speak of, and explain, positive
aspects of their own society to outsiders. The West's positive assessment
of Japanese schooling has reinforced the views of some Japanese people.
Such views are congruent with the traditional Confucian belief in the
essentially virtuous nature of learning. This common-sense understanding is indeed appealing: schools enable individuals to acquire the
knowledge and skills (often unavailable in families) they need to lead
fulfilling adult lives, and, as a consequence, allow the society to maintain
and promote stability, efficiency, productivity and, perhaps, democracy.
The ready acceptance of such an optimistic understanding of schooling
has in part been due to the economic prosperity and relative social
stability that the Japanese public have enjoyed in the last four decades.

This picture is not invalid, but it is grossly incomplete. Not only does
schooling perform (both by design and otherwise) roles other than
those mentioned above, but what it provides means different things to
different people. That is, individuals attach varying meanings to schools
as institutions and to the education that they provide. Even if relatively
uniform education is provided by schools, it is likely to be consumed and
utilised to varying degrees and in varying ways by people located in
diverse social positions. What people obtain from schools is consequently
likely to vary, with some benefiting more than others. In this case, the
assumption of equality of opportunity in education based on merit needs
re-examination.

While the post-war system of schooling has provided valuable ingredients for economic success and social stability, as mentioned above, these have been accompanied by unfavourable developments. Examples include what critics see as the excessively competitive examinations for entry into higher schools; the uniformity that some claim stifles individual development; bullying and school refusal. Post-war schooling has maintained monocultural orientations (as distinct from multiculturalism), which assume that all students are from a single ethnic group (Japanese), and mean that state-sponsored schools cater almost exclusively for their needs. This approach has not only undervalued what 'others' might bring to school and undermined their self-esteem; it may also have helped 'mainstream' (i.e. urban middle-class) children to develop a distorted view of the world. The practice of schooling continues to reproduce, rather than eliminate, family disadvantages. Within Japan there is a pool of studies on these negative aspects, which, naturally, exhibit research orientations that are distinct from those underlying studies on Japanese schooling published in English. We will attempt to integrate these studies, which have been conducted by 'insiders' and presented for the domestic audience, in this book.

The book has three aims. First, it will illustrate the *practice* of schooling at the macroscopic level of policy and the institutional school systems, and at the microscopic level of the schooling process. Second, it will discuss what modern schooling has brought to the society and to individuals, and how individuals, social groups and the state in turn have influenced the shaping of schooling practice. Third, it will enhance our understanding of the complex relationship between the society, schooling and individuals by discussing the above from a range of sociological perspectives.

Our central questions are as follows. What has modern schooling brought to Japanese society at large, and to individuals in diverse social locations? How have the major players (students and teachers) experienced schooling? Have they all equally received the fruits of the so-called 'successful' schooling praised by outsiders? If not, are there any patterns of variation in the experiences and benefits gained from schooling? To what extent have students, teachers and various social groups maintained autonomy in their ability (however limited) to influence the shaping of schooling practice? Where has the state stood in these dynamic processes? In what ways have students, teachers, parents, divergent social groups and the state struggled to exert influence in shaping school practice, at both the policy-making level and the level of schooling practice?

Our starting assumption is that opportunities and resources are not distributed equally to everybody; and that even when the same opportunity is given, one needs to be equipped with certain types, and a certain amount, of resources to be able to utilise that opportunity most effectively. Consequently, individuals (both students and teachers) in varied social locations (in the configuration made up of class, gender, minority status, region, etc.) undergo divergent experiences of schooling, and obtain differential benefits from it. In return, divergent social groups (some more powerful than others) and the state struggle to exert influence in shaping schooling practice at both macroscopic and microscopic levels.

The theme that will run through the book is the interplay of family, schooling and the wider social forces (including the state) that influence them. We consider that the structure of social relations is hierarchical, in that resources and power are unequally distributed; and that families are the main connection between students and the larger social structure. It is mainly the family that socialises children into class-specific culture, and directly provides resources (economic, cultural and social) for them. An individual student's school experience needs to be comprehended in relation to social processes on a larger scale, while such social processes at the structural level can most effectively be understood through the way they affect particular lives.

The book is based on a critical review of research published to date in both English and Japanese. We have inevitably brought in our own past research in various fields of education. We have tried to refer to the research published in English as much as possible, so that the reader can pursue topics of interest beyond this book. At the same time, we have tried to incorporate research published in the Japanese language in order to introduce the reader (who may not possess sufficient Japanese language proficiency) to a sample of the vast pool of research in the field of education that is available there.

Our extensive use of ethnographic research, and children's and teachers' own accounts of schooling (in Chapters 3, 4 and 5), is deliberate. We want to bring major participants in the schooling process to the centre stage, so that they can make their voices heard and, so that you, the reader, can make sense of their accounts. Naturally, we, as the researchers and authors of the book, present our own interpretations of these ethnographies and actors' accounts; but we also want to share with you these first-hand accounts and invite your own interpretation of them. If at the end of this book you can envision the many diverse faces of children and teachers we have tried to represent, we will consider that one of our aims has been achieved.

We hope that the differences that each of us brings to this book will be to its benefit. Our differences in gender, age, place of residence (Australia and Japan) and past career path have given rise to differences in perspective, which could sometimes be difficult to reconcile(!). There are also differences in our academic disciplinary backgrounds. One of us received research training in Japan in the 1960s, and has worked on school systems, policies and the history of modern Japanese education. His substantive areas of research are teachers (union movements, teacher education and certification), educational reforms, and, more recently, 'children's rights'. The other author undertook postgraduate studies in the sociology of education in the late 1980s in Australia and New Zealand, where she was a secondary-school teacher, and has focused on the practice of schooling at the microscopic level, and on the theories of inequality and education. Her substantive research areas have been working-class students and the school-to-work transition.

Our perspectives shape our perceptions, which inevitably involve screening and selection. Each of us perceives Japanese schooling from differing social positions, and we discussed our perceptions in the process of producing this book. We also tried to capitalise on the strengths of each other's past research experience, in deciding who would be the major author of each chapter. In some chapters we contributed equally. In all cases, drafts were discussed. One of us, familiar with the literature and research concerns in the Anglophone world, performed the task of writing the work in English, so that we could most effectively communicate our discussions to the reader. The end product, we hope, will provide a more comprehensive and balanced examination of Japanese schooling than a book that one or the other of us might have written alone. We must confess that both of us have learned enormously from the process of producing this book. We enjoyed it as much.

We wrote this book with two audience groups in mind. One consists of students and researchers of Japanese society, who are interested in knowing more about its practice of schooling in order to enhance their understanding of the society as a whole. The other group comprises students and researchers of education (in particular the fields of comparative education and the sociology and anthropology of education). They will be interested in the case of Japanese schooling as an example of education in 'another society', which may provide insights into a particular aspect of education that they are studying. For beginning students in both groups, we have attached a list of further reading at the end of each chapter.

The opening chapter introduces the reader to analytical frameworks for understanding the school's relationship to the society and individuals it serves, drawing on sociology of education. Chapter 2 examines the main developments of modern schooling in Japan, from the beginning of the Meiji era up to the present. The following two chapters are devoted to an examination of the practice of schooling as experienced by students. Chapter 3 examines first 'mainstream' education, and then the schooling experienced by five different groups of students, namely girls, the poor, the male elites, youth in correspondence schools and rural youth from farming families. Chapter 4 then focuses on the schooling that minority groups experience (third-generation Koreans, *buraku* children and children of newcomers). In these two chapters we examine the nature of the varying relationships that respective groups develop with schools, and explore the consequences for individual students' life chances.

In Chapter 5, the focus shifts to the other major participants in the schooling process, the teachers. We examine the institutional systems that produce them and impose constraints on what they do, teachers' daily realities, and the culture of teaching. We also introduce three examples of the practice of teaching that Japanese teachers idealise, and present three teachers' life histories. Chapter 6 first examines the so-called pathological phenomena (bullying, school refusal and corporal punishment) that have given political justification for major educational reforms. We then scrutinise the policy proposals and the implementation of reforms in education during the 1980s and 1990s.

We are indebted to our colleagues in both Australia and Japan and, in particular, to the anonymous reviewers and to the editors at Cambridge University Press. Their critical and insightful comments have contributed to a much refined final product. Co-authoring across a long distance has not been easy. We have benefited from an Australian Research Council grant; and from Okano's sabbatical leave and La Trobe University's travel assistance, which provided us with excellent opportunities to work together at a late stage of production. Finally, we would like to thank our respective families, Fukuko, Kaoru and Maki, and David and Yukiko, for their support. Yukiko arrived during the gestation of the book, providing her parents with a new challenge as well as many pleasurable and needed distractions from excessive concentration on authorship.

CHAPTER 1

Analytical Frameworks: Schooling and Society

The purpose of this brief chapter is to present you with some of the major theoretical frameworks that are currently being, or have been, applied in research on schooling and society, which we hope will enhance your understanding of Japanese schooling. Drawing on developments in the sociology of education, we will appraise the relative merits of such theories in relation to the study of Japanese schooling, while reviewing the major existing studies in English and Japanese. We begin by briefly examining some of the general properties of a theory: what it is and is not, how it can be used to extend our knowledge of a given research topic or subject area, and some of the pitfalls of theoretical analysis.

General Properties of a Sociological Theory

The notion of a theory is not exclusively the property of academic research. A theory is, simply stated, a way of seeing and knowing the world around us. It consists of a set of assumptions and concepts, which together may constitute a grand theory, a medium-range theory or a theory about a specific event. All theories (even grand theories) are, by their nature, tentative, and remain hypotheses to be refuted, modified and refined. That is to say, when a proposed hypothesis is refuted, it is modified to some degree, and the modified version of the hypothesis is presented as a new hypothesis to be tested again. This process of 'knowing' occurs both in academic research and in our daily lives (in particular, when one enters a new environment). Since it is an arbitrary matter to determine at which precise stage of this process a casual interpretation of events or observations becomes a so-called hypothesis, we will refer to 'theories' in their broadest sense (all of which are tentative).

1

The theories that people form about a particular event or situation are often based on assumptions of their own, which they may have taken for granted, or even be completely unaware of. For example, consider the common observation by outsiders that Japanese primary school classroom teachers give relatively few directions to the children in their charge. An observer who is interested in Confucianism may form a theory that Japanese school children do not require their teacher to provide them with constant direction because they have internalised the Confucian ideal of learning. Another observer, who has studied teacher–pupil interactions at a Japanese nursery school, may say that Japanese children are more secure as a result of very intimate relationships with their teachers, who encourage a nurturing environment for learning. Having formed such theories, people often happily leave a situation without actively seeking to further test and refine them through a deliberate process of conjecture and refutation. Consequently some 'theories' are naturally more valid and helpful than others in explaining an aspect of the world or a particular phenomenon. Our understanding of Japanese schooling is subject to change, since further research will bring new insights. The practice of Japanese schooling is also inevitably impacted by change.

Why use sociological theories here? Even without them, you could learn about, and form a particular understanding of, Japanese schooling by reading factual information, life histories, ethnographies, media reports and so forth. Such an understanding would inevitably be influenced by your taken-for-granted assumptions, which might derive from, for example, what you have previously read, experiences with Japanese exchange students or teachers, or from what you may have heard about Japanese children. This is because when you perceive an event or phenomenon, your perception and interpretation (which often occur simultaneously) are bound to be screened by your existing theory (a set of assumptions). Having a knowledge of several representative theories about education and society (sociological theories), which we present below, will keep you conscious of your own theories in relation to other ways of perceiving Japanese schooling, by encouraging you to interpret it from multiple perspectives.

There are downsides to theories as well. The contrastive set of theories about schooling and society (consensus and conflict theories) that we present below is exaggerated and polar. These theories are highly abstract constructs developed in line with Western traditional logic, and present us with a neat depiction of schooling and society. Sceptics would argue that such neat pictures are the creations of academics removed from the microlevel practice of schooling. What we intend to do in this book is not merely to impose a neat (and simplistic) picture onto what is in reality complex and elusive, by drawing on these theories, but to emphasise the complex processes and realities of Japanese schooling and society. The theoretical frameworks presented in this chapter are meant to help our understanding by offering us signposts.

English-language Studies of Japanese Schooling

To date, most studies available in the English language have discussed Japan's modern schooling in terms of its contribution to the country's modernisation and economic development. Among them are seven books that cover Japanese education in general (Beauchamp 1978, 1991; Kobayashi 1976; Leestma et al. 1987; Lynn 1988; Simmons 1990; White 1987). The West has been informed that schooling during the Meiji modernisation and in the post-war period was particularly effective. The education system has raised the population's literacy and numeracy, transmitted modern skills and knowledge, provided equal opportunity of education, conducted meritocratic selection of the nation's young people, and allocated them to appropriate places in the adult society. The popular focus on schooling's role in modernisation and economic development derives, at least partly, from the West's preoccupation with understanding the unprecedented 'success' of Japan's modernisation. Western academics and policy makers have also been interested in Japan's modern schooling because it appears to offer long-awaited 'evidence' that schools have the potential to transform a society, rather than preserve the existing social relations.

The Four Roles

We see four major direct roles in which schools provide for young people. Modern schools perform these roles simultaneously, but each of them receives varying priorities at different points in time, according to the people involved. Different groups of students are affected in different ways, as we shall discuss in the following chapters. At the national policy level, priorities have shifted over the years. Interest groups assert their views on where priorities should lie. Teachers do not always agree on the nationally set priorities. Individual schools may have priorities different from the national ones, in order to meet particular needs of the local student population. Certain educational roles affect the lives of young people from specific backgrounds more than others, as in, for example, the case of girls not obtaining the same benefit as boys from 'merit-based' selection.

Transmission of Knowledge

First, schools transmit 'useful' knowledge to children. Children acquire basic literacy and numeracy, knowledge and skills, which assist them in fulfilling their potential and in becoming adult members of the society. Studies have argued that Japanese schools have been successful in promoting such cognitive development. Literacy and numeracy rates are claimed to be higher in Japan than anywhere else (e.g. Duke 1986:60). High average achievement and low variation in Japanese children's performance in international mathematics and science achievement surveys are often quoted to demonstrate high cognitive development among Japanese children, and the reasons for such 'success' have been sought (Cummings 1980, 1982:17–25; Lynn 1988:121–44; Simmons and Wade 1988; Duke 1986). It has been claimed that a highly educated population has contributed to the high quality of the workforce. Others have argued that vocational preparation is effectively conducted in the schooling system, noting that the breadth of technological overview given to students at vocational high schools provides the flexible foundation upon which to build when they receive specific training from employers; and that Japanese five-year technical colleges (*kōtō senmongakkō*) and vocational high schools produce 10–20 times as many technicians per head of the workforce as the education system in the UK (Prais 1987:50).

Socialisation and Acculturation

Second, schools socialise and acculturate children for the adult Japanese world, both through explicit instructions and by means of a 'hidden curriculum'. The routine process of schooling and the interaction between teachers and students instil particular values and behavioural dispositions that are deemed desirable by the dominant society. A particular view of the way the society operates is also learned. At the most basic level, children learn to follow the set school routine with punctuality, and to maintain cooperative relationships with peers. By the end of schooling, students will have learnt that selection to higher schools is based on 'merit' and is therefore 'fair'; that equal opportunity of education enables everyone who works hard to achieve their goals; and, by implication, that those who fail at school and beyond have only themselves to blame. This message of 'fair' schools for everyone is also present in other advanced societies.

The socialisation of young children in families has been studied in psychological research, which showed how Japanese families socialise infants and young children from birth. Several comparative studies of Japan and the US, based on experimental methods, observations and interviews, revealed differences in the internal dynamics of Japanese and American families, and, in particular, the ways in which young children are reared before their entry into preschool educational institutions (Chen and Miyake 1986; Hess et al. 1986). Of particular note is Azuma's assertion

(1986:6–8) that Japanese mothers' indulgent devotion to their children socialises young children into *amae* (dependency) relationships, in which the children internalise their mothers' wishes for them, and consequently are susceptible to being educated in the ways the mothers want.

In regard to socialisation within educational institutions, the authors of studies such as those quoted below have focused on what are considered to be 'uniquely Japanese' features, and have sought explanations of such features in terms of 'Japanese culture and traditions'. There are others who disagree with such culturalist explanations and insist on social–institutional explanations. In this view, the education system 'developed in tandem with the labour market practice', and the school, students and parents respond rationally to the education–labour market link to maximise their own interest (Brinton 1993:221). Both groups argue that schools effectively prepare youth for the adult society, which requires of its members such values and dispositions.

The socialisation of Japanese children has been studied at nursery school and kindergarten levels (Tobin et al. 1987; Hendry 1986; Peak 1991), primary level (Lewis 1988; Cummings 1980; Duke 1986), secondary level (Rohlen 1983; Shimahara 1979; Okano 1993), post-secondary level (Tsukada 1991) and in general (White 1987). Classroom management encourages students to be loyal to groups, and to persevere through hardships to achieve goals (Duke 1986). Emphasis on activities in small heterogeneous ability groups promotes cooperation and understanding (Duke 1986; Tsuneyoshi 1994). The notorious competitive examination for entry into university can be understood as a preparation for the adult world, a 'rite of passage', in that it teaches young people to develop self-discipline and defer gratification (Shimahara 1979). Such dispositions, it is claimed, make Japanese young people desirable employees, and contribute to the high productivity and efficiency of the economy. They also create law-abiding citizens. While many of these studies tend to examine Japanese students as a whole, emphasising common socialisation features, close observation would suggest that students' socialisation experiences are highly influenced by peer groups and/or subcultures that they construct and continuously reconstruct, a point that we will shortly take up.

Selection and Differentiation

Third, schooling selects young people based on their academic achievement, and prepares them for 'appropriate' positions in the workforce and in society generally; for instance, identifying some for leadership positions and others for subordinate positions. The well-publicised competitive nature of the university entrance examination exemplifies this selection function of Japanese schools. Some argue that the selection is based on 'objective' merits (Shimahara 1979; Cummings 1980). More recently, others have argued against such a view, contending that students' academic achievement is significantly related to their family backgrounds, and that family-derived privileges have come to advantage the child to a greater extent in the last two decades (Rohlen 1983; Brinton 1993; Okano 1993).

Legitimation of Knowledge

Fourth, schools legitimate what they teach to students simply by teaching it. By transmitting a certain collection of knowledge to students as the school curriculum, schools legitimate that version of knowledge as 'true' and 'neutral'. The Japanese government's textbook screening system is one of the most overt examples of this process. More subtle forms of knowledge legitimation also exist. By socialising and acculturating students, schools legitimate particular sets of dispositions that are considered to be desirable (such as perseverance), a particular world view, and a system of values, as being universally virtuous, 'correct' and equally valuable for everyone. As will be discussed shortly, disagreement exists as to whether what schools teach is indeed based on consensus and works equally well for everyone.

Multiple Interpretations of Schooling and Society

Modern schools perform the four roles simultaneously: transmitting cognitive knowledge, socialising and acculturating, selecting and differentiating young people, and legitimating what they teach. This simultaneous operation of the four functions can be interpreted in divergent ways. Consensus theories and conflict theories provide a contrastive (and therefore exaggerated, but nonetheless useful) set of assumptions and ways to observe schooling. Let us introduce the two in turn.

Structuralist Interpretations: Consensus and Conflict Theories

Consensus Theories

Consensus theories stress the relative stability and harmonious nature of Japanese society. This stability is explained in terms of 'consensus', that is, shared norms and values in the society. For instance, consensus theorists claim that across diverse social groups, a relative consensus exists that education is necessary for one's adult life; and that schooling offers all children an opportunity to move up the social ladder if they are willing to work hard. These theories originate from a structural–functionalist view of the society. Such a view assumes that society consists of parts, each of which contributes to the overall societal structure; and is interested in each part's function in maintaining the whole. For example, a small suburban community is made up of such parts as retail shops, garbage collectors, church groups, children's play groups, elderly people, meals-on-wheels, an unemployed youth group that does voluntary gardening, and a primary school; and each of them plays a role in maintaining the healthy operation of the community.

Although 'problems' may sometimes occur, because some parts do not function properly, or because individuals fail to accept the social norms and become 'deviant' due to poor socialisation, consensus theories assume that the society can recover its healthy operation through 'appropriate adjustments'. In the case of the small suburban community, imagine that the community's garbage has not recently been cleared because the system simply cannot cope with the increased amounts of rubbish produced by a growing population. The community may solve this problem by employing unemployed youth on a temporary basis until a more permanent arrangement is established by the community council.

Consider also the case where some children develop school phobia. One would explain that these children fail to develop self-esteem and interpersonal skills in an overtly competitive environment. The delinquent behaviour of some children might be attributed to their socialisation in a family headed by an alcoholic father. To resolve these 'problems' the school might try to create a more caring environment. Children from 'problematic' families could be sent to institutional care.

Consensus theories do not rule out the existence of conflict or disagreement. Some members of the society may disagree, but there is a consensus as to the rules and procedures to be applied when such disagreement occurs. For instance, in order to overcome disagreement as to how to manage school phobia, a committee might be set up to investigate the phenomenon and to report its findings to the public. There might also be conflict in the form of competition, but competition increases efficiency and satisfaction, and provides an arena where aggressions can legitimately be displayed.

Seen in this view, schools are performing the four important functions in order to maintain the present state of social relations, or, as in Japan in the late 1940s, to develop a renewed society as agreed on by members of the society. Schools provide children with the knowledge required for membership of adult society and of the workforce. They socialise young people to fit into adult Japanese society, instilling 'appropriate' social values, and assisting in forming 'appropriate' social identities in children from different social backgrounds. Schools identify the talents of children, and prepare them to fulfil 'appropriate' roles in adult society and to accept their allocation (e.g. to professional or to subordinate roles). This supposedly leads to a 'match' of talents and positions, with, for instance, the most 'talented' being channelled into the most 'important' positions. There is believed to be a consensus as to what constitutes 'appropriate' social identities, values and roles, and what are the most 'talented' and 'important' positions, a point that conflict theories challenge. The success or otherwise of these educational functions is mainly seen in terms of economic performance (productivity, economic growth, income distribution), and the modernisation process, at both the personal and the societal level.

Conflict Theories

In contrast, conflict theories, which are based on various versions of Marxist approaches, understand Japanese society quite differently. The society is considered to be *temporarily* stable because of a 'consensus' in which many of the society's members accept certain norms and values, although these norms and values operate not in the interest of the majority but only for the benefit of small groups of the powerful. This consensus is called the *ideology*. The presence of this ideology conceals the fact that social relations are based on 'domination' rather than on harmony, and hides from the society's members the real nature of social stability, which exploits, and is contrary to the interests of, the majority. The economic base is seen to play a pivotal role in the maintenance of the social structure: the structure of production in the economy systematically differentiates individuals' access to resources and opportunities. The existing social relations are preserved, it is argued, as a result of the penetration of the dominant ideology through all levels of society. When those who are exploited accept the ideology that marginalises them, they are said to be living in 'false consciousness'. Some conflict theories interpret the entire process as a deliberate control of people by the state (e.g. Horio 1988; Yamazumi 1987; Miliband 1969), while others argue that the control is not a conspiracy but a consequence of overall structural forces inherent in capitalist society (Althusser 1971). The former interpretation has been dominant amongst union teachers and academics in education in Japan.

Conflict theories acknowledge the presence of stability and consensus, but differ radically from the consensus theories in their understanding of the nature of such consensus and social stability. They question whether a prevailing consensus is in fact serving the interests of all members of society, and ask how such a consensus is maintained despite the fact that it brings little benefit to the majority.

Schooling, in the view of conflict theorists, socialises children to accept the dominant ideology. First, schools teach a version of knowledge, values and world view (often that held by the dominant groups) as if they were 'true' and 'universal'. Consider the controversial school history book that described Japan's actions in Asia during the Second World War as an 'advance' and the 'liberation of Asia from Western colonialism', as opposed to an 'invasion' and the 'exploitation of Asia'. Second, schools recognise and reward certain types of 'ability' in children, conduct differentiation based on what the schools define as 'merits', and prepare some for leadership or professional positions and others for subordinate positions in the adult society. Imagine two girls named Aya and Kimi. Aya, self-assured, outgoing and articulate, has excelled in reading and writing since she was small. The school recognises Aya's high level of language skills, encourages her development by providing extra reading materials and encouragement, and recommends that she pursue a legal career that would utilise her valued abilities. On the other hand, Kimi is a self-effacing and compassionate girl, who loves and is good at making things with her hands, such as craft work, sewing and cooking (which some would call 'soft' options or non-academic subjects). Kimi chooses a domestic science course at a vocational high school, which the school happily endorses. It may not be a coincidence that Aya comes from a family where both parents are tertiary-educated professionals, who have created an environment that promotes Aya's interest in academic subjects. Kimi may have lacked such an influence.

The schools thus make people believe that the selection of young people is 'fair' since it is based on individual achievement and schools provide equal opportunities to everybody. As a result, they legitimate existing inequalities in such a way that the powerful maintain, and even enhance, their resources and power. Their enhanced power is, in return, utilised through various institutions to legitimate the powerful's position. To conflict theorists, schooling is a key process that preserves both the dominant ideology and inequality across generations.

The consensus and conflict theories correspond to the often con-trastive interpretations by the Japanese Ministry of Education (MOE) and the major teachers' union of policies and events in post-war education, as Chapter 2 will reveal. The union and intellectuals on the political left interpreted many of the government's initiatives to 'adjust' schooling to the perceived needs of the society, as deliberate measures to 'control' the practice of schooling to satisfy the government's aims, with damaging consequences for the human development of pupils and to what they saw as democratic ideals. Many of the government's reform proposals in the 1980s and 1990s faced similar criticisms from the left (as discussed in Chapter 6). The two contrastive theories attach different significance to the differences in educational experiences of divergent social groups (to be examined in Chapters 3 and 4). A teacher's adoption of either a consensus or a conflict theory approach in relation to educational practice is likely to shape his or her professional career; the balance of the two within a school is likely to affect the culture of teaching, as shown in Chapter 5.

Adding Interactionist Interpretations: Macroscopic and Microscopic Understandings

The consensus and conflict theories are similar in that both focus on social structure and the part that schools play in that structure. Both see structural forces and the needs of the society as directly determining what occurs in schools and, in turn, regard what schools do as contributing to the maintenance of the existing society. That is to say, both see schools as effectively doing what they are meant to: either preparing children for a harmonious adult society through meritocratic selection (consensus theories), or instilling the dominant ideology in children so that they accept a society based on domination (conflict theories). In this regard, both theories adopt a particular version of the structuralist approach.

While these theories present very neat pictures of schooling and society, closer observation would show that schools have not been as successful in implementing their assigned tasks as their proponents would have us believe. Schools have also done other things, which are not expected in either theory. For example, even strict consensus theorists would acknowledge that the most talented are not always in positions where they can make optimal use of their talent for the society's good. In reality, what schools do and the outcomes of schooling are more diverse than either type of theory make us believe. The relations among schools, families and society are more complex, problematic, and even unpredictable.

The process of schooling involves various participants: teachers, school administrators, students and their families. None of them are passive role players who stringently follow what the state (or the powerful) prescribes that they do. The premise of *interactionist* approaches (Woods 1983) is that individual participants make their own sense of a particular event and act on their own accord. Students, teachers, parents and others are active in attaching particular meaning to an event, and in creating their own experience. Participants' actions are naturally constrained by external factors, and the extent of these constraints is not fixed but depends on the circumstances surrounding an event. The significance to be attached to the power of external constraints is open to disagreement, depending on one's theoretical stance.

Imagine a decision by a Japanese high-school student not to proceed to tertiary education, although she has always been at the top of her class. Her teacher considers this to be tragic, since he believes that tertiary education will enhance her life chances (which he considers everyone wants), and tries hard to persuade her to change her mind. Her parents might say to their daughter that they would support her if she wanted to pursue tertiary education, although they might secretly think that university education would not bring much benefit to a girl and that they would rather save the resources for her younger brother. The student might have come to such a decision simply because she has had enough of studying and wants to have a change, thinking that she would be able to return to study in future if she so desired. A researcher of gender inequality might interpret this case as one of the student's undervaluing her ability because she is female.

A focus on microlevel interactions among students, teachers and other significant players in schooling has revealed a fascinating picture of how diverse meanings are created and experienced, and has directed us to the indeterminate nature of what occurs in Japanese schools (e.g. Miyazaki 1993; Shimahara and Sakai 1995; LeTendre 1994). While closely focused microscopic research has its own merit, attempts to interpret the micro-interactions at the classroom level in relation to macrostructural theories have also been fruitful (Willis 1977; Walker 1988; Connell et al. 1982; Okano 1993). These studies of industrial societies have suggested that the mechanical processes of schooling pictured by both consensus and conflict theories are far from the reality of the schooling process. Participants (children and families, teachers) with diverse characteristics *interact* with the school and make sense of schooling. This affects the process in which the school selects and differentiates students for the adult society. In interacting with the school authorities, teachers, their families and other students, students constantly create and reconstruct relationships with the other participants (and subcultures), through which they experience schooling. Teachers do the same. It is the nature of these relationships that determines participants' experience of schooling, what each of them obtains from it, and consequently what schooling offers to social groups and the society as a whole.

What we seek to do in our detailed analysis of Japanese schooling is to utilise the existing theoretical frameworks to enhance our understanding of Japanese schooling, and to present a more refined 'theory' of Japanese schooling by revealing and examining what consensus and conflict theories do not show. Macrostructural approaches (including both consensus and conflict interpretations) give us a particular structural map of the society that helps explain the role (often normative, in our view) of schooling in the society. Micro-interactionist approaches that closely examine schooling practice at the individual level illustrate how diverse individuals and groups experience the schooling process. Drawing on the two types of approach, we will examine participants' different experiences of Japanese schooling in relation to the structural map of Japanese society.

Our focus will be the diversity in the major players' (students and teachers) experiences of schooling, and in the roles that schooling plays for the society and for individuals in various social locations. We intend to explain such diversities, in relation to both social inequality and the level of autonomy that the players maintain in contemporary Japanese society. First, however, we will briefly survey the development of modern Japanese education, in order to examine the historical background to the present realities of schooling.

Further Reading

Ballantine, Jeanne H. (1989). *The Sociology of Education* (2nd edn). Englewood Cliffs, NJ: Prentice Hall.

Beauchamp, Edward R. (ed.) (1991). *Windows on Japanese Education.* Westport, CT: Greenwood Press.

Blackledge, David and Hunt, Barry (1985). *Sociological Interpretations of Education.* London: Routledge.

Leestma, Robert, Bennett, William J., George, B. and Peak, Lois (1987). *Japanese Education Today.* Washington, DC: US Department of Education.

Simmons, Cyril (1990). *Growing Up and Going to School in Japan: Tradition and trends.* Milton Keynes: Open University Press.

White, Merry I. (1987). *The Japanese Educational Challenge: A commitment to children.* New York: The Free Press.

CHAPTER 2

The Development of Modern Schooling

Except for the totalitarian states, no modern nation has used the schools so systematically for purposes of political indoctrination as Japan. Although the early builders of the modern school system spoke a utilitarian language, they did not for a moment forget problems of morality and patriotism. (Passin 1982:149)

The contemporary system and practice of modern schooling in Japan bears the legacy of its 130-year history. This chapter surveys the development of modern schooling, including both the national policies and institutions and the realities that the major participants (students and teachers) experienced at the level of the school. We believe that these participants have not been passive recipients of what the state gave them, even though the state no doubt had its own agenda, as the above quotation suggests. We will examine the development of Japanese education as critics of the system and the government's intentions for it.

Radical reforms marked the beginning of both the pre-war period of nationalist schooling (1868–1945) and the post-war one of democratic education (1945–present). The former period saw the introduction of the system of modern schooling by the imperial state, which aimed to nurture a sense of nationhood and to serve the needs of the emerging nation-state. The reforms of the latter, implemented by the Allied Occupation, were a well-planned attempt to overhaul the pre-war nationalist system and to introduce so-called democratic education. Moderate changes took place between these radical reforms and have continued to occur up to the present. The series of reforms initiated by the Ad-Hoc Council in the 1980s (to be covered in Chapter 6) was among these.

Nationalist Schooling up to 1945

In the latter half of the 19th century, the Meiji government tried to build the basis for a centralised imperial state. The Tokugawa shōgunate opened the country's doors to the West and handed over its 250-year-old political power to the emperor in 1868. The new state was to resist pressures from the Western powers (which were then expanding in various parts of Asia) and to achieve an ethnic independence and modernisation.[1]

Meiji schooling was a radical departure from the pre-modern education that had existed in the Tokugawa feudal era.[2] Under the Tokugawa feudal system, approximately 280 feudal domains maintained relative autonomy, with the Tokugawa shōgunate clan at the peak of the hierarchy. The respective domains and the shōgunate government maintained their own schooling for the sons of *samurai*. Under the rigid class divisions of the feudal system, where schools existed they were operated and sponsored by the respective classes for the benefit of their members.

The noble class provided their own schools in Kyoto. For the *samurai* class, shōgunate schools offered education for the future ruling elite. In the case of *samurai* other than the Tokugawa families, each feudal lord had at least one domain school (*hankō*) for its *samurai* class, which centred on Confucian learning. There were also local schools (*gōgaku*), which accommodated the *samurai* class residing outside feudal capitals. Private academies (*shijuku*) were also available for the *samurai* class.[3] By the late Tokugawa era, both domain schools and private academies were accepting a limited number of commoners wishing to enter academic professions. For the commoners, temple schools (*terakoya*) offered children the 'three Rs' and basic skills they would need to become merchants, artisans and farmers. *Terakoya* education was informal, often held in the local temple and private homes. All of these institutions, except for the *terakoya*, accepted only boys. The *terakoya* enrolment was approximately one-quarter female, and boys and girls were educated separately beyond age seven, following Confucian teachings (Osada 1961:123–4). Thus the education that children received was to equip them with the knowledge and skills that they would require in performing the tasks of their respective classes when they reached adulthood.

In contrast, Meiji schooling was to be open to every child in the country, regardless of their place of residence and class background. It thereby aimed to create a national identity, or a shared sense of nationhood, among people who had until then associated themselves with their respective feudal lords, and to train people for the building of a modern nation-state.

The Beginning of Modern Schooling

The ambitious master plan for modern schooling was created by the 1872 Education Law (*Gakusei*). Schooling was to form an important part of the state policies of 'rich nation and strong army' (*fukoku kyōhei*) and 'increase in production and founding of industries' (*shokusan kōgyō*), along with land reform and the new conscription system. The government believed that a rich nation required Western civilisation and educated citizens. It set out four principles for the new education system: (1) to eliminate feudalistic barriers and open educational opportunities to all citizens; (2) to consider the individual's success in life and enlightenment as the goals of study and education; (3) to emphasise the three Rs and other practical studies (e.g. medicine and engineering); and (4) to leave the cost of education to individuals. The country was to be divided into eight university zones, each having one university, 32 middle schools and 6720 primary schools, totalling 256 middle schools and 53,760 primary schools. Children were to receive eight years of compulsory education. Besides the institutional system, Western pedagogical principles and teaching methods (e.g. student-centred 'developmental education') were also introduced to normal schools, to be transmitted to schools across the nation (Lincicome 1995).

The early implementation of the *Gakusei* was not as successful as the government had hoped. By 1876 only 25,000 primary schools were operating. Over 70 per cent were single-class schools, which held lessons in local temples and private homes, just like the Tokugawa *terakoya*. The enrolment rate was about 30 per cent. Textbooks included those translated into Japanese from American primary-school textbooks and general books for enlightenment, which people in villages found irrelevant to their own lives. People in rural communities were dissatisfied with the imposed schooling, the cost of which was borne by individual families. Farming families could no longer rely on their children's labour. In some villages, people damaged school buildings and demanded the abolition of school levies.

The development of Meiji schooling should not be understood as a simple transplantation of Western civilisation into feudal Japan, and as a one-sided departure from the indigenous practice of education (Passin 1982). In late Tokugawa Japan, an institutionalised form of education had been enjoyed by a considerable portion of the male populace. Almost all *samurai* were highly literate, and even among commoners, the school attendance rate was 40 per cent for boys and 15 per cent for girls (Passin 1982:54). Mixed schooling for *samurai* and commoners had started to emerge at some domain schools and private academies (Passin

1982:54). Tokugawa schooling thus laid the groundwork for the rapid development of Meiji modern schooling (Passin 1982:54). The legacy of Tokugawa education contributed, at least partly, to the rapid creation of a modern industrial state (Dore 1965:291–316).

The Freedom and People's Rights Movement

The Freedom and People's Rights Movement (*Jiyū Minken Undō*) (1874–90) was a political movement against the government. It called for a *Diet* (Japanese parliament) and a democratic constitution, as well as urging the recognition of basic human rights, revision of treaties that disadvantaged Japan and land tax reform. A wide range of people (e.g. landowners, peasants and teachers) were involved.

The movement criticised the interventionist nature of the *Gakusei* education system and espoused freedom of education. The government acknowledged the limitations of the *Gakusei* and announced a change in 1879. This so-called 'liberal education' system introduced local governance of schooling, following the American example; shortened compulsory schooling to four years; and left school management to local representatives. Although this resulted in a lower attendance rate, it encouraged local people to establish their own schooling, and 'enlightenment' occurred in the villages, as reflected, for example, in the success of private schools which provided high-quality secondary education in some areas (Miyahara 1963:92).

However, the 1879 liberal education system was abandoned only one year later. Within the government, critics attacked the Westernisation policy in education, and suggested that the traditional Japanese Confucian values should underpin the nation's educational philosophy. The government tried to contain the influence of the civil movements. In 1880 the government banned teachers and students from attending political meetings, and prohibited the use of some textbooks which it considered 'inappropriate'. The revised education ordinance in the following year gave the Ministry of Education (MOE) more power to intervene in the running of schools. For example, moral education (*shūshin*) was placed at the centre of the primary-school curriculum. Prefectural governors were now to determine school rules, subject to approval from the MOE. The MOE set official guidelines for teachers' behaviour and thoughts. Co-education beyond primary schools was formally abolished, which deprived girls of opportunities to attend public middle schools, another regressive move away from the early *Gakusei* (Hara 1995:98–9)

Mori's Nationalist Education

Arinori Mori, the first Minister of Education, appointed in 1885, charted the map of the education system that was to continue until the end of the Second World War.[4] In 1886 Mori presented his master plan for a multi-track system of national education by issuing several major ordinances (the Imperial Universities Ordinance, the Middle Schools Ordinance, the Primary Schools Ordinance and the Normal Schools Ordinance). Mori's plan introduced overt nationalist schooling, which was expected to aid successful competition with the Western powers, and the countering of the civil movements, as well as the nurturing of filial imperial subjects.

Mori made a clear distinction between 'academic study' (*gakumon*) and 'education' (*kyōiku*). He believed that the two were qualitatively different, and that those who would become the leaders of the state should pursue academic study at imperial universities, while the remainder should receive 'only' education. In academic study, students explored 'the truth' in science and technology and the study of Western civilisation. Education, on the other hand, provided the three Rs and moral education, which would turn individuals into filial imperial subjects. Primary schools provided education, but middle schools and universities allowed students to pursue academic study.

At the apex of academic study was Tokyo University, the only university that had existed prior to the 1886 Ordinance. The value that the MOE attached to Tokyo University for nation-building can be seen by its allocation of the MOE's budget (in 1880 as much as 40 per cent). Private institutions for higher learning were also established but were not granted university status: Yukichi Fukuzawa's Keiō Gijuku (the present Keiō University) in 1885, and Shigenobu Ōkuma's Tokyo Senmongakkō (which later became Waseda University) in 1882. With the Imperial Universities Ordinance, Tokyo University changed its name to Tokyo Imperial University. The government granted financial assistance to its students, exempted them from conscription, and allowed the graduates in law to become probationary higher government officers.

Normal schools, which trained primary-school teachers, differed greatly from the universities. Mori attached a unique position and characteristics to the normal schools. The government provided financially for their students. Normal schools emphasised trainees' personal character over achievement in academic subjects, and required trainees to reside in the school's dormitories. They embodied a military style of education, adopting, for example, military patterns of group organisation and marching. Normal-school education produced the so-called 'normal-school type' teachers who single-mindedly pursued nationalistic schooling. However, not all trainees from normal schools became the kind of teachers that Mori had hoped for, as we shall see later when discussing teachers' resistance to nationalist schooling.

The Imperial Rescript on Education (Kyōiku Chokugo)

Mori's nationalist school system was completed by the 1890 Imperial Rescript on Education. The Rescript confirmed the absolute moral status of the emperor, in addition to the legal sovereignty that the 1889 Imperial Constitution conferred. The Rescript was the emperor's direct announcement, the supreme moral basis beyond legislation, and remained (along with the Rescript on the Army) the state ideology until the end of the Second World War. The Rescript preached Confucian morals on family relationships (e.g. between parents and children, among siblings, and between husband and wife) on one hand; and the morals of the modern nation on the other, including public benefits, public duties, a national constitution and national legislation. The morals of the family and the nation were integrated in the sacrifice of individuals in the service of the imperial state. The basis for girls' education was 'education to be good wives and wise mothers'. The duty of Japanese women was to serve their men and families and to maintain the continuity of the Japanese patriarchal family system (Hara 1995:97)

At the individual school level, the Rescript placed more emphasis on moral education. Besides the three Rs, pupils learned about the unique characteristics of Japan. A copy of the Rescript and a photograph of the emperor and empress, which were distributed to all schools, formed the basis of nationalistic rituals, designed to instil a view among students and their parents that education was for the state rather than for individuals. Failure to defer to the Rescript resulted in official punishment. Below is an ex-pupil's recollection of the Rescript in the early 1930s.

> . . . we used to have assembly every morning out of doors, in front of the school shrine. The school had its own little shrine in the courtyard, and inside it there was a picture of the emperor and a scroll containing the Imperial Rescript on Education. Every morning we had to line up before the shrine, and the headmaster – he was what you might call a fanatical Shintoist – used to come and chant a long litany. I can hear his great booming voice even now. Of course we didn't understand a word he said . . . but I can still remember parts of it to this day, phrases about the first emperor coming from heaven to govern the nation, and so on. (Morris-Suzuki 1984:18)

After the Rescript on Education was issued, the MOE increased its control on the school curriculum and from 1903 produced textbooks on moral education, and Japanese language, history and geography, which, until then, had only required approval from the MOE. Intellectuals and teachers accused the state of virtually designating particular knowledge as the 'truth' and of constraining the freedom of academic study. Anything in the school curriculum that contradicted the Rescript on Education was challenged by the state, which not only requested that it be rectified, but also punished the person concerned.

Expansion of Schooling: Primary, Vocational and Tertiary

Japan's industrialisation progressed during the Sino-Japanese War (1894–5) and the Russo-Japanese War (1904–5). The government's project to achieve an imperial power status commensurate with those of the Western powers was well under way. While enhancing the ideological aspects of schooling through the Rescript, the MOE endeavoured to improve the nation's capacity to manage advanced technology. This involved extending the period of compulsory schooling from four to six years (in 1907), and expanding post-primary vocational education and tertiary education. Growing economic prosperity enabled these attempts to be implemented.

In 1905, 86.9 per cent of children attended four-year compulsory schooling, up from 52 per cent in 1896.[5] This suggests that by this time Japan was turning the majority of school-aged children into imperial subjects through primary education. The increased school attendance was a result of industrialisation, which brought relative economic prosperity to many ordinary people. Industrialisation provided more urban employment opportunities, and motivated individuals to obtain higher levels of schooling. The economic prosperity also enabled the government to provide subsidies to individual schools and for teachers' salaries, and, most importantly, to introduce free primary schooling for all. Consequently, primary-school attendance was further enhanced.

Recognising an urgent need for medium- and lower-level technicians in industry, the government reorganised post-primary schooling for non-elites, through the Vocational Schools Ordinance of 1899 (*Jitsugyōgakkō-rei*) and the Specialised Schools Ordinance of 1903 (*Senmongakkō-rei*). The government provided subsidies to promote these schools. The existing multiple-track schooling (academic education which led to universities, and vocational education) was further consolidated by an expansion of the university sector (four more imperial universities) and of higher schools (*kōtōgakkō*), which were created to offer preparatory courses for entry to the imperial universities (see Figure 2.1).

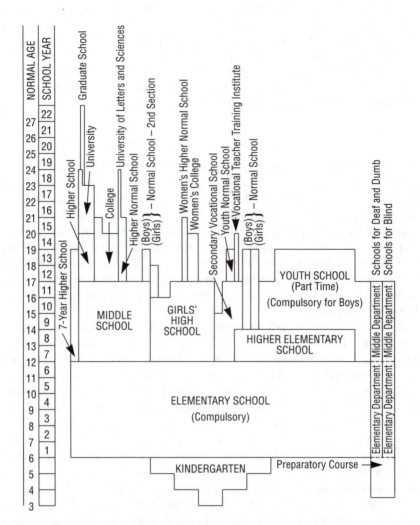

Figure 2.1 The Japanese school system in 1937
Source: Passin (1982), p. 308 (© 1982 Kodansha International Ltd. Reprinted by permission. All rights reserved.)

Post-primary Schooling for Girls

Girls were denied access to middle schools that would eventually lead to universities where the nation's elites were educated. Post-primary schooling for girls was separate from that for boys. After completing primary education, girls could choose to attend normal schools, private secondary schools, or government girls' secondary schools.

In the 1870s missionaries established several post-primary schools for girls in various parts of Japan, providing teachers from Anglo-Western countries. The early Meiji leaders also had a liberal vision for girls' education, and established a public post-primary Tokyo School for Girls in 1872, with assistance from American women teachers. It was closed down five years later and the students were absorbed into the Normal School for Women (Usui 1994:172). By the mid-1890s, however, there were eight public high schools for girls. In 1900 the central government requested the local governments to establish at least one secondary school for girls in each prefecture. This move, as well as the country's growing industrialisation, resulted in 156 public and 53 private secondary schools for girls by 1912, and 487 public and 176 private secondary schools for girls by 1926 (Hara 1995:99). The philosophy of secondary education for girls at the time was primarily 'good wives and wise mothers'.

The multi-track system of schooling based on gender meant that girls did not have access to universities. At the turn of the century, the only tertiary educational institution open to girls was the government Higher Normal School for Women in Tokyo (the present Ochanomizu Women's University). Private tertiary educational institutions for women were established by various prominent individuals. Ms Ume Tsuda established the forerunner of the present Tsuda Women's College in 1900, and Mr Jinzō Naruse, a Christian minister educated in the US, the Japan Women's University in 1901 (Nakajima 1989). A women's medical school and a school for fine arts were also established around this time. Tsuda was one of the five young girls that the early government (1871) sent to the US over a ten-year period to study. On her return to Japan, Tsuda was disappointed with the type of education available to girls ('good wife and wise mother'), and started Tsuda College to provide professional and academic education for women (Yamazaki 1989).

Taishō Liberalism and Educational Reform

Taishō Democracy refers to the relatively liberal political tendencies that emerged after the establishment of the Taishō emperor in 1912. Recession and the rising cost of living led to the formation of various civil movements (e.g. a movement for the protection of the Constitution, labour unions, and the suffrage movement), which argued for greater participation by ordinary people in politics. While their demands were within the framework of the Imperial Constitution, the government feared that they might develop into a socialist movement, and issued the Peace Preservation Law (*Chian Iji Hō*) in 1925 in order to restrict freedom of thought and belief. Workers and farmers still created nationwide organisations in support of their interests.

The Extraordinary Education Committee (*Rinji Kyōiku Kaigi*), established in 1917 in order to meet the new needs of the changing society, introduced two major changes. One was an adjustment of the education system to meet the needs of the growing industrial sector; and the other was an increased emphasis on militaristic nationalist education.

First, education for industrial needs was strengthened at all levels of education. Vocational subjects (e.g. abacus, drawing) were made compulsory at upper-primary schools. Girls were required to study sewing and domestic science. Existing private post-secondary institutions (often professional and vocational in nature) were granted university status in 1918. The government established ten higher schools, six higher technical schools, four higher agricultural schools and seven higher commerce schools. In order to meet industrial requirements, and in the face of the increased number of middle-school graduates, the educational track for the elite was consolidated. Higher schools, which had been preparatory schools attached to imperial universities, became separate general education institutions. Higher schools not only prepared selected young men academically; like the British public schools, they also provided gentlemanly cultivation through a distinctive student culture (Roden 1980). Higher schools started accepting those who had skipped a year at middle school, shortening the length of study required for university graduation; and seven-year higher schools were established. Concurrent with the expansion of the university sector, the imperial universities called for autonomy.

Second, the government devised measures that enabled it to use education more effectively for its political agenda. At primary schools moral education was strengthened. Drilling by military officers was introduced to schools, and military service for normal-school graduates was increased from six weeks to one year. Military service for students of middle schools or above, who had largely been exempt, was now only deferred. While the MOE offered to pay a portion of primary-school teachers' salaries (which had until now been borne by local governments), it in return expected teachers to discharge their 'national' duty to educate the imperial subjects. The MOE decided to use adult education programs (*shakai kyōiku*, literally 'social education') in order to cultivate patriarchal family values and the imperial education ideology, which it hoped would limit civil movements. The existing young men's associations (*seinen-dan*) were integrated under a national body. Much later the MOE and Ministry of Defence established a youth training institute for working youth with primary-school education, which emphasised military training.

The Taishō 'New Education' Movement

Taishō liberalism prompted grassroots-level liberal movements in education. Liberal educationalists espoused the so-called New Education (*Shin Kyōiku*), and introduced Western educational theories and practices. Deploring uniformity, teacher-centred schooling and the emphasis on the mechanical transmission of prescribed knowledge in the existing schooling, the proponents of New Education believed that children were innately good; and urged schools to respect children's individual characters, initiative and creative capacities.

Examples of liberal education abound. Besides numerous existing schools that adopted the New Education approach, experimental private schools were established by individuals such as Masatarō Sawayanagi[6] (Seijō School in 1917) and Motoko Hani (Jiyū Gakuen in 1921). The experience of one such school, Tomoe Gakuen, is vividly described in an ex-pupil's book, which has been popular with young people both within and outside Japan:

> . . . But here (at Tomoe Gakuen) it was quite different. At the beginning of the first period, the teacher made a list of all the problems and questions in the subjects to be studied that day. Then she would say, 'Now, start with any of these you like.' So whether you started on Japanese or arithmetic or something else didn't matter at all. Someone who liked composition might be writing something, while behind you someone who liked physics might be boiling something in a flask over an alcohol burner, so that a small explosion was liable to occur in any of the classrooms . . . As for the pupils, they loved being able to start with their favourite subject, and the fact that they had all day to cope with the subjects they disliked meant they could usually manage them somehow . . . (Kuroyanagi 1982:29)

Like-minded educationalists established the Century of Education Group, the core group for liberal education movements, and Children's Hamlet Primary School, which implemented its principles. These attempts had a significant influence on teaching methods and schooling generally.

Girls' education benefited from the prevailing New Education philosophy. Hara (1995:100–2) recounts her own experience of a Tokyo public secondary school for girls, which she entered in 1928. The school was highly influenced by the New Education movement. It offered modern facilities and teaching methods, which stressed independence, self-study and self-reliance, under a principal who was an advocate of women's rights.

The influence of the New Education movement was largely limited to private schools, some government schools and to those attached to normal schools, which mainly took children from wealthy families. They did not address contradictions in the wider society, or directly challenge the state control of schooling. Their avoidance of overtly challenging the official education policy was likely to have been deliberate, since such a challenge would have prompted government suppression. Tomoe Gakuen (1937–45) avoided publicising its own practices to avoid attracting the authorities' attention (Kuroyanagi 1982:192).

The First Teachers' Union: Keimeikai

Another liberal move in education in this period was the establishment of teacher unions. Although teachers participated in the movement for a modern parliament and demanded higher wages and status as early as the 1880s, it was in the midst of labour disputes after World War One that teachers formed small-scale unions across the country in the name of defending their living standards. One of them, *Keimeikai*, formed by primary-school teachers in Saitama prefecture in 1919 with Yasaburō Shimonaka as its leader (Nakano 1989), later extended its activities nationally.

The *Keimeikai* issued 'four principles for educational reform': popularisation of education, equal educational opportunities, autonomy of education, and dynamic educational organisations. Progressive at the time, the union stated that 'the right to receive education is a basic human right. Education is not an individual duty but a societal one, and equal educational opportunities should be pursued'. It demanded 'public funding for education from primary to tertiary levels (fees, school textbooks, minimum living expenses)', proclaimed that it is 'the national (not local) government's responsibility for providing educational expenditure', and advocated that 'universities open up to the public and allow the admission of women'. It proposed that teachers' autonomous unions form education boards and democratise educational adminis-tration, and that education boards (both local and central) be involved in drafting educational legislation (Tsuchiya 1995).

The *Keimeikai* opposed uniform imperial education and sought democ-ratisation of educational administration, while obtaining basic rights for teachers. The *Keimeikai* won a degree of influence (its bulletin had over 2000 readers at one time), but it eventually disbanded in 1927. This was in part because it failed to meet the members' demand for improved working conditions and suffered from organisational weaknesses (Tsuchiya 1995).

Ultranationalism and Militarism in Education

External expansion of its territory into Asia and the horrific oppression of its own people within the country were two measures that the government adopted to counter the fallout of the world depression. Education was to play a crucial role in effecting the state control of thought, both within and outside schools. The government effectively used schooling as a political means to mobilise the people for the military expansion.

Research at universities faced increasing restrictions from the government. In the late 1920s several Marxist scholars were expelled from universities. The government established a committee (*Kyōgaku Sasshin Hyōgikai*) to seek measures to further consolidate the imperial ideology through education, and to develop manpower for national security. The Bureau of Thought (created within the MOE in 1934) issued the Principles of the National Policy (*Kokutai no Hongi*) in 1937, and the 'Ways of Japanese Subjecthood' (1941). The MOE's National Spiritual Mobilisation Policy (*Kokumin Seishin Sōdōin*) enhanced the place of military drills within schools, and a vigorous dissemination of the imperial ideology was conducted through school education and adult education groups. By the late 1930s this initiative involved local administrative offices. With the establishment of the Imperial Rule Assistance Association (*Taiseiyokusan-kai*) in 1940, indoctrination took even more intensified forms.

The military intervened in the MOE's role of designing school curricula, and demanded that it include the principles of the security of the imperial state and basic military science. The following extract describes the military drills at a middle school in the then colonial Taiwan:

> . . . The (middle) school employed an ex-army officer, now on the reserve list, to look after their training programme, and there was also a serving army captain who came in once a week to put the boys through their paces. During the first three years the drill consisted mainly of square-bashing and exercises with wooden model guns, but from the fourth year onwards they were trained in the use of real weapons. For all their love of war games, the boys found the novelty of military exercises soon wore off. Week after week there were the same repetitive drills to go through, the same dusty parade ground was filled with the same sweaty, reluctant teenagers . . . (Morris-Suzuki 1984:29)

By 1941 military drills had become compulsory from primary school to university.

In March 1941 national schools (*kokumingakkō*), which aimed at 'providing general education and basic training in accordance with the way of imperial state', replaced primary schools. The curriculum centred on the imperial ideology, focusing on cultivating the personal attributes of the ideal subject. Textbooks were full of patriotism and the need for national security, while the majority of music textbooks contained military songs.

To what extent moral education across the curriculum was effective in instilling loyalty to the imperial state amongst individual youths is open to debate. One can only assume that it largely succeeded in preventing most of them from expressing overt disagreement with the state, but that there were individuals who secretly did not accept it. Below is a passage that describes how boys were making decisions about their futures in mid-1940:

> . . . A lot of boys decided at that time to specialize in science subjects, because they reckoned that science students would be the last ones to be called up if it came to all-out war. Although I'd admired the soldiers and pilots whom I'd met in Taiwan, I was no more keen on the thought of joining the army than the rest of the boys . . . (Morris-Suzuki 1984:40).

Quiet resistance to the state's expectations was also visible among teachers at individual school levels, a point we take up next.

Resistance: The Essay Writing Education Movement

The government's concerted efforts to promulgate the official ideology through schooling were unable to eliminate all opposition to it. Resistance to the government ideology was observable at the individual school level. One initiative was the Essay Writing Education Movement, which posed an indirect challenge to what the state advocated. The other was a more direct attack on the state education policy by (unofficially) unionised teachers.

The Essay Writing Education Movement (*Seikatsu Tsuzurikata Kyōiku Undō*) refers to a diverse grassroots educational movement of the 1930s. Although essay writing had always been a part of the study of Japanese, individual teachers were able to exploit the absence of official textbooks in essay writing and to shift the focus from formalism in writing towards greater creativity. Teachers encouraged students to learn to write about their immediate lives, and in so doing to develop the ability to comprehend the present realities in a critical way. In describing the immediate reality, students learned to be critical of the situation (as well as improving their writing skills), and obtained the motivation and the practical capacity to enrich their own daily lives. For instance, peasants' children were then suffering from the impact of the rural recession. While illustrating their immediate experience of the poverty and struggles of their families, children saw that there was something wrong with their lives and explored the causes of the problems. Like-minded teachers published professional journals such as *Tsuzurikata Seikatsu* (1929), exchanged a collection of student essays, formed an association, and organised study group meetings. Approximately 10,000 teachers were estimated to have participated in this movement (four per cent of all primary teachers at the time). In promoting this critical spirit across the curriculum, the movement challenged a uniform and oppressive education imposed by the state.

The Essay Writing Education Movement presented a subtle challenge to, and a criticism of, the state-imposed schooling. The government left the movement to flourish until it sensed the danger inherent in its existence. Although the government suppressed teachers active in the movement, the tradition of the movement was later revived by a dedicated teacher who started a journal called *Yamabiko Gakkō* shortly after the war (Muchaku 1951; Kokubun 1951).

Resistance: Teachers' Opposition

Another form of resistance to the state's imperial education program was a continuation of the direct and vocal attack on the state policy by unionised teachers. Since labour unions were illegal, teachers formed their own in an unofficial capacity in 1930 (*Nihon Kyōiku Rōdōsha Kumiai, Kyōrō* in short), with 26 prefectural branches. The union's journal was read nationally, as well as in Korea and Taiwan. *Kyōrō* maintained contact with an international organisation of educational workers (the Education Workers International) and won support from the Japan Congress of Labour Unions (*Nihon Rōdō Kumiai Zenkoku Kyōgikai*).

Kyōrō announced its socialist-oriented platforms,[7] and presented 92 concrete demands in the areas of economy, conscription, education, children and politics. For example, it opposed the government certification of school textbooks, and called for teacher autonomy to select subjects and textbooks, 40-pupil classes, and provision by the national government of clothing, lunches and educational necessities to poor children. The union also called for basic labour rights for teachers: the freedom to participate in union and political activities, and the right to strike.

The union's research institute, the New Educational Research Institute (*Shinkō Kyōiku Kenkyūsho*), actively conducted group projects that centred on a critique of nationalist state education and the state-authored textbooks, which were undergoing their third revision. Union activities were later curtailed by the government, which prohibited several issues of the Institute's bulletin and dismissed active teachers. The union then went underground until the end of the war, but formed a basis for the post-war development of teacher union movements, as we shall see later. Although the union's activities were thus transitory on the public scene, they were significant in that the union presented some resistance to the expansionist policies and imperial ideology in schooling (Tsuchiya 1995).

Schooling During World War Two

The beginning of the Pacific War in December 1941 was followed by the announcement of the Education Policy for Greater East Asia (1942). The Policy aimed at turning the whole population into the loyal subjects who would lead the construction of the Greater East Asia Co-prosperity Sphere. It proposed concrete measures to create the manpower required for the national defence and associated industries. As a result of the war situation, the government postponed the implementation of eight-year national schooling; it now required a shorter period of middle schooling for higher levels of education, as well as military service for students of higher schools, higher specialist schools and universities; and took fewer numbers of university students in the arts. By late 1943 university students were in active military service.

In 1944 the student mobilisation into labour service became permanent. An ex-pupil at a girls' school in then colonial Korea remembers her contribution to the war effort in 1944:

> So from the Third Form onwards Ayako spent almost half her time in silk-reeling factories or on farms, where her task was to catch grasshoppers – not only to protect the crops from their ravages, but also because grasshoppers, boiled with soy-sauce and sugar, make a strongly flavoured and protein-filled sweetmeat. (Morris-Suzuki 1984:148)

Students' working hours were later extended to 12 hours a day; and those over 16 years old started to work overnight. Schooling thus ceased to function altogether at this point. Fearing an imminent attack on mainland cities, the government evacuated pupils to villages. In March 1945 schools stopped operating completely. In May the government issued the Wartime Education Ordinance, which urged each school to organise a fighting unit. Atomic explosions over Hiroshima and Nagasaki were followed by Japan's unconditional surrender on 15 August 1945. The defeat was a military defeat of imperial Japan and of imperial education.

Colonial Education in Taiwan and Korea

Modern Japan is the only non-Western nation that held colonial territories. Japan's colonial education was an extension of its domestic education policy, which tried to produce loyal imperial subjects and consolidate the power of the ruling establishment. Colonial education also sought to 'Japanise' people in colonial territories so that, the government claimed, local people would enjoy the benefit of the imperial state. This meant that local people were to adopt Japanese cultural mores and abandon their own heritage.

Taiwan became Japanese territory in 1895. In the beginning the colonial office taught Japanese language and moral education at Japanese Language Schools. In 1898 common schools (*kōgakkō*) were established for basic primary education of six years for children over eight years old. Twenty years later schools for secondary education (four-year higher schools and three-year higher schools for girls) were established, along with vocational schools, normal schools and specialised colleges. In 1922 the so-called integration was initiated, whereby Taiwanese and Japanese children would attend the same schools. In reality, however, separate schools operated on the basis of Japanese language proficiency, and schools above secondary education institutions had a quota for Taiwanese students.

As the Sino-Japanese War expanded, the colonial authority intensified measures to 'Japanise' Taiwanese children. Use of Japanese language and visits to Shintoist shrines (then the official religion of the state) were required. Common schools were renamed national schools, as in mainland Japan. Branches of the Imperial Subject Service Society (*Kōmin Hōkō Kai*) were established all over the island in order to promulgate the ideology through adult education. From 1942 many young Taiwanese men were mobilised as Japanese imperial soldiers to South East Asia and the South Pacific islands. Tsurumi (1977) provides a detailed study of Japanese colonial education in Taiwan.

Although a similar system of colonial education existed in Korea, the Koreans resisted more vigorously, and maintained a greater anti-Japan sentiment than their Taiwanese counterparts. Korea became Japan's protectorate in 1905 and was annexed in 1910. The 1911 Ordinance made education for Korean children separate from that for Japanese children in Korea. Schooling for Korean children emphasised ethics, Japanese language, and Japanese history and geography, while denying them the opportunity to study Korean language and history.

In 1919 the Korean people's independence movement forced the authority to reconsider its policy. The 1922 revised Ordinance announced that formal discrimination was to be abolished, and that Korean and Japanese children were to be integrated into 'the same school system'. The 'equality of opportunity' embodied in the 1922 education reform denied Korean children education in their mother tongue, as well as studies of their history and culture. The overt assimilation policy was strengthened further. With the 1938 revised Ordinance, students were expected to use only Japanese language at school. Adults were expected to recite the 'Imperial Subjects' Oath'. The National Spiritual Mobilisation Association set up branches all over the peninsula. Korean people were forced to adopt Japanese names, and drafted into both military and labour service.

Post-war Education

Post-war schooling started amid social chaos. Cities contained many homeless orphans, and children fortunate enough to have families were in danger of starvation. Many schools had been destroyed. Some children attended classes outdoors, while others participated in one of the three daily shifts of classes. The MOE was desperate to restore the operation of schooling, and issued, as early as mid-September 1945, a new education policy that advocated 'maintenance of the national policy' and 'construction of a peaceful nation'.

By the end of 1945, the General Headquarters of the occupation forces (GHQ) ordered that militarist and nationalist ideology be removed from the school curriculum and textbooks; that world peace and human rights (such as freedom of thought, speech and belief) be taught; and that militarist and nationalist teachers be removed from service. These moves were decisive. Schools immediately stopped teaching moral education, Japanese history and geography. The MOE instructed that certain parts of textbooks be censored with black ink. To children and teachers the ink-painted textbooks symbolised defeat in war and the upcoming change that was to take place in education.

The Occupation Authorities' Agenda: The US Education Mission

At the GHQ's request, the US sent the 27-member US Education Mission to Japan to advise on the new education system in March 1946. The Mission's report received complete endorsement from the GHQ. The report stated that the problems of the pre-war education lay in: (1) excessive centralisation; (2) multi-track schooling, which advantaged the elites; (3) uniformity and knowledge-dissemination-based teaching; (4) bureaucratic authoritarian administration; and (5) the complexity of the Japanese writing systems.

It recommended that the following directions be considered for the new education:

1 that schools respect the individuality of children, provide equal opportunity based on ability, and remove standardisation of the curriculum and teaching methods;

2 that schools adopt the Japanese phonetic alphabet, as well as the roman alphabet, restricting the number of Chinese characters;

3 that the MOE establish a single-line 6-3-3 school system (i.e. six primary, three middle-school and three high-school years) with nine-year compulsory education and co-educational settings, accommodate

all those who wish to pursue upper-secondary education, exempt tuition fees, and adopt publicly elected education boards;

4 that schools introduce new teaching methods and a new subject called 'social studies'; and that current teachers be retrained and granted the freedom to organise themselves. New teachers are to be educated at universities;

5 that the MOE encourage adult education; and

6 that universities be open to the public, and emphasise general education.

The report's democratic principles were mostly welcomed by teachers and education officials, and were to exert a profound influence.

The Committee of Educational Professionals (*Kyōiku Senmonka Iinkai*), established by the Japanese government, supported most of the Mission's recommendations. There were a few differences. One was the Committee's request for a new Rescript on Education to replace the old one, which would set out a new direction for democratic education. The other was that the teachers' organisation be a non-labour union.

The MOE, originally not enthusiastic about the coming reforms, issued a document called 'New Guidelines for Education'. These acknowledged the limitations of pre-war education, and stressed respect for humanity, individuality and democracy. Teachers supported the MOE's new approach in the guidelines, not so much in the content as in the fact that the MOE did not impose the guidelines but encouraged teachers to use them as a point of discussion. In this respect, the document did have some impact at the school level.

The Education Reform Council (*Kyōiku Sasshin Iinkai*) was established as an advisory body to the Prime Minister in August 1946 at the request of GHQ, which by then had received the US Mission's report. Many of the new Council's members came from the Committee of Educational Professionals mentioned above. The Council was not only the first post-war education-related council reporting to the cabinet, but also an autonomous body free from bureaucracy. The Council submitted 35 reports and two recommendations over a six-year period, which became the basis for much of the central legislation regarding post-war education.

The 1947 Fundamental Education Law

On 31 March 1947 the Fundamental Education Law (*Kyōiku Kihonhō*) was issued, establishing new directions for education that would replace the pre-war Rescript on Education, and setting out the principles of the education reform that would be based on the new Constitution.

The most serious hindrance to the process of establishing the Fundamental Education Law was people in the bureaucracy and the government (including the Prime Minister and the Minister of Education in
November 1945) who publicly acknowledged the merits, and supported
the maintenance, of the Rescript on Education. This is not surprising if
one recalls the MOE's first post-war announcement, which supported the
coexistence of 'national policies' and a 'peaceful nation'. Support for the
Rescript continued to be announced, however, even after the GHQ
issued various ordinances in criticism of the system of pre-war militarist
education. For instance, the Head of the Bureau of School Education
within the MOE stated as late as February 1946 that the Rescript was
consistent with core universal morals.

The GHQ also agonised over what to do with the Rescript. The
Australian Foreign Ministry (which took the toughest stance on imperial
Japan in the war criminal courts) sent to the US government a memo
entitled 'Re-education of the Japanese People: Unofficial Notes'
(October 1945) which urged that the Rescript be either rewritten
completely or discarded. The Civil Information and Education Bureau
(CIEB), on the other hand, concluded that the Rescript itself was not at
fault but that its use by the militarist government was; and recommended
that the rituals associated with the Rescript, but not the Rescript itself, be
abandoned. Consequently, it decided to consider a new Rescript on
Education which would deny the divine nature of the emperor, rather
than discarding it altogether. Following this, drafts for a Rescript were
prepared. The Head of the CIEB and the then Minister of Education
agreed that a new Rescript would be most effective in providing spiritual
guidance for the Japanese people.

The US Mission report did not directly criticise the Rescript, only
suggesting the abolition of the Rescript-related rituals. Its avoidance of
an overt critique of the Rescript might have been due to its consideration
of the US's emerging policy to support the continuation of the emperorship as an institution. The Committee of Educational Professionals
argued that the Rescript was not essentially wrong but inappropriate as
spiritual guidance for the people in the changing circumstances, and
advocated a new Rescript that would set out new educational directions
for a peaceful nation. Against these views, major newspapers (e.g. *Asahi
Shinbun* and *Yomiuri Shinbun*) presented a staunch critique of maintaining a Rescript for that purpose.

Against this background, the fate of the Rescript on Education
remained a topic for lasting debate by the two camps within the Education
Reform Council. One group gave a positive valuation to the Rescript as a
source of traditional Japanese morals, while the other argued that its
feudalism was inappropriate for the democratic society that the state

was seeking to build. In the end, the majority vote in September 1946 decided that a new Rescript on Education would not be issued, and that the new Constitution (to be promulgated within two months) would state that the fundamental principles of future education must be in accordance with the Constitution. In the following month, the MOE issued an instruction that all Rescript-related rituals be stopped in schools.

The Fundamental Education Law was developed in close conformity to the new Constitution. The Constitution, issued in November 1946, adopted three principles: sovereignty of the people, fundamental human rights and abandonment of war. Article 26 specified that everyone possesses the right to receive education as a fundamental human right. The Fundamental Education Law is like the educational constitution, 'the post-war declaration on education', as it was aptly described by the then Education Minister on its submission to the Parliament. All legislation related to education now had to conform to the Law. It repudiated the pre-war education based on the old Rescript, and set out new democratic principles of education, peace and human rights. Although the Fundamental Education Law legally nullified the pre-war Rescript, there remained a considerable number of people in the government bureaucracy who supported the Rescript. It is interesting that a bill to confirm the invalidity of the Rescript had to be passed through both the upper and lower houses as late as June 1948, 15 months after the Law was issued. The government then started to retrieve the imperial Rescripts from the schools.

The Realities of the New Education

The 1947 School Education Law set out a single-track 6-3-3-4 system of schooling (i.e. the 6-3-3 system plus four years of university; see Figure 2.2). The most serious problem was the economic and material conditions that made the daily operation of compulsory schooling almost impossible. The restoration of school buildings progressed only slowly, and there was a constant lack of teachers. Children were malnourished. Besides, the new institution of middle schools (which now offered compulsory education) meant that the total number of classrooms was grossly insufficient to accommodate a further one million children. Further, the government reduced the budget for implementing the 6-3 component of schooling by a factor of eight. The new education system therefore had to rely on donations, voluntary labour and the sale of village properties.

In 1948 the new system of upper-secondary education integrated pre-war middle and vocational schools and pre-war girls' high schools under the term 'high school' (*kōtōgakkō*), and the same status was accorded to

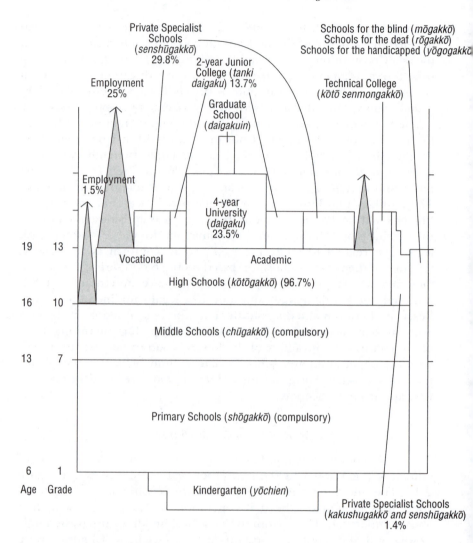

Figure 2.2 The Japanese school system in 1995
Sources: Japan, Monbushō (1994), p. 14; Japan, Monbushō (1995a), pp. 26, 27, 596, 608, 609

all. Co-education and the comprehensive high-school format were adopted by many. In the following year the new system of tertiary education integrated several types of pre-war tertiary education institutions (imperial universities, national and public colleges, normal schools, private universities and professional schools), under the broad headings of four-year university and two-year junior colleges. Educational administration was radically decentralised. Local education boards, elected by local residents, now took over from the MOE a considerable portion of the decisions (such as teacher appointment) relating to the daily operation of schools.

Not only new teaching methods (such as discussions) but also new lesson content appeared in schools. In 1947 the MOE issued the Course of Study (*Gakushū shidō yōryō* – an outline of curriculum), which delineated the aims and a set of standards for the content that teachers were expected to cover. It encouraged the independence of individual teachers in planning and implementing lessons. The Course of Study was to be used as a 'guideline' – it was not a requirement imposed from above. Teachers were expected to arrange the curriculum to suit the realities of the local community and its children. Such attempts later led to the development of regional educational planning. The subject in the new curriculum that attracted the most attention was social studies, introduced for the first time in 1947.

The Japan Teachers' Union (Nikkyōso)

By 1946 there were 1200 unions in Japan, involving over 40 per cent of workers. This trend influenced teachers, who were trying to cope with the scale of change brought to post-war education. Teachers formed two separate unions, the All Japan Teachers Union (*Zenkoku Nihon Kyōin Kumiai*, or *Zenkyō*) and the Japan Educationalist Union (*Nihon Kyōikusha Kumiai*, or *Nikkyō*).

Zenkyō was formed by members of the pre-war *Kyōrō*, the teachers involved in the Essay Writing Education Movement (*Seikatsu Tsuzurikata Kyōiku*), research groups and the Young Teachers' Association. The *Zenkyō* platforms were: 'removal of militarist and ultranationalist education, and contribution to democratic education'; 'higher social, economic and political status for teachers'; and 'establishment of a national union of teachers, and solidarity with the International Union of Teachers'. On the other hand, the more conservative *Nikkyō* consisted mainly of middle-school principals, supported the maintenance of the emperorship and the Japan Socialist Party, and refused *Zenkyō*'s invitation to form a unified national union.

In late 1946 teachers mobilised themselves in support of minimum working conditions. This initiative was eventually absorbed into a larger movement covering public employees. The largest nationwide strike up to that time was planned, but at the last moment cancelled on instructions from the Head of GHQ. The attempt, however, resulted in improved working conditions for all public employees, and laid the ground for the united labour movements to come.

In March 1947 an historic labour agreement was reached between two major teachers' unions and the MOE. As a result, the MOE now recognised teachers' unions as agents for collective bargaining. The agreement included working conditions (such as the prohibition of gender-based discrimination, 42 working hours per week, 16 weeks of maternity leave, and a wage structure determined by the union representatives), and recognised the freedom of unions to pursue their role and of members to be engaged in political activities. This development led to similar labour agreements at the prefectural level.

In June 1947 the Japan Teachers' Union (*Nihon Kyōshokuin Kumiai*, or *Nikkyōso*) was formed from three existing unions. Its platforms were to advance the 'economic, social and political status of teachers' and 'democratic education and the freedom to conduct research', and to 'stand together for the creation of a democratic state'. The priority issue was 'compulsory education for all funded by the national government'. *Nikkyōso* succeeded in gaining an increase in the government's education budget, in diminishing wage differences between regions, and in ameliorating gender discrimination. It issued a white paper on education, and was an active player in the Education Rehabilitation Conference, which consisted of 81 organisations including political parties, labour unions, farmers' unions, students and intellectuals.

The Beginning of Conservatism and Liberal Opposition

The amicable relationship between the MOE and the union did not last long, however. In 1948 the government unilaterally deprived government employees of the right to bargain collectively and to strike. The MOE issued notice that teachers' unions would no longer be able to bargain collectively with the MOE, and that the previous labour agreement was now invalid. With the backdrop of the expansion of communism on the Asian continent, the Occupation decided to restrict labour movements involving public employees, which had been flourishing in post-war Japan, assuming that the unions had socialist ideological foundations and would pose a potential danger to Japan's stability. Against these government moves, educationalists and intellectuals took up the importance of peace education. Collective statements were released by both a group of scientists and the Japan Society of Pedagogy. *Nikkyōso* announced five platforms on peace in 1950: 'establishment of democratic rights, opposition to military bases, independence of ethnic groups, signing of the peace treaty, and the establishment of effective peace education'.

In the 1950s the government tried to increase its 'influence' over educational practice through a series of initiatives. *Nikkyōso* and other progressive organisations interpreted these initiatives (from a conflict theory perspective) as a government conspiracy to increase 'control' over the practice of education, and launched a mobilised opposition. This was the beginning of the liberal opposition to conservatism in the field of education. Education in fact became one of the topics most frequently discussed in the public arena, and we will explore why this has been the case in a summary of this chapter, but for now we turn to an examination of specific conservative initiatives and the opposition to them generated (in particular by *Nikkyōso*) during the 1950s. These include the MOE's attempts to restrict teachers' freedom, to monitor their performance, to dismantle decentralised educational adminis-tration and to standardise textbooks.

First, the 1951 Ordinance Review Committee was formed within the cabinet to examine and modify, if necessary, the institutional systems that were established during the Occupation period. The Committee's proposals on education included the separation of academic courses and vocational courses at the middle-school level; the dismantling of com-prehensive high schools; the abolition of school zoning; the division of two- to three-year specialised tertiary institutions and four-year academic universities; the state's creation of standard textbooks; and the replacement of publicly elected education boards with ones appointed by prefectural governors.

The dominant reaction to the Committee's recommendations among teachers, intellectuals and parents was alarm that the changes would compromise the new system of education that they had accepted with enthusiasm. They recalled the pre-war experience whereby teachers were used to inculcate innocent youths for the benefit of the state, and in 1951 coined the slogan 'We will not send our students to battlefields'. *Nikkyōso* also presented the details of what it considered to be 'an ideal teacher' in a document entitled 'A Code of Ethics for Teachers' (*Kyōshi no Rinri Yōkō*, 1952).[8] Such a strong reaction was raised by two of the recommendations in particular – the appointed education board and the state's creation of textbooks – and by the fact that the Committee failed to address desperate concerns held by parents and teachers at the time (e.g. inadequate buildings for newly introduced middle schools, charges for compulsory schooling, and an inadequate number of high schools). The introduction of vocational education at middle schools and the reorganisation of tertiary education were seen to address the practical needs of the society.

Second, the government commenced to restrict the freedom of teachers. In 1953 the government changed the status of teachers in the compulsory education system to that of national government employees, in order to restrict their political freedom. In 1954, in the name of 'the neutrality of education', the government introduced two bills to revise teacher-related legislation (the so-called 'Two Education Bills'), which would prohibit all political activities of teachers and impose a fine or imprisonment on those who invited others to support or oppose particular political parties. Although *Nikkyōso* organised the first nationwide struggles to oppose the bills in 1954, the government pushed them through after calling the police to the Parliament.

Third, the government introduced the 'Three Education Bills' to the Diet in 1956. These were the bill to establish the Ad-Hoc Council on Education (to consider a revision to the existing education system), the bill on appointed local education boards, and the bill on school textbooks. The opposition to the three bills involved a wide range of people and organisations, including the Association of Primary and Middle School Principals, intellectuals and women's groups, *Nikkyōso*, a group of university presidents, and academic societies. The government again pushed through the bills, having called the police to the Parliament, and eventually established the appointment system for members of local education boards.

The government's fourth conservative move was the Teacher Performance Assessment Program. Under this scheme, principals were to assess individual teachers in terms of their work (on 46 criteria, such as classroom management, student guidance, and clerical work), and their characteristics and abilities (36 criteria, such as honesty, sense of responsibility, and pedagogical effectiveness). The principals were then to submit the assessment to the local education board so that it could be used for future personnel planning. *Nikkyōso* understood that the Program aimed at differentiating teachers and increasing the administration's control, so that the new policies would be implemented effectively. *Nikkyōso* convened an extraordinary meeting and organised a one-day strike. For instance, about 40,000 members of the Tokyo Metropolitan Teachers' Union protested to the Tokyo Education Board, which resulted in a police raid on union executives. A court case stemming from this incident was to follow. Struggles to stop the Program involved other workers and citizens. The 'Citizens' Meeting to Oppose the Teacher Performance Assessment and to Defend Democratic Education' held in August 1958 was the scene of assaults by the police and right-wing groups, and over 100 participants were injured. When *Nikkyōso* organised a nationally coordinated campaign in December 1958, over 440,000 teachers across 40 prefectures participated in it, as well as over two million workers from labour unions in *Sōhyō* (the then largest peak union body, consisting mainly of public employees). The government attempted to contain these moves. The secretary of *Nikkyōso* was assaulted, and some prefectural governments threatened to remove union members and cut their wages. The struggles to oppose the Program represented the largest-scale campaign in the history of education.

Other moves were the MOE's stricter authorisation of school text-books, revision of the social studies curriculum, the introduction of moral education, and the new Course of Study (an outline of curriculum to be covered), which became more prescriptive in nature. The new social studies curriculum was to stress the status of the emperor. The MOE announced that moral education was to be conducted by homeroom teachers once a week, and organised in-service education to advise this. In 1955 the new Course of Study was no longer presented as a tentative plan, but as legally binding.

Education and Economic Growth

In the 1960s the focus of educational policies shifted from the justification of the post-war democratic society and the socialisation of the population towards such a society, to the development of human capital for the nation's economic growth. Since the early 1950s, industrial and business circles had been requesting that education be reorganised to suit the needs of industry. In 1952 the Japan Federation of Employers (*Nikkeiren*) urged that vocational education be strengthened at secondary and tertiary levels. The rapid growth of heavy industry in the late 1950s required effective training of engineers and young workers.

The National Income Doubling Plan (1960) stated that the system of education was to be a means to develop the human resources required for the targeted economic growth. The plan was based on the then popular human capital theory, which assessed education in terms of its contribution to the economy, but which undervalued individual human development. The education budget was thus allocated to the areas that were considered to maximise economic output; and educational costs were borne by individuals (i.e. parents) who, the theory claimed, would receive due return from the education that they invested in. Consequently, educational expenditure by parents increased twofold for primary and middle-school students over the period 1961 to 1964.

The Central Education Council, pressured by the Economic Council (*Keizai Shingi-kai*), announced that schools would take up the development of human resources (for the economy) as a priority task. It distinguished 'low-level human resources' from 'high-level human resources' (which would be five per cent of the population), and decided that the system of schooling would prioritise the training of 'high-level human resources'. The system of education would also aim to inculcate a sense of roles according to the level of human talents, founded on 'merit-based' education. These moves were manifested in the diversification of high schools. In 1962 the system of five-year public technical colleges (*kōtō senmongakkō*) was established to train medium-level technicians by combining high-school and two-year tertiary-level studies. Tertiary programs for science and engineering were expanded to produce a larger number of graduates in these fields.

Another notable initiative by the Central Education Council was to attempt to define what makes the ideal Japanese person, in a document entitled 'The Image of the Ideal Japanese Person' (*Kitai Sareru Ningenzō*, 1966). This included the requirements for the ideal Japanese citizen, which listed respect for the emperor and patriotism. As expected, the report was perceived to signal a revival of pre-war nationalism by *Nikkyōso* and leftist intellectuals, who vigorously opposed it.

In order to effectively implement its human resource plans, the government considered that changes to the system of university management were necessary. However, its draft bill on university administration was abandoned because of nationwide opposition from university staff in 1963. Impetus for the change came from an unexpected source, namely radical student movements on campuses. As a result of the rapid expansion in high-school enrolments, the number of university students doubled and the student/teacher ratio increased from 14 to 18 in the 1960s. The expansion in enrolments was mainly accommodated by private universities, which suffered from poor teaching conditions, and they were forced to raise their fees. By the mid-1960s, students were expressing their disillusionment with the realities of university education (e.g. fees, large classes), and with the government policies that they perceived to be compromising the post-war democracy (e.g. the security treaty, more control over education). Students across the country demanded democratic management of universities and an autonomy based on collaboration among the teaching staff, general staff and students of an institution. Some radical elements insisted on the dismantling of universities, and adopted violence against other groups with different platforms. This provided a justification for the government to legalise its intervention into the management of universities.

Civil Movements in Education

In the 1960s and 1970s, teachers, parents and interested citizens organised grassroots or school-level movements to pursue what they believed to be democratic education. They mounted a successful opposition to the National Academic Achievement Test, demanded 'high school education for all', and challenged the government's textbook authorisation system.

The National Academic Achievement Test

The National Academic Achievement Test was implemented at primary and middle schools between 1961 and 1964. The Test, so the MOE claimed, aimed to examine the relationship between learning conditions and academic achievement and provide data that could be used for improving teaching. The most controversial Test was that for middle schools. All 11th- and 12th-graders were to take the same examinations in five major subjects simultaneously across the country, and the results were to be recorded in the students' school records and kept for 20 years. Teachers argued that the Test would cause middle schools to concentrate overtly on preparation for the Test, and, with parent organisations, started opposing the move.

Opposition to the Test was widespread. For example, over 90 per cent of schools in Iwate prefecture and 80 per cent in Fukuoka prefecture defied the MOE's instruction to implement the Test. The government, in an attempt to contain *Nikkyōso*'s opposition, accused teachers and the union executives, as well as other workers who supported the opposition movement, of criminal responsibility for interfering with government officials in the execution of their duties. Twenty staff members were dismissed. In several prefectures, teachers and parents went to court over the legality of the Test. The early verdicts of local and prefectural high courts were that the Test was illegal, but a 1976 Supreme Court verdict held that the National Academic Achievement Test was an administrative survey conducted by the MOE, and that the MOE's request to local governments to provide the survey results did not contradict the principle of local self-governance of education. These verdicts presented a public critique of bureaucratic intervention in the content of schooling and of the state administration of education. Continued opposition to the Test caused the MOE to implement it in only a sample of schools (20 per cent) from 1965. The Test was to be conducted three-yearly from 1967, but was eventually abandoned in 1969.

The 'High Schooling for Everybody Who Desires It' Movement

A movement called 'high schooling for everybody who desires it' resulted from an increased demand for high schooling by parents and the public in general. This was enabled by the single-track 6-3 system of compulsory schooling and the economic recovery of the 1950s.

Local groups of mothers initiated the demands for 'high school education for anybody who desires it', and eventually organised a national conference (*Kōkō Zen'in Nyūgaku Mondai Zenkoku Kyōgikai*, or *Zen'nyūkyō*) in association with union teachers. The conference demanded the creation of new public high schools, government subsidies to private high schools (many of which had been accepting more students than they could accommodate in order to meet the demand), and an expansion of government financial assistance to needy students. One influential group in this movement was a nationwide non-governmental organisation of mothers and female teachers, *Zenkoku Hahaoya Renrakukai*. Since holding its first national meeting in June 1955, this group has acted on various educational and social issues that they have seen as being important (e.g. free school textbooks; childcare facilities for working parents; educational opportunities for the poor, the handicapped and *buraku* children; free vaccinations; and maternal and child health). The group continues to hold annual meetings at national, prefectural and local levels.

Although parents hoped for an increased number of 'academic' high schools to accommodate all who desired a high-school education, the government established more vocational high schools than academic ones over this period, in accordance with the national policy for economic development. Like many conservatives in the fields of education, the MOE maintained the view that upper-secondary education was to be provided only to 'suitable' youth, and it therefore adopted 'appropriate' selection mechanisms.

The movement did increase the retention rate to high schools (from 57.7 per cent in 1960 to 82.1 per cent in 1970). This outcome, however, was not welcomed by all, and the diverse views on the movement revealed particular positions that various groups held at the time. The idea that upper-secondary education was to be provided to all without entrance examination was not easily accepted by those who held the traditional view that only selected students should receive such education. Not all high-school teachers welcomed the wide range of students entering their schools, which caused practical difficulties that they now had to face. The Association of High School Principals did not provide official endorsement of the movement. Neither did any education-related academic societies, although some individuals gave enthusiastic support to the progressive movement.

Textbook Authorisation

Concerns with the system of state authorisation of textbooks had always existed among teachers and intellectuals. Professor Saburō Ienaga challenged the MOE's system of textbook authorisation in three court cases. In the first case (1965), Ienaga argued that the system was inconsistent with the Constitution and the Fundamental Education Law. In support he cited the fact that his high-school history textbook was not approved in 1963, but that when the same manuscript was submitted in the following year, the MOE requested that over 300 sections be revised. In a 1974 decision the Tokyo District Court found in the MOE's favour. When this decision was appealed in 1986, the Tokyo High Court ordered that Ienaga withdraw his request. In 1993 the Supreme Court confirmed that the MOE's authorisation was legal.

In the second case (1967), Ienaga requested that this 1964 disapproval be overturned and that the sections in the textbook removed under the MOE's authorisation in 1964 be reinstated. This case followed a different path. In 1970 the Tokyo District Court judged that the textbook authorisation system was unjust, on the grounds that people have a right to education and that the state should not engage in unwarranted interference in this right, and supported the plaintiff's demand that the disapproval of the textbook concerned be overturned. The MOE appealed, and the subsequent 1975 Tokyo High Court verdict was also in Ienaga's favour. The case then went to the Supreme Court, which refrained from passing judgement and in 1982 requested the Tokyo High Court to consider the case again. However, in 1989 the Tokyo High Court also refrained from passing judgement, stating that there was little benefit to be gained from considering events which had taken place in the 1960s.

The third case (1984) also challenged the legality of the system in removing a textbook's description of the Japanese army's brutality (in the Nanking massacre, etc.), amid criticism of such censorship from Asian nations. Concerned people, encouraged by Ienaga's move, created a nationwide organisation to support his case, and these movements became major critics of the state control over textbooks and education policies at the time. In a 1989 hearing, the Tokyo District Court gave a verdict only partially in favour of Ienaga, but in 1993 the Tokyo High Court overturned the verdict, judging that some descriptions in the textbook (e.g. the Nanking massacre) were unjust. In August 1997 the Supreme Court handed Ienaga another partial victory. It judged that the authorisation system itself conformed to the Constitution but that the system could produce an illegal outcome if implemented in an unjust way; for example, if it involved excessive government intervention in the details of the textbook's content. The Court ruled that Ienaga was not required to rewrite four of the eight sections in the textbook that the MOE had demanded be modified in order for it to receive authorisation.

One concrete outcome of the citizen-level movement was observed in Tokyo's Nakano Ward. In 1979 residents successfully established a system whereby the local education board members were appointed by the governor through a residents' election. This enabled residents to participate in local educational administration.[9]

Heightened Awareness of Human Rights in the 1970s

Throughout the 1970s human rights emerged as a prominent issue in education. This heightened awareness of human rights in education came from two directions. On the one hand, a series of civil movements and court cases in relation to education in the 1960s caused lively discussions about students' rights to education, and teachers' rights in relation to the state's intervention. On the other hand, the powerful activism of a minority organisation, the Buraku Liberation League, forced schools to re-examine their assumptions and educational practices in relation to *buraku* students (see below) at first, and then to reconsider the human rights of students generally. We will cover the rights of minorities and students with disabilities here, leaving a discussion of students' and teachers' rights to Chapter 5.

The most influential factors in the rise of human rights on the educational agenda were the continued disadvantage that *buraku* children faced, and the *buraku* organisation that mobilised to launch a direct attack on the establishment, including the system of education which it believed marginalised their children. *Buraku* people are descended from the outcastes of the feudal class system. Although the institutional class system was abandoned in the late 19th century, prejudice and discrimination remains strong in employment and marriage. There are said to be approximately three million *buraku* people living in 6000 communities throughout Japan (Takagi 1991:286). Civil rights movements initiated by *buraku* organisations have brought improvements to the *buraku* people in terms of living conditions and in the educational achievement of their young people.[10] Other minority groups (such as Korean residents) have also benefited from the actions of, and gains won by, *buraku* organisations.

The Buraku Liberation League (BLL) is a nationwide *buraku* organisation established in 1955, taking over from a *buraku* liberation committee formed in 1946. The BLL pursued the elimination of discrimination against *buraku* people, both by denouncing individuals or organisations for discriminating against *buraku* people, and by advocating government policies (local and national) to improve social and material conditions for *buraku* people. Its alliance with the Japan Communist Party and the Japan Socialist Party widened its political base. These moves resulted in the Special Measures for Regional Improvement Law (*Tokubetsu Chiiki Kaihatsu Sochi-hō*) in 1969, in which the national government gave financial support for the improvement of *buraku* people's living conditions (e.g. housing, health and welfare) and the educational attainment of *buraku* children over the next 10 years. The Law was renewed every decade thereafter, and was effective for 26 years.

In March 1997, however, it was decided that the Law would not be renewed again, on the basis that sufficient improvements had been achieved.

In education, the so-called *Dōwa* Education programs (egalitarian or assimilation education) were implemented. Initiatives were already under way in 1953 when the national organisation of *Dōwa* Education was established. The 1969 Law then put *Dōwa* Education on the national agenda, and required the government to fund the implementation of programs in the schools. *Dōwa* Education includes a wide variety of activities that aim to redress the discrimination that *buraku* people face. One direction is to improve *buraku* children's school attendance, academic achievement and employment opportunities. Funding was provided for employing extra teachers for schools with high concentrations of *buraku* children. Scholarships were offered to enable children to continue schooling. Another initiative is to educate both *buraku* and non-*buraku* people about the nature of the *buraku* communities and the injustices they suffer, to change the deep-rooted prejudice against *buraku* people. We will refer to *buraku* children's schooling in more detail in Chapter 4.

Education for children with disabilities also emerged in discussions in the 1970s. Although education for disabled children and their adaptation to adult society were discussed by some teachers in the 1950s, it was in 1967, when *Nikkyōso* took them up as a research agenda and created a special study group for them, that the rights of disabled children were first seriously explored. The dominant interpretation became that any child with a disability possessed a potential for development (even if limited); and that they should be given the content and methods of education that would develop that potential. This led to an interpretation that children have a right to receive education according to their individual needs for development, rather than according to their abilities. Concerned teachers and parents demanded appropriate education, welfare and medical treatment to enable the realisation of the potential of every disabled child.

Changes Since 1970

Both the government and business circles wanted a stronger state role in managing the social problems that emerged in the 1970s (e.g. the increased cost of living, heavy taxation and population concentration in the cities). Their expectation of state education was no exception.

Among the Central Education Council's recommendations of 1971, the following changes were implemented. First, the position of vice-principal, with a separate salary scale, became legally recognised in 1974.

Second, it was decided that a new type of university in terms of management and internal organisation, Tsukuba University, was to be established. Third, new graduate colleges of education were established to offer graduate studies for existing teachers.

Nikkyōso, as usual, saw the above changes as attempts by the government to strengthen its control over schooling, and consequently as a threat to democratic education. One needs to understand, at this point, that the relationship between the government (the MOE) and *Nikkyōso* had been based on a deep-rooted mistrust and characterised by constant conflict since a brief amicable period after the war. Any move by the MOE to change the existing education system was interpreted as a threat to the original system of post-war education that *Nikkyōso* upheld as universally democratic. In 1971 *Nikkyōso* established a citizens' federation to promote democratic education, which involved other labour unions and educational organisations. The federation organised branches at prefectural, municipal, town and village levels, and opposed the Central Education Council's recommendations. Another notable move by *Nikkyōso* was the establishment of an independent committee (consisting of academics and practitioners), which examined the existing education system and made suggestions on the future direction of education in several reports. The latest report, entitled 'Education Reform in Japan' (1983), proposed that schools shift their focus from selecting and differentiating pupils to letting them make their own decisions concerning their schooling (e.g. the choice of school, subjects, courses); that rights to lifelong education be guaranteed; that changes to education be initiated by local residents; and that schools maintain an autonomy. These reports provided teachers and other practitioners with reference points for discussion, and in that sense were influential. However, the 1983 report was to be the last significant contribution of the 'old *Nikkyōso*', which had already started to lose influence among teachers. *Nikkyōso* then became embroiled in the reorganisation of peak union bodies, and eventually split into two groups. We will elaborate on this in Chapter 5.

From the beginning of the 1980s the conservative Liberal Democratic Party (LDP) discussed, and made recommendations for, changes to the education system. These suggestions were to be considered by the Ad-Hoc Education Council, as we shall see in Chapter 6.

Textbooks continued to be a topic of controversy in the 1980s. The LDP's bulletin in the first half of 1980 claimed that the descriptions of some issues (e.g. self-defence force, human rights, nuclear power plants, environmental pollution and multinational corporations) in existing textbooks were 'biased' (towards the left). This led to a series of critiques of the LDP's position by the authors of social science textbooks, by groups of academics, and by *Nikkyōso*. Public awareness of the contents of the textbooks was heightened. However, it was international pressure (mainly from Asian nations) that eventually led the government to issue a public statement regarding the criteria for textbook authorisation. The media in China and Korea reported on the history textbook descriptions of events that took place during the Second World War (which underrated the atrocities of the Japanese army); Chinese and Korean citizens and their respective governments protested that these descriptions were not accurate. The MOE recommended that 'more consideration be given in relation to the treatment of historical events in Asia in textbooks, in order to promote international understanding and cooperation'. The textbook issue continues tò be a controversial one.

Summary

The development of modern schooling in Japan over the last 130 years saw two major junctures. One was the initial introduction of modern schooling by the imperial state in the late 19th century, with the transplantation of a few Western models at first, and then later the creation of the kind of 'Japanese' schooling that the state believed to be most effective for the needs of the emerging state. The second was the radical reform of schooling implemented under the supervision of the Allied Occupation authorities after the war. Meiji schooling's foremost goal was to create human resources for the state. The state's nationalist schooling system experienced some resistance (ranging from public demonstrations and announcements by unionised teachers and intellectuals, to essay writing movements conducted at the individual school level); but survived with its philosophy intact until the end of the Second World War. The post-war reforms aimed to dismantle such nationalist elements in schooling, and to pursue a new democratic education system with an emphasis on individual development. The Imperial Rescript on Education, an ideological underpinning of pre-war education, was replaced by the Fundamental Education Law.

The radical departure of the post-war education system from the pre-war one was accompanied by some continuities. At the level of philosophy, policies and systems of education, the post-war education reform was a complete denial and overhaul of the old system. The Rescript was abandoned. Schooling was to be for individual development (rather than purely for that of the state), was open to everybody, and was to work as an agency for democratisation and demilitarisation amongst a confused populace. To receive education became an individual right, rather than a duty. At the level of practice, however, there were continuities. Participation in schooling continued to rise, and the number of educational institutions continued to expand. Japanese schools continued to play more significant roles for aspects of education other than cognitive development (e.g. personal development, manners) than their American counterparts, as we discuss in the following chapter.

At various stages of the development of modern schooling, emphasis was placed on distinctive functions of schooling. Recall the four major functions of modern schooling that we presented in Chapter 1: transmission of knowledge, socialisation, selection and differentiation of people, and legitimation of a particular version of knowledge and a particular system. While modern schooling has always performed all these four functions simultaneously, differences are observable in their priorities at different points in time. Below we have devised six phases to illuminate these changing priorities.

The first phase, the beginning of Meiji schooling (1872–90), emphasised knowledge dissemination and, to a lesser degree, selection of the nation's elites. The government tried to transmit the knowledge required for modernisation by bringing 'enlightenment' to all children (regardless of their backgrounds) through primary schools all over the country. It also offered Western and utilitarian knowledge (e.g. law, engineering, economics) to the select few who were to lead the state as the core members of the central government.

In the second phase (1890–1917), the selection of human resources remained a prominent concern, but this time for medium-level positions in the government, business and industry (rather than the top-level bureaucrats) to assist in rapid industrialisation. A system of multi-track post-primary education (e.g. vocational schools and girls' high schools) was established and expanded. Although the 1890 Imperial Rescript on Education underlined the ideological side of education, it was not until the next phase that the state ideology dominated education at the level of the individual school.

The third phase (1918–45) was characterised by nationalism and militarism. By this time the Rescript on Education's influence on the practice of schooling was profound. State schooling focused on the legitimation of the state ideology and the socialisation of youth for service to the imperial state until the end of the Second World War. It should be noted that various forms of resistance to this focus also existed.

Defeat in the war led to the fourth phase (1945–59). The Allied Occupation force tried to overhaul the pre-war nationalist society and to install democracy in all aspects of the state institutions. Since schooling was utilised as an agent for such a radical change of the whole society, its priority was to legitimate the newly envisaged democracy and to socialise youth towards that democratic society. Another priority was to expand educational opportunities by extending the compulsory schooling period to nine years, so that more people received basic knowledge.

By 1960, however, priorities had shifted to the dissemination of knowledge and the selection of human resources to meet the emerging needs in the economy, which had by then started to 'take off' (fifth phase, 1960–80). This was in part because the post-war democracy was considered to have taken root to a sufficient degree, and in part because business circles became vocal about the kind of schooling they considered necessary. The emphasis on these two aspects of schooling remained strong into the 1980s (sixth phase). Discussions centred on what kind of knowledge was to be taught and what types of human resources were required for the new industrial structure and globalising trends. In addition, the 1980s saw neonationalist views (such as an emphasis on distinctive Japanese characteristics) and a refocusing on past values (e.g. then Prime Minister Yasuhiro Nakasone's education reforms).

Throughout the post-war period, education has been a focus of the liberal opposition, as well as one of the most publicly debated social issues. The liberal opposition to conservative moves (particularly in relation to increased government intervention in schooling) started in 1948 when the MOE began to restrict teachers' labour rights. While the MOE's initial moves derived mainly from the changes in American foreign policy in relation to Japan at that time, the government's subsequent initiatives reflected the sort of education it considered socially necessary. Many of these initiatives have met with fierce opposition from the left, and caused wide discussion among the public.

We suspect that the focus of the liberal opposition on education has arisen because, on one hand, the public have high expectations of schooling, and, on the other, teachers' unions were influential in the post-war union movements and brought their concerns to the centre stage of public discussions. In the first place, nearly all people are involved in state schooling at some stage of their lives, both directly and indirectly (e.g. as mothers demanding that textbooks be free in the 1960s, as elderly pondering over their grandchildren's future education). Second, many individuals (but not all, as we will discuss later in the book) tend to see education as an instrument by which they can attempt to raise their standard of living or obtain self-fulfilment and social status. We saw this in the 'high school for everyone who desires it' movement. Third, the state and business circles have maintained vested interests in schooling in order to achieve an effective selection of human resources for the economy and the public service. Fourth, the state is interested in people's social awareness, that is, how the general public thinks about and sees the world, in order to maintain what it considers to be a harmonious society (e.g. people's consciousness about the self-defence force and world peace). Lastly, the vocal and visible teachers' unions (which have maintained an acrimonious relationship with the MOE) have been able to maintain a heightened public awareness of what occurs at school, by launching constant attacks on government initiatives.

Interpretations of post-war schooling are located on the continuum between two extremes. At one end of the continuum is the position that interprets the so-called 'reverse course' initiatives in the 1950s (e.g. centralisation and the reintroduction of moral education and patriotism) as legitimate and appropriate measures to rectify 'excesses' introduced by the authorities in the late 1940s (e.g. Aso and Amano 1983, Beauchamp and Vardaman 1994). Some of those who take this view consider that many of the changes introduced then were 'imposed' by the Americans, who dominated the Allied Occupation forces; and that such changes were unsuitable for Japan, which possesses different characteristics to the US (e.g. ex-Prime Minister Nakasone). At the other end of the continuum is the position that vigorously upholds the universal virtue of the initial post-war education reform, and contends that subsequent changes to it have been regressive in terms of their perception of democratic education (e.g. Horio 1988). Supporters of this view are inclined to deny the validity of changes made to the original post-war system.

Somewhere in the middle are those who selectively appreciate or reject the changes, depending on the specific circumstances and their own specific interests at the time. For example, some considered that the abandonment of direct election of local education boards was necessary because the practical conditions were not ready for such a nationwide system at that time, although they supported the philosophy of local participation. In 1979, when conditions were considered favourable, Tokyo's Nakano Ward introduced local elections for education board members within the existing legal framework, by passing an ordinance in the Ward's council. The Supreme Court's verdict in August 1997 on the Ienaga case also reflected a position of this type. It considered that the textbook authorisation system itself is legal but can become illegal if it permits excessive government intervention in the determination of the detailed content of textbooks. This judgement generated considerably positive reactions.

The map of the post-war struggles over the practice of education in Japan has been dominated by two mutually antagonistic camps, the MOE, which has proposed a series of educational policies, and *Nikkyōso*, which has provided opposition to these initiatives. However, participation in these struggles by other interest groups independent of the MOE or *Nikkyōso* (e.g. parents' groups, professional associations, local governments) have introduced complexities to this basic picture. The 'high-school education for all' movement and the civil movements surrounding textbook authorisation illustrate this complexity most succinctly.

We will take up this discussion again in Chapter 6, which focuses on changes in educational policies and systems in the 1980s and 1990s. Before that, we will examine contemporary schooling as it is experienced by students (Chapters 3 and 4) and by teachers (Chapter 5).

Further Reading

Amano, Ikuo (1990). *Education and Examination in Modern Japan.* Tokyo: Tokyo University Press.
Duke, Benjamin (ed.) (1989). *The Great Educators of Modern Japan.* Tokyo: Tokyo University Press.
Passin, Herbert (1982, first published 1965). *Society and Education in Japan.* Tokyo: Kodansha International Ltd.
Rose, B. (1992). *Tsuda Umeko and Women's Education in Japan.* New Haven, CT: Yale University Press.

Notes

1 Because of space limitations, we are unable to provide a fuller history of modern Japan. See Hunter (1989) for an introduction to the history of Modern Japan.
2 See Dore (1965) for details.
3 Rubinger (1982) provides an excellent study on this.
4 Hall (1973) provides a biography of Mori.
5 See Aso and Amano (1983:33–8) for detailed statistics on the expansion in school attendance.
6 See Mizuuchi (1989) for the details.
7 *Kyōrō's* platforms were: (1) to defend the educational workers' right to a decent living; (2) to remove reactionary education which favoured capitalists and landlords, and to construct education for the proletariat; (3) to cooperate with other labour unions and farmers' unions; and (4) to cooperate with other teachers' unions both nationally and internationally.
8 The code read that teachers: (1) shall work with the youth of the country in fulfilling the tasks of society; (2) shall fight for equal opportunity in education; (3) shall protect peace; (4) shall act on behalf of scientific truth; (5) shall allow no infringements on freedom in education; (6) shall seek after proper government; (7) shall fight side by side with parents against corruption in society and shall create a new culture; (8) are labourers; (9) shall defend their rights to maintain a minimum standard of living; and (10) shall unite. (English version from Beauchamp and Vardaman 1994:31–4) Despite government criticism of the code, it has been maintained. The World Conference of Teachers (1953) later adopted this as applicable to the

teaching profession throughout the world, along with the 'World Teachers' Charter' (*Sekai Kyōin Kenshō*).

9 The system of direct election of local education board members was abolished in January 1994 when the conservatives gained power in the Nakano Ward Council. This development reflected general trends in the national politics.

10 Shimahara (1991a) and Hawkins (1983) examine in detail the civil movements and the development of government policies in relation to *buraku* people. Both assess the outcomes of the movements and of government policy in a positive light.

CHAPTER 3

Students' Experiences of Schooling, Part 1: Social Groups

There are many actors involved in schooling: students, teachers, administrators, caretakers, parents, policy makers and researchers. All of these actors experience the schooling process quite differently, since the variations in their assigned roles and social positions in the educational system inevitably lead them to perceive the same process from different angles. These actors are not equally equipped, either culturally or socially, to make their voices heard in expressing their perceptions of schooling. It would be fair to say that policy makers, researchers (like ourselves) and administrators are more likely to make their voices heard in public. The voices of students (i.e. children and young people) are not the most powerful, although, it might be argued, they are the most important actors in the schooling process.

In the next two chapters we seek to make the voices of students heard by focusing on their experiences of schooling. Our aims are (1) to show that students from families in varied social locations (in the configuration made up of class, gender, minority status and region) bring different characteristics and expectations to schools, and consequently experience schooling differently; (2) to discuss such diverse experiences in relation to the social processes at the structural level; and (3) to explore the two-way relationships between the microlevel practice of schooling and the external social forces, that is, how and why various social groups obtain differential benefits from schooling. We will do this by introducing many case studies, in particular, observational studies of schools from both English and Japanese sources.

To a large degree post-war Japan has achieved the 'provision' of equal opportunities in education; and many would agree that education is one area in which individuals face the least overt institutionalised discrimination, and where individual achievement largely determines reward. There is, however, a gap between the provision of educational opportunities and the 'consumption' of them, since providing the same opportunities does not lead every young person to use them most effectively to their advantage. We would suggest that patterns exist in their use of educational opportunities. One needs to perceive the personal value of taking up such opportunities, and to be equipped with a certain type and volume of resources, in order to appropriate what 'mainstream' schools (i.e. those that cater mainly for the urban middle class) offer. As we will show, people have different perceptions of the use of schooling, since the instrumental (as distinct from intrinsic) values of schooling for post-school lives vary for individuals belonging to different social groups. People also possess different kinds and levels of resources, due to their family locations in the social hierarchy, and certain kinds of resources (most often those possessed by the urban middle class) are more congruent to, and therefore more helpful in utilising, what schools offer.

Individual children have diverse experiences of, and obtain different benefits from, Japanese schooling, as in any modern Anglo-Western industrial society. We are also aware that there are features of learning and teaching that may be particular to Japanese schools, in comparison with the Anglo-West. Rohlen and LeTendre (1996), for example, provide an excellent collection of teaching and learning processes that occur in diverse settings (e.g. Zen Buddhist monastery learning and the Suzuki music method) throughout the lifespan of Japanese people. Many observational studies of Japanese schools published to date in English have examined those in urban middle-class settings, depicting the characteristic practices that are considered to be 'Japanese' as distinct from Anglo-Western ones, and attempting to explain the reasons for, and the consequences of, such practices. Explanations have been sought in traditional dispositions such as the Confucian ideal, and/or in institutional arrangements and constraints that derive from the fact that Japan was a late developer. The consequences of such 'Japanese' practices have been discussed in terms of both individual development (e.g. cognitive and emotional), and their contribution to the well-being of the society as a whole. We have, however, decided to go beyond this sort of approach, and to emphasise the variations within the students' experiences of schooling. We believe that an emphasis on diversity is more inclusive to the whole population under study than a search for common features, since the latter often results in a simplification and an exclusion of the special features of some groups. We also hope that this approach will bring readers closer to the various actors involved in schooling.

In this chapter, we will first provide a statistical sketch of schooling, and then illustrate features of mainstream schooling processes at the primary, middle- and high-school levels, drawing on several ethnographic studies that are available in English. Readers who are interested in detailed descriptions of classroom-level schooling processes in these schools are encouraged to read the observational studies in English listed as Further Reading at the end of this chapter. Second, we will examine schooling processes as they are experienced by particular social groups (namely girls, the poor, privileged families, youth in correspondence schools, and rural youth), drawing on studies published in Japanese. In so doing we will illuminate differences between these groups in their experiences of schooling and the benefits (if any) that they obtained. In the next chapter, we will focus on the experiences of so-called minority students (Koreans, *buraku* people, and the children of newcomers).

A Statistical Sketch of Japanese Schooling

Before going further, consideration of a statistical sketch of the present state of Japanese schools may be helpful (Japan, Monbushō 1994, 1995a).[1] Japanese children attend primary school for six years from age six. Over 99 per cent of primary schools are government co-educational institutions. The average class size of the nation has become smaller over the last decade, reaching 28.4 pupils in 1995, but typical suburban schools continue to have 35 to 40 pupils in one class. The number of primary pupils has been declining since 1982. School sizes vary, from large suburban schools with over 1000 pupils to rural single-class schools. Mixed-age homeroom classes exist in small rural schools, constituting 2.3 per cent of the total homeroom classes in the country. Around 19 per cent of schools are designated as 'remote rural schools' (*hekichigakkō*), but the number of such schools has been declining due to amalgamation and closure. The number of female teachers has increased to 61.2 per cent.

Of all primary schools, 43 per cent maintain so-called special education homeroom classes (*tokushu gakkyū* or *75-jō no gakkyū*)[2] within the school. These classes accept intellectually and physically handicapped children, as well as those who are physically weak, weak-sighted, or hard of hearing, and those who have speech problems, or are emotionally disturbed. Just over five per cent of all homeroom classes at primary schools are special education classes, accommodating 0.5 per cent of the pupil population. Children who exhibit more serious difficulties attend special education institutions, namely schools for the deaf (*rōgakkō*), schools for the blind (*mōgakkō*) and those that serve students with other significant disabilities (*yōgogakkō*). All of them cater for children of primary, middle and high-school age. Prefectural governments have been required to establish these institutions by national legislation. There are currently 70 schools for the blind, 107 schools for the deaf and 790 schools for the otherwise handicapped. The numbers of the first two types of schools have been in decline.

At age 12, children proceed to middle schools, which are still part of compulsory education. At this point a small number of students start to attend private schools (5.7 per cent), which often allow their students direct entry into their high schools (precluding the need to undergo the formal selection procedure). The average class size is 33.3 students. Around 15 per cent of middle schools are designated as 'remote rural schools'. Forty per cent of middle-school teachers are female, and this percentage has been increasing. About 47 per cent of all middle schools maintain special education homeroom classes. This statistic also shows an upward trend.

The majority of middle-school graduates go on to high schools (96.7 per cent). If those who choose further education at private specialist institutions are included, over 98 per cent of 15-year-olds continue on to further education. The retention rate to high schools varies across regions, ranging from 91.9 per cent in Okinawa prefecture to 98.8 per cent in Toyama prefecture. Given that the vast majority of students complete high-school education, a high-school diploma is a prerequisite for the attainment of even modest aspirations. When students gain admission to high schools by passing the entrance examinations, differentiation of students emerges concretely. One-quarter of students attend private high schools, a handful of which are elite academic high schools. Most high schools are co-educational. Over 97 per cent of high-school students attend day high schools; the remaining few study at evening high schools. Of all high-school students, about 75 per cent are enrolled in academic courses. There are 93 correspondence high schools, and 342 high schools that support correspondence courses. Unlike the situation in primary and middle schools, female teachers account for only 23 per cent of all high-school teachers.

About 38 per cent of high-school graduates go on to tertiary education, which includes four-year universities and two-year junior colleges. Thirty per cent proceed to private specialist vocational institutions (senshūgakkō and kakushugakkō), with the remaining 25 per cent entering employment. The male retention rate to tertiary education is 30 per cent, and for females 45 per cent. Since 1974 more girls have gone on to tertiary education than boys, but as many as 60 per cent of girls in tertiary education study at two-year junior colleges.

There are 534 four-year universities. Almost three-quarters of students are enrolled at private universities. Female students constitute 30 per cent of four-year university students, studying almost exclusively humanities, social sciences, home science and education. The majority of students at the nation's 595 two-year junior colleges are female, and over 90 per cent of junior college students attend private colleges. In contrast to undergraduate education, national universities dominate in post-graduate studies.

Mainstream Schooling

Outsiders are often confused by two contrasting images of Japanese schooling processes presented by the media. On one hand, we hear about monotonous lecture-based learning geared towards the competitive examinations, youngsters attending after-school classes to increase their advantage in exams, an extensive coverage of academic subjects, high levels of achievement in mathematics, and the hierarchical classification of schools and universities that affects students' employment prospects. On the other hand, we hear about noisy classes with little supervision from teachers, where multi-ability small-group activities foster cooperative, carefree and caring relationships among students, and where teachers emphasise egalitarianism. In fact both are accurate illustrations of schooling processes in contemporary Japan: the former depicts high schools, while the latter images are from preschools and primary schools. In between lies the three-year middle school (grades 7 to 9), in which students acquire new skills and attitudes to equip them for the gradual progression to the high school, where lecture-centred and systematic learning and an intensive selection process occur.

Why such a contrast? Is this contrast peculiar to contemporary Japan? We do not think so, although it may be more sharply evident in Japanese schools. As we will illustrate below, the contrast seems to derive from the inherent nature of modern schooling, which is expected to conduct several functions simultaneously. Recall the four functions of schooling that we discussed in Chapter 1. Schools transmit a version of knowledge and culture; socialise children to the adult world; select the young, based on the supposed achievements of individuals, for different positions in the adult society; and legitimate the knowledge and culture that is transmitted in that process. Each stage of schooling emphasises different functions, and consequently displays distinctive, if somewhat contradictory, characteristics.

We will now take you on a brief trip to classrooms at primary, middle, and high schools that mainstream Japanese experience, in order to explore teaching and learning processes. Readers will see the distinctive features at each level of schooling, which reflect the expectations of progressive stages of the transition from childhood to adulthood, as defined by the dominant Japanese society.

Primary Schools: Caring and Egalitarianism

Outsiders immediately notice that the typical class size of urban Japanese primary schools is much larger than in Anglo-Western schools (35 to 40 students in one class with one teacher in charge). Classrooms are noisy and a wide range of behaviours are tolerated, although there seems to be order during classes. Classroom walls are full of posters that convey non-academic 'goals', bearing exhortations such as 'keep the room clean', 'do not forget to bring necessary things to school' and 'be kind to your classmates' (Lewis 1988; Cummings 1980). The absence rate of around one per cent is low compared to that in American schools (Cummings 1980:113). There is virtually no skipping of grades, nor of repeating, unless the student is absent from school for an extended period. There are monthly observation days, which every parent is invited to attend.

Primary schools maintain a cooperative, nurturing and creative learning environment, where every student is made to feel relaxed and is encouraged to find his or her own place. There is virtually no ability-based streaming and little sign of individual competition at this level. Emphasis is placed on 'full participation' in each activity by everyone in the class (Sato 1993; Cummings 1980). Teachers believe that these approaches contribute to a desirable learning environment. Individual academic achievement is not considered to be as important as the collective achievement of the class's non-academic goals.

The primary school's main task is to provide 'whole person' education (Sato 1993; Lewis 1988). This whole person education is conducted both in 'moral education' classes held once a week and, more effectively, as part of school routine, such as through the daily interaction that students experience with their teachers and classmates, classroom cleaning and school lunch responsibilities (Cummings 1980; Tsuneyoshi 1994). When moral education was officially reintroduced into the primary school curriculum in 1959, union teachers held a heated debate and expressed serious concern that it might be a revival of the pre-war nationalistic moral education. However, Cummings (1980) reports that these classes are of a general nature, teaching, for example, respect for all occupations and an egalitarian ethos. Moral education through the school routine is made effective by the long-term and fruitful relationship that a teacher is expected to develop with all of his or her charges. A teacher is normally responsible for the same class over a two-year period. Teachers say, 'The first year, you look and listen, the second year, you can act and do.' (Sato 1993:128). Teachers repeatedly emphasise and practise with their classes 'procedural skills' or 'non-academic and physical skills' (e.g. how to arrange desk contents, how to greet people, how to wash one's hands and correct classroom behaviour); set out weekly and monthly class goals; and review the students' progress towards them. Thus non-academic activities are conducted for whole person education in order to develop and nurture cooperative attitudes, responsibility for one's own possessions, basic procedural skills and group responsibility.

An American educator (Sato 1993) who conducted an ethnographic study of Japanese primary schools expressed surprise at the absence of teacher supervision and at the effective use of 'peer supervision' in various classroom activities. Rather than controlling the students themselves, teachers often delegate authority, roles and responsibilities to class members (Sato 1993; Cummings 1980; Lewis 1988:162; Tsuneyoshi 1994:123). Various class duties are delegated to students on a rotational basis (e.g. health, library liaison, checking classroom cleaning). Everyone is at some time the chief monitor, who ensures that the blackboard is clean after each class and who maintains the class diary, amongst other assorted tasks.

The use of small groups (*han*) in classes both for classroom management and for academic activities is another characteristic of primary-school interaction. These groups comprise a mixture of abilities in that they may include children with leadership qualities, problem children, caring children, and both fast and slow learners. Each member of a small group is expected to contribute to the whole group (Sato 1994; Cummings 1980; Lewis 1988), since teachers believe that one's effort, rather than one's ability, determines academic achievement. Students are also involved in the evaluation of each other's work; for instance, teachers encourage students to applaud a classmate who performs well (Lewis 1988; Cummings 1980). Once the working relationships in these small groups have been established, teachers can rely on these groups as a basis for teaching academic subjects. The routine nature of small-group activities, and the clearly specified roles and procedures, enable teachers to delegate some authority to these groups in order to manage classes. Well-managed classes based on *han* activities, peer supervision and trustful teacher–pupil relationships allow more time for educational programs, since teachers need not spend as much time on classroom management (Peak 1991:191).

The regular curriculum (excluding moral education and special activities such as athletics meetings) covers Japanese, social studies, mathematics, science, music, arts and handicrafts, homemaking and physical education. Seventy per cent of teachers teach all eight subjects, since specialist teachers are rare at the primary level. A larger number of school days per year (240 days in Japan, compared to 180 days in the US) means that the coverage is extensive (Sato 1993:116). Japanese primary schools spend a relatively smaller proportion of total educational time on Japanese, and relatively more time on music, fine arts and physical education. Through these regular subjects, as well as small-group activities and delegation of various responsibilities to students, teachers conduct 'whole person' education.

Ninety-nine per cent of primary pupils attended government schools in 1995 (Japan, Monbushō 1995a:34). There are differences across schools, but such differences are less visible than in the case of middle and high schools. Some primary schools suffer from 'problems' such as bullying, school refusal, and *juku* (private after-school supplementary school) attendance. *Juku* was attended by 23.6 per cent of primary pupils (59.5 per cent of middle-school students), according to the MOE's 1993 survey (*Asahi Shinbun* 17 June 1996). The majority attended small-scale family-run *juku*, which supplement schoolwork, rather than large-scale cram school chains, which offer intensive preparation for exams. Some *juku* actively cater for those who suffer from school refusal (*Asahi Shinbun* 17 June 1996). Chapter 6 will examine bullying, school refusal and physical punishment in more detail. For interested readers, rich descriptions of Japanese primary schools are available in English (Cummings 1980; Duke 1986; Lewis 1988; Sato 1993; Tsuneyoshi 1994).

Middle Schools: Transition to Academic Studies

Middle schools (grades 7–9) take in 12- to 14-year-olds and complete their compulsory education. Until the end of middle school, education is relatively homogeneous, at least across government schools, in comparison to the differentiated schooling that high schools offer at the next stage. Ninety-five per cent of middle-school students attended government schools in 1995 (Japan, Monbushō 1995a:97). It is a transitional period from the caring and nurturing primary-school environment to the systematic academic studies of high school. Middle schools prepare students for high-school entrance examinations, the imminent point of major differentiation in their life courses, while still offering the whole person development that is pursued at primary schools. There is no ability tracking, nor are elective subjects offered. Middle schools still allocate proportionately more time to non-academic subjects and activities than do American schools (Fukuzawa 1994:69).

Students start receiving lessons from specialist subject teachers. Subject teachers are less likely to rely on the kind of intense and long-term relationships that primary-school teachers develop. The curriculum includes Japanese, mathematics, social studies, science, English, music, art, physical education, field trips, clubs and homeroom time. Unlike in primary schools, instruction is intense, fact-filled, and routine-based (Fukuzawa 1994:66); and *han* are no longer common in academic subjects. Teachers adhere to the texts because the amount of material

'Kikuchi, I've lost my Maths homework paper. Can you let me have a look at yours?'

'Sure.'

'Haven't you done it?'

'Not yet.'

'In that case I don't need it.'

'But, haven't you lost yours?'

'I've lost my motivation.'

Source: *Asahi Shinbun* 5 June 1997 © Hisaichi Ishii

that needs to be covered for the high-school entrance examination allows little time for diversion. The peer evaluation that primary schools encourage is replaced by tests that assess the individual's mastery of material in the texts (Fukuzawa 1994).

At middle schools the relationships among students in different grades become more hierarchical. Clubs exemplify the emphasis on hierarchy through senior–junior relations (LeTendre 1994:47). The senior–junior relations are open for abuse by seniors, as is so vividly illustrated by LeTendre's case study (1994). Hierarchy is also observed in the ways teachers and students manage schools through various committees (e.g. health, cultural festival, sports), where students learn to operate in highly organised and hierarchically patterned work environments (LeTendre 1994).

A preoccupation in middle schools with the development of 'the whole person' is observable in 'lifestyle guidance' (*seikatsushidō* or *seitoshidō*). This aims at developing in students 'proper' lifestyles and attitudes, both in and out of school (e.g. use of time, appearance, manners) (Fukuzawa 1994:69; Shimizu 1992), and is based on a close personal relationship between student and homeroom teacher. Teachers try to understand students and to detect 'problems' at an early stage; for example, by having students keep individual 'daily life notebooks', which are reviewed regularly; by circulating a small-group notebook in which *han* members record their thoughts; or by conducting a survey of students' eating habits (Fukuzawa 1994:71–4). As in primary schools, middle-school teachers visit students' homes annually, and parents are invited to the annual Classroom Observation Day (Fukuzawa 1994:76–7).

The organised and disciplined lifestyle thus learned at middle school builds on students' internalisation of social norms, and is required for the study environment at high school (Fukuzawa 1994:85). What middle schools consider to be an 'ideal student' therefore takes on a different focus to what primary schools consider 'ideal' in their students (e.g. liveliness, energy, cooperativeness, carefreeness and a caring nature).

Three recent ethnographic studies are available in English if readers are interested in more vivid descriptions of middle-school experiences (Fukuzawa 1994; LeTendre 1994; Shimizu 1992). Singleton (1967) provides an insight into schooling processes at a middle school in the 1960s.

High Schools: Differentiation

The entry point into high school marks the most important juncture of differentiation for young Japanese. Individual students decide on their preferred schools, and sit for entrance examinations held by local governments, who run the schools in a school district, or by individual

Table 3.1 National distribution of high-school students, 1995
(Unit: 1000 students)

	Total	National	Local govt.	Private	
Day high schools					
Academic	3,428,327	8,516	2,282,880	1,136,931	71.4%
Vocational					22.7%
Agricultural	130,010	304	129,534	172	
Technical	394,653	579	313,817	80,257	
Commerce	439,001	–	316,040	122,961	
Fishery	13,216	–	13,162	54	
Home Science	89,754	40	59,994	29,720	
Nursing	22,540	–	9,479	13,061	
Others	87,382	154	52,934	34,294	1.8%
Day high school total	4,604,883	9,593	3,177,840	1,417,450	
Evening high schools	107,331				2.2%
Correspondence high schools	77,921				1.6%
Schools for the handicapped					0.2%
High school division					
The blind	3,011				
The deaf	2,231				
Others	5,410				
Total	10,652				
Total high school enrolment	4,806,179				99.9%

Source: Japan, Monbushō 1995a, pp. 168, 188–94, 208–29, 306, 324, 352, 379.

private schools. Given that over 96 per cent of the age cohort proceed to high schools, the high-school diploma itself no longer differentiates young Japanese. It is the nature and ranking of high schools that strongly influence students' future life chances. In each school district there is an elaborate hierarchy of high schools, based on the relative difficulty of gaining admission. Different high schools hold distinctive missions, in particular in relation to preparation for their students' post-school destinations. Because of this, different high schools develop distinctive subcultures, in contrast to the relative homogeneity observed across middle schools. Table 3.1 displays the nationwide numerical distribution of students in different kinds of high schools for 1995.

What follows is a typology of high-school education that seeks to explain differences in terms of likely post-school destinations, student background, and student culture (see Table 3.2). While other differences, such

Table 3.2 Typology of high schools

Type 1	Elite academic high schools
Type 2	Non-elite academic high schools
Type 3	Vocational high schools
Type 4	Evening high schools
Type 5	Correspondence high schools
Type 6	High-school departments of the schools for the blind, the deaf and the otherwise handicapped

as private versus government, rural and urban, and co-educational versus single-sex schooling, are important, we do not use them as discerning factors for this typology, although we touch on these differences throughout this chapter.

The distinction between academic high schools and vocational high schools is, perhaps, the most important one. For academic high schools the focus is on preparing students for the university entrance examination and/or further studies elsewhere, and in the case of vocational high schools, preparation for entry into the workforce. Over 70 per cent of those enrolled in high school attend day academic high schools (public and private). Among 1995 academic high-school graduates, 29.7 per cent entered four-year universities, 16.2 per cent two-year junior colleges, and 33.5 per cent private specialist schools (which offer both technical and general education courses); 13.4 per cent went to full-time employment, and the remainder went to other types of educational institution or to part-time employment or unemployment (Japan, Monbushō 1995a:602–3, 608–9) (see Table 3.3).

These nationwide figures, however, do not show important differences within academic high schools. We emphasise the distinction between 'elite' (Type 1 below) and 'non-elite' (Type 2) academic high schools, and the diversity within non-elite academic high schools.

Type 1: Elite Academic High Schools

Type 1 covers the elite academic high schools, which accept the cream of the age cohort in terms of academic excellence and send the majority of its graduates to the nation's top universities. There are only a few Type 1 schools – they are the top prefectural and national academic high schools in urban centres, and a handful of private high schools. Almost all national academic high schools are attached to the Faculty of Education of a national university. We will examine the case of Nada High School (a private school) later in this chapter, as an example of a Type 1 high school.

Table 3.3 Post-school destinations of 1995 graduates of academic high schools and vocational high schools (day schools)

	Academic high-school graduates	Vocational high-school graduates
4-year university	29.7%	4.3%
2-year junior college	16.2	6.6
Senshūgakkō (private specialist school)	33.5	22.5
Full-time employment	13.4	59.7
Others	7.2	6.9

Source: Japan, Monbushō 1995a, pp. 602–3, 608–9

Type 2: Non-elite Academic High Schools

Type 2 represents non-elite academic high schools, which aim to prepare students for less prestigious universities and junior colleges but which in reality send a considerable proportion of their students to private specialist schools (*senshūgakkō*), which teach subjects such as book-keeping, languages and computer programming. These schools constitute the majority of the so-called academic high schools. We estimate that non-elite academic high schools accommodate the largest proportion of the high-school population, and therefore constitute the mainstream high schooling. We will elaborate on non-academic high schools later in this chapter.

Type 3: Vocational High Schools

Type 3 covers vocational high schools, both government and private. About 23 per cent of high-school students attend vocational high schools. There are vocational courses in commerce, technical subjects, agriculture, home science, nursing and fishery (in descending order of number of enrolled students in 1995). Most private vocational high schools are commerce schools, since other types require more expensive facilities. Vocational high schools generally rank lower, and therefore are easier to gain admission to, than academic high schools. Vocational high schools aim to prepare students for immediate employment, although recently greater numbers of students have come to choose further education at *senshūgakkō*. Among 1995 vocational high-school graduates nationwide, 4.3 per cent entered four-year universities, 6.6 per cent two-year junior colleges, 22.5 per cent *senshūgakkō*; 59.7 per cent went to full-time employment, with the remainder going to other types of educational institutions or into unemployment (Japan, Monbushō 1995a:602–3, 608–9). Choices of vocational courses are highly gender-specific. Boys are dominant in technical courses, and girls in commerce, home science and nursing, although technical high schools enrol more girls now than before. We will present a case study of rural agricultural high schools later in this chapter.

Type 4: Evening High Schools

Type 4 covers evening high schools, which 2.2 per cent of high-school students attended in 1995. Evening schools used to serve poor but ambitious and able students who supported themselves while receiving education. Although this type of student still exists, many of the students at Type 4 schools go there after missing out on places at day schools. Four years of study are required to obtain a high-school diploma. In Rohlen's (1983) study of Sakura Evening High School, one class had, officially, 17 students, but the absentee rate was about 50 per cent. School started after 5:30 pm when students finished a day's work, although some students were unemployed during the day. Many could not read the Chinese characters in the easiest level of Japanese literature textbook approved by the MOE for use in high schools – evening high schools generally enrolled students from the lowest two percentiles of the age cohort in terms of academic achievement (Rohlen 1983:31). Both students and teachers were aware of the gap between the students' ability and the curriculum. Students constantly complained but the teachers (who Rohlen considers to be the most skilled and devoted) managed classes with good humour.

Type 5: Correspondence High Schools

Type 5 denotes correspondence high schools. These schools offer a flexible form of schooling for those who missed out on high schooling when they were young, those who cannot regularly attend school for medical reasons, and those who could not adjust to, or chose to opt out of, regular day school. Approximately 1.6 per cent of those enrolled in high school received this form of schooling in 1995. A case study is included later in this chapter.

Type 6: Schools for the Handicapped

Type 6 comprises the high-school departments of the schools for the blind, the deaf and the otherwise handicapped, serving 0.2 per cent of the high-school enrolment in 1995. Many of these students undergo primary, middle and high schooling in the same schools.

The rankings of the first four types of schools are based purely on students' academic achievement at the end point of compulsory education. The ranking of schools also reflects the family backgrounds of students. Students from more privileged family backgrounds (in terms of parents' occupations and income) concentrate at the higher-ranked schools and those from less privileged backgrounds at the lower-ranked schools (Rohlen 1983; Okano 1993:62–77). The differences in academic achievement among students at these four types of schools, the distinctive missions that different schools set out, the strategies that they devise to achieve their missions, and the influences and attitudes that students bring to school from home all contribute to the distinctive 'school culture' or 'peer group culture' created at these schools. These attitudes in turn reinforce the differences in academic achievement and future ambitions that characterise individual students at the commencement of high school. The differentiation among young people is almost complete when they leave high school.

Non-elite Academic High Schools: Mainstream High Schooling

Accommodating the largest number of high-school students, non-elite academic high schools are diverse in their practice despite having shared missions. Non-elite academic high schools can be anywhere on the continuum between higher-ranked schools, which send over a half of their graduates to four-year universities, and lower-ranked schools, which send the majority of their graduates to private specialist schools or employment while managing to find places for university aspirants in fourth-grade universities through 'entry by recommendation' (*suisen nyūgaku*).

Exactly what proportion of the so-called academic high schools fit into the category of 'non-elite academic high schools', and the diversity within the non-elite academic high schools, are difficult to estimate from the nationwide statistics. An interesting picture of academic high schools emerges in the statistics of the post-school destinations of 1997 graduates listed by individual schools and courses (in the case of comprehensive high schools) in Kobe city. The list was compiled by the Hyōgo Prefecture High School Head Guidance Teachers' Association (*Hyōgoken Kōtōgakkō Shinroshidō Kenkyūkai*).

Among 51 academic high schools (including general academic, English, mathematics and science courses, and international studies courses at comprehensive high schools), only seven schools had over 70 per cent of their students directly entering four-year universities, and 16 schools between 50 and 70 per cent. Eight schools had between 30 and 50 per cent of their graduates going on to four-year universities, while as many as 20 schools sent under 30 per cent (see Figure 3.1). That is to say, almost three-fifths of so-called academic high schools send *less than half* of their graduates to four-year universities. Not all academic high schools focus on academic preparation for the university entrance examination, with some focusing on preparing students for entry to two-year junior colleges or private specialist schools.

While the proportion of graduates directly entering four-year universities indicates a school's academic orientation, the schools with the highest percentages of their graduates going directly to four-year universities are not necessarily Type 1 elite academic high schools. This is because the choice of university is often gender-specific, and also because the most ambitious are willing to remain unemployed for a year in order to attempt entry to the top universities. In the above survey, the five schools that sent the largest percentage of their students to four-year universities were three private girls' high schools (90.4, 76.7 and 72.2 per cent), a government high school's English course (89.2 per cent), and a

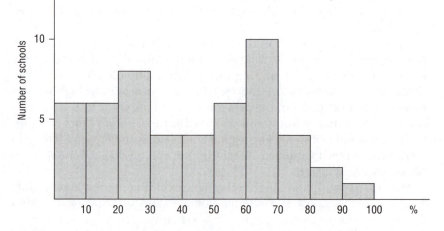

Figure 3.1 Interschool differences in the percentage of academic high-school graduates directly entering four-year universities
Source: Unpublished document compiled by *Hyōgoken Kōtōgakkō Shinroshidō Kenkyūkai* (1997)

private boys' high school's mathematics and science course (75.6 per cent). In fact, Nada High, a private boys' high school nationally renowned for its success, and three top prefectural co-ed high schools sent only 50 to 65 per cent of their students directly to four-year universities. The graduates of these high schools (in particular boys) were prepared to spend an extra year to gain entry to elite universities. Girls at private schools, on the other hand, were more likely to settle on the kind of universities that they could gain admission to at the time. Indeed the schools that had over 30 per cent of their graduates opting for an extra year of study are three elite private boys' academic high schools and the three top prefectural co-ed high schools. In contrast, at the three above-mentioned private girls' high schools that sent the largest percentage of their students to four-year universities, fewer opted for another year of pre-university preparation (6.2, 15.5 and 7 per cent).

Nada High School and two other private boys' high schools and the top three prefectural academic high schools comprise Kobe city's Type 1 elite academic high schools, sending the majority of their students to top-ranking four-year universities through open competition. Type 1 elite academic high schools accounted for approximately 10 per cent of Kobe city's academic high-school students in March 1997. The remaining 90 per cent of them were at non-elite academic high schools.

The diversity within non-elite academic high schools is shown by Figure 3.1, in terms of the four-year university entry figures. Some of them (private girls' academic high schools) send over 50 per cent of their graduates directly to two-year junior colleges, while relatively higher-ranked co-ed schools send very few to these institutions. The proportions of graduates entering *senshūgakkō* range school by school from almost nonexistent to 33 per cent of graduates. The equivalent figure for those entering employment ranges from almost nonexistent to 45 per cent of graduates. Lower-ranked academic high schools send more students to *senshūgakkō* than to four-year universities, and manage to find places for university aspirants in fourth-grade universities through entry by recommendation. Table 3.4 lists a range of non-elite academic high schools in Kobe city. The first three schools have been studied by ethnographers (Rohlen 1983; Okano 1993); the research is discussed below. The data for A High, B High, C Girls' High and D Boys' High are derived from a survey (unpublished) by the Hyōgo Prefecture High School Head Guidance Teachers' Association (*Hyōgoken Kōtōgakkō Shinroshidō Kenkyūkai*). A High and B High are both government co-ed schools, while C Girls' High and D Boys' High are both large private academic high schools.

Rohlen (1983) describes two non-elite academic schools, Okada and Otani. Okada, a prefectural academic school, sees its mission as

Table 3.4 Distribution of graduates of selected non-elite academic high schools

	Four-year university %	Two-year junior college %	Senshūgakkō %	Employment %	Others %
Rohlen's Okada High (government)	72	14	data unavailable		
Rohlen's Otani High (government)	62	25	data unavailable		
A High (government)	41	20	14	1	24
B High (government)	25	26	24	7	18
Okano's Sasaki High (academic course) (government)	13	20	27	27	14
C Girls' High (private)	5	27	14	45	6
D Boys' High (private)	10	3	31	36	19

Errors due to rounding.
Sources: Unpublished document compiled by *Hyōgoken Kōtōgakkō Shinroshidō Kenkyūkai* (1997); Rohlen (1983:44); Okano (1993:71)

preparing students for university entrance examinations, with nearly all its students proceeding to tertiary education. But unlike elite academic schools, only 10 per cent of Okada students make it to national universities. Okada's timetable in the final year is organised in such a way as to enable those who aim at science courses to study more science subjects, and those who aim for arts courses to take more arts subjects. Otani, the next in the ranking in Rohlen's study, is a municipal academic high school, which also focuses on preparation for entrance examinations, but for less prestigious universities. Almost all of Otani's graduates proceed to tertiary education, but the percentage of girls opting for two-year junior colleges (instead of four-year universities) is larger than at Okada.

Okada and Otani are representative of schools where the kind of socialisation for university entrance examinations described by Shimahara (1979) takes place. While Okada and Otani look almost identical to casual observers, students, teachers and parents are acutely aware of the difference between the two in terms of their ranking and the future prospects that they offer. Both Otani and Okada offer well-prepared conventional one-hour lecture-style classes with little diversion from texts. Neither school has disciplinary problems. During breaks and after school students are engaged in high-spirited activities, as Rohlen describes below:

> When the bell announces the end of the hour and the teacher leaves, pandemonium breaks loose. Some girls scurry for the door to meet their girlfriends in the hall. Some head for the washroom. A boy in a stairwell begins practising his trumpet. A Japanese chess game is brought out from under a desk and two students pick up their match where they left off after the last period. Several others look on. A small group gathers at another desk to study a car magazine. Two boys are at the blackboard working out a physics assignment. The hallways are full of smiling, noisy kids. Then suddenly it's all over. Ten minutes have passed. (Rohlen 1983:13)

Okada and Otani are not mere examination preparation machines. About half the students are active in after-school clubs (e.g. sports, a rock band, the English Speaking Society). These students actually enjoy school, finding ways to express their energy and enthusiasm at breaks and after school. On average, Japanese high schools maintain a higher level of order without undue exercise of authority, and students comply with the basic rules that protect classroom instruction, compared with American schools (Rohlen 1983:18).

Academic schools ranked lower than the above two send fewer students to four-year universities. Among the graduates of the academic course at Sasaki High, a municipal comprehensive high school that Okano (1993) investigated, only 12.5 per cent went on to four-year universities, 20.2 per cent to two-year junior colleges, 27.0 per cent to *senshūgakkō*, 27.0 per cent to full-time employment, and 13.5 per cent either became *rōnin* (literally 'masterless *samurai*', i.e. students who spend one or two extra years preparing for the next round of entrance examinations) or remained undecided in March 1990 (Okano 1993:71). Students were fully aware, from the school's past record, that entry to a national university was virtually impossible, and aimed at the universities that they considered 'appropriate to their level'. Some chose to make use of the school's entry-by-recommendation system to secure a place at a university or a two-year junior college. Some chose to enter tertiary institutions through their sport club activities, while others were simply happy to enter any university or junior college. Most students were discouraged by teachers from spending an extra year preparing for the following year's entrance examination as *rōnin*, since, teachers explained, Sasaki High's past record indicated that *rōnin* students usually did not manage to significantly improve their academic performance. Over a quarter of the students opted for *senshūgakkō* in order to obtain a particular technical skill, instead of aiming at university education. Perhaps because of the lower emphasis placed on preparation for examinations, students were relaxed and enjoyed school, spending a longer time with friends and teachers after school.

Aspirants to academic high schools who do not perform well enough to enter their chosen government high schools attend non-elite private academic high schools like C Girls' High and D Boys' High in Table 3.4. An urban private girls' academic high school that Miyazaki (1993) studied streamed its students tightly according to their likely post-school destinations, ranging from four-year university to employment and private specialist schools. In the school distinctive peer groups were observable, with at one extreme a studious group, who conformed to the school's expectations, and at the other the most 'carefree' group, who enjoyed wearing makeup, smoking, drinking and sexual activities; other groups occurred in the middle (Miyazaki 1993). The most 'carefree' group in Miyazaki's description resembles the non-conformist students that Rohlen (1983) and Okano (1993) describe in respect of vocational high-school students.

We suspect that the lowest-ranking non-elite academic high schools (private institutions in Kobe city, like C Girls' High and D Boys' High in Table 3.4) develop similar student cultures to those at urban vocational high schools. The post-school destinations of the majority of the students at these non-elite academic high schools do not require academic preparation for entrance examinations, and are not radically different from those at vocational schools. The following section illustrates the culture of urban vocational high schools, which we see as resembling that observed at the lowest-ranked non-elite academic high schools.

Urban Vocational High Schools

A municipal commerce high school, Yama, that Rohlen (1983) studied sends 80 per cent of its students directly into the workforce. Like many other vocational high schools in the city, its students occupy the bottom half of the age cohort in terms of academic achievement at grade-nine level. Many students come to Yama because they could not enter academic high schools, which creates a low level of morale among both students and teachers. Some do make it to third- or fourth-grade private universities, often through a teacher's recommendation. Rohlen (1983) observed various disciplinary and delinquency problems (although he admits their nature is mild in comparison to those in the US), such as skipping classes, leaving the school grounds during school hours, smoking, and vandalism. At Yama, students have fewer organisational skills, and less self-confidence than those at academic high schools.

Among the students in a commerce course and a data-processing course at Sasaki High, a municipal comprehensive school that Okano (1993) studied, over 80 per cent of the graduates of both courses entered employment directly. Okano (1993:66–8) reveals that the relatively high achievers of the age cohort, who had sufficient academic merit to enter second-rank academic high schools such as Rohlen's Okada, chose the data-processing course, contrary to the public belief that academic merit determines one's high school. She argues that these students chose the data-processing course (instead of entering academic high school) because they had already decided to go straight into employment after graduating from high school when they entered high school; and that such decisions resulted from their past experience and family circumstances, both directly (e.g. financial reasons) and indirectly (e.g. no immediate role models) (Okano 1993:66–8).

Imai Tech High, a municipal technical high school that Okano (1993) studied, was male-dominated among both students and staff members. Over 90 per cent of Imai students entered employment directly, with 5 per cent proceeding to four-year universities and two-year junior colleges (Okano 1993:76). Just over 17 per cent of the entrants dropped out over the three-year period of high schooling (Okano 1993:74), a much higher figure than the average for all high schools in the city. Okano observed various activities on the part of students that violated the school rules (in particular, the school's prohibition of part-time work after school, the bans on smoking, drinking and the riding of motor-bikes, and school dress codes). However, the students' conduct was not overtly confrontational to the school authorities, unlike the 'lads' in Willis's (1977) study of British working-class males:

> ... it was 'cool' to be engaged in oppositional activities in a 'tactful' (*youryougaii*) way without being caught. They enjoyed testing school authority to see how far they could 'bend the rules', but always only to the extent that they did not face confrontation with teachers. The capacity to estimate the 'right' extent was important, and was the essence of 'tactful' strategies. (Okano 1993:198)

The situation can be interpreted as a form of conflict or struggle between teachers and students over what students can or cannot do, but students were not so serious as to make a commitment to the struggle. Rather, it was a game the students enjoyed playing. Okano describes a typical class in progress:

> ... only about 10 students out of the total 37 listened attentively to the teacher. The class was not noisy, neither was it silent, several students chatting with one another in low voices. At least 10 students were asleep, about three read comics under their desk, a few girls combed their hair, and a few copied

other subjects notes taken by 'brainy' students. The extent of these activities differed depending on the subject teacher. Teachers were aware of a small proportion of these non-study activities, but did not seem to care, as long as those students were not disturbing the motivated students. Almost at the end of the class some of these inattentive students suddenly got notes from others and copied them. Others did not bother. (Okano 1993:198)

For these students the purpose of coming to school was not to study but to have a good time with friends. But since the school required students to work, they made 'creative' adjustments to 'manage' the school routine according to their own outlook.

Despite low academic achievement and occasional delinquent behaviour, almost all of Imai's graduates obtain 'proper' full-time jobs when they leave school, since vocational high schools take it as their duty to ensure that every student has a starting place in the workforce by providing highly elaborate, personalised and systematic job referral services for their students (Okano 1993). Okano's ethnographic study (1993) illustrates this nuance-filled process, whereby schools provide more elaborate guidance and assistance to the more 'problematic' and less able students, akin to that provided in middle schools (Shimizu 1992:125–6).

The Forgotten 50 per cent: Girls

The meritocratic nature of educational participation in contemporary Japan applies only to the male half of the population.[3] Although the post-war US occupation performed a remarkable task in trying to abolish the pre-war education system, which rigidly institutionalised sex segregation by the type and level of schooling available, gender-specific educational participation still occurs at present. This section has two aims. The first is to examine the forms of, and reasons for, the continued sex-specific female educational participation. The second is to go beyond the female–male dichotomy and to explore the diversity among women in their participation in, and appropriation of, schooling.

Gendered Value and the Meaning of Schooling

The meaning and values of schooling are not identical for Japanese men and women. 'Competition' in schooling is driven by the close link between schooling and 'desirable' careers in large firms and in government, at least for male graduates. This is most vividly demonstrated by the example of boys from an elite private school, Nada, which we take up in a later case study. Women cannot enjoy this link (Brinton 1993). In fact, a Japanese woman's level of education explains little about her

Table 3.5 Gender-specific differences in post-secondary education

	Male %	Female %
Four-year university	26.5	18.7
Two-year junior college	1.8	24.3
Senshūgakkō	18.7	7.6

Source: Japan, Monbushō 1995a, pp. 598, 600, 609, 610, 612, 613

lifetime employment trajectory (Brinton 1993:199). The restricted opportunity structure in the labour market for women, along with gender-specific expectations concerning family roles, means that the value attached to schooling for women is quite different from that for men. Based on an understanding of the gender-specific meaning and value of schooling, girls and their parents conduct 'rational decision making' regarding their education.

Gender-specific differences become striking at the tertiary education level. The main tertiary track for women is two-year junior colleges (24.3 per cent of female high-school graduates) rather than four-year universities (18.7 per cent), while 26.5 per cent of high-school graduate males directly entered four-year universities in 1995 (Japan, Monbushō 1995a) (see Table 3.5). Female enrolment at four-year universities is lower than that in any Western industrialised nation (Nakata and Mosk 1987). Women are also less represented in Japan's top universities (Brinton 1993:202). Women's major subject choices are heavily biased towards 'general education' areas, such as humanities and fine arts, and typically female areas such as home economics and education (Japan, Monbushō 1994:44).

Why are there such striking differences? Given that few institutional barriers exist for girls in schooling, we would suggest that gender-specific educational participation results from 'choices' made by girls and their parents.

First, girls make decisions about their educational participation based on their perception of the use of education for their post-school lives, in particular, in relation to employment. Except in a few occupations in which women have traditionally been engaged (e.g. teaching), four-year university female graduates have extremely limited employment opportunities, in comparison to their male counterparts and to two-year junior college female graduates (Fujimura-Fanselow 1995:133). Employers have hired young women out of high school or two-year junior colleges for clerical tasks on the assumption that they would quit upon marriage or childbirth; and avoided university-educated women for similar tasks since they are more expensive and have fewer years to work for them. Women have been denied promotion and wages based on length of consecutive service within a particular company. Although the 1986 Equal Opportunity Act widened the range of career options for women (e.g. career-track positions, or *sōgōshoku*), the employment and promotion practices as well as the cultures of workplaces remain hurdles for women to overcome (Shimizu 1994; Takeuchi 1994). As well, the economic downturn in the early 1990s has resulted in cutbacks in job opportunities for four-year university-educated women. As of June 1996, the number of positions for male graduates in 1997 that employers are seeking to fill amount to 1.8 times the expected number of graduates, while the equivalent figure for females is 0.64 (*Asahi Shinbun* 17 July 1996).

Compared with those of men, women's educational qualifications possess a symbolic value (higher social status and level of cultural sophistication) rather than a practical value (in terms of employment opportunities) (Amano 1988:280). Men's educational qualifications have a more powerful 'instrumental value' in acquiring high-status, powerful and well-paid positions in the employment market. Women, granted few opportunities to convert their educational resources into jobs relevant to their qualifications, turn out to use them, perhaps quite unintentionally, as a symbolic commodity.

Second, apart from employment and promotion opportunities, other institutional arrangement such as adequate and acceptable facilities for the care of dependants (both children and the elderly) are not in place. Furthermore, the long working hours and transfers expected of those with a long-term career commitment make it difficult for women to combine a career and family responsibilities. Such flexibility has always been expected of their male counterparts, whose wives take care of household responsibilities.

Young women observe objective realities such as those mentioned above. It is not surprising then that they are hesitant in pursuing work on a continuous and long-term basis, choose their educational paths accordingly, and perhaps receive tertiary education, if any, for purposes different from those of men, a point that we will touch upon again.

Third, parents make an economic calculation of financial return on the investment of family resources (Brinton 1993:209). Since more education for a son brings more benefits in the employment and marriage markets, parents give preferential allocation of their resources to their sons rather than to their daughters, for whom university education is not perceived as being as beneficial in these terms (Brinton 1993:210). For instance, Iwai (1990:155–84) reveals that over half of women in their early thirties are out of the labour force, regardless of their education level (high school, two-year college, and four-year university), and that by age 35, high-school and two-year college graduates are likely to return to work, but not four-year university graduates. When parents allocate their family resources to daughters, they tend to spend them in different ways; for instance, by providing for cultural and artistic classes and activities such as music, rather than academic *juku* or private tutors (Brinton 1993:217–20). Parents are likely to rely financially on their sons in their old age. It makes sense then that the extent of gender-specific educational participation depends on the parents' perceptions of the labour market restrictions for women, and also on whether the parents are to rely financially on their daughters.

A fourth factor is the societal and parental expectations of sex-specific life trajectories, and the dominant notion of femininity. Many Japanese parents believe that their daughters and sons should be socialised to acquire sex-specific roles, and femininity (*onnarashisa*) and masculinity (*otokorashisa*). International comparison illustrates that the proportion of Japanese parents who support sex-based (as opposed to sex-neutral) socialisation is much higher (62.6 per cent) than in other industrial societies (e.g. 20 per cent in England, 31.3 per cent in the US and 6 per cent in Sweden) (Japan, Sōrifu 1982). Japanese parents are less critical of bringing up daughters as *onnarashiku* (13.5 per cent) than their UK counterparts (32.1 per cent), but in both countries mothers are more critical than fathers (Japan, Sōrifu, Seishōnen Taisakuhonbu, 1982:44–5). Indeed, Kanda's (1985) review of three major surveys conducted in the 1980s reveals that parents bring up their sons and daughters quite differently, based on their own notions of femininity and masculinity, and expect life courses to be strongly influenced by gender. This is despite the fact that sex-specific role expectations have softened over the post-war period (Kanda 1985; Nakayama 1985), particularly in relation to the proposition of 'men as breadwinners and women at home', attitudes towards married women at work, and the participation of husbands in domestic chores (Azuma and Suzuki 1991).

Lastly, schools also make a difference. In comparison to families and the society as a whole, gender-specific restrictions and expectations are less prevalent at school. That high-achieving female university students perceive gender discrimination for the first time when seeking employment demonstrates this point (Yoshihara 1995:117–20). Gendered socialisation within the school setting has been identified in terms of curriculum (home economics and martial arts) (Ujihara 1994) and in student–teacher interaction (Miyazaki 1991). Female student cultures are also said to have internalised gender-specific expectations to a large degree, exhibiting 'typically female' characteristics, such as high adaptability to changing circumstances (Takeuchi 1985). Some schools have taken initiatives in promoting non-sexist education, by devising new curricula and teaching materials (Kishizawa 1993), and by implementing a non-sexist policy across the curriculum (Yanagi 1982). The success of these initiatives, although limited, can be observed in the outcomes: schools that advocated 'career women' paths produced more career-minded graduates than those schools with a 'traditional wife and mother' perspective (Nakanishi 1993).

Nonetheless, girls still receive contradictory messages from schooling. The school on the one hand conveys the dominant achievement ideology, which espouses academic excellence and its reward in post-school life, and egalitarianism; and on the other hand a sexist ideology that supports the dominant view of gender-specific roles and life trajectories. Girls are aware, to varying degrees, that their academic excellence does not translate into rewards in post-school life in the same way that it does for boys; and that they are expected to perform 'women's roles' once married. Decisions on the part of high-achieving girls about further education and post-school destinations are not based purely on their academic merit to the same extent as those of their male counterparts. Gender (i.e. socially constructed and inevitably arbitrary views on sex roles), gender-specific social practices (as in the employment market), and the girls' own perceptions intervene in their decision making. Minority groups (e.g. ethnic groups, new migrants) also conduct decision making by considering factors other than their academic achievements (e.g. subcultural norms, or their perception of a job ceiling), as we will discuss in the following chapter.

Diversity Among Women

While we have emphasised that girls participate in and benefit from schooling differently from men, girls themselves hold diverse views. A recent survey suggests that one of the most striking characteristics of younger women (at university) is the diversity in their views on gender roles and career plans, as opposed to a unanimous challenging of the traditional sex-specific roles (Ochi et al. 1992:122). We suspect that family class location and minority status affect the ways in which girls participate in education; and that the notion of femininity is likely to differ across classes in Japan, as is observed in Britain (McRobbie 1978). However, few studies to date have explored the intersection between gender and class, and that between gender and ethnic minorities in Japan. When diversity is emphasised, it is often among girls at university and academic high schools.

Girls vary in reacting to the schools' messages. Kimura (1990:159–60) identifies four types of girls in terms of how they respond to the two contradictory school messages of achievement ideology and gender-specific roles. These are: (1) 'elegant high achievers', who never attempt to compete with boys and want to be the full-time housewives of elite husbands; (2) 'career-oriented high achievers', who are prepared to compete with men in pursuing their own careers and independence; (3) 'ordinary girls', the majority of whom opt out of the competition with men and seek 'female' options (which can be either becoming full-time housewives or entering typically 'female' occupations); and (4) 'school resisters', who reject the two messages of the school and resort to 'deviant' behaviour.

Differences were observed in 157 middle-school and high-school girls' plans on post-marital employment and in their views on the jobs 'suitable to women'. The girls' responses were strongly influenced by their individual understanding of the labour market restrictions facing women (Kameda 1977). Among female university students too there is diversity in their perception of labour market realities and assumed sex-specific roles, and their future plans (Ochi et al. 1992). The latter study draws on 999 female students at four-year universities and two-year junior colleges, and suggests that women's strategies vary; and that even when a particular strategy is chosen, the reasons for that strategy are not necessarily uniform. Since this is one of the most recent and extensive studies of young women, we elaborate on it below.

Female university students' career decisions are strongly influenced by their views on marriage (i.e. the importance attached to it and its timing). The majority of young Japanese women no longer see marriage as compulsory. Among 20–29 year old women in 1990, 24 per cent considered that women were better off married, while 75 per cent answered that it depends on individual circumstances (Ochi et al. 1992:130). Amongst Ochi et al.'s female university students, only 35 per cent sought to marry before the average marriage age of 25 years (Ochi et al. 1992:130). Female university students devise strategies to 'manage' their career commitment and impending marriage. Those who desire career-track positions (sōgōshoku) in mass communications, and teachers (two of the most popular 'career' choices for female university graduates) tend to want 'later marriage', while over half of the non-career-track position (ippanshoku) seekers opt for 'early marriage' (Ochi et al. 1992:131). For these women considerations such as economic base (from a husband's income) or the emotional benefits of having children and partner may be more important than whether marriage would fit into any career plans they might have (Ochi et al. 1992:137). For more career-oriented women, their career plans often determine the kind of marriage that they seek. In either case, plans for marriage and/or career are an individual construct, both pragmatic and strategic, which the individual believes will enable what they consider to be a happy life.

In young women's career decisions, the question of whether employment options are 'suitable for women' is also important. Interestingly, many of the survey respondents considered that their desired occupations fell into this category: 65 per cent of those who sought jobs as teachers or librarians, 64 per cent of those seeking jobs in mass communications, 63 per cent of those who wished for *sōgōshoku* positions, and 78 per cent of those seeking *ippanshoku* positions (Ochi et al. 1992:132). Some saw the 'domesticity' inherent in occupations such as nursing and teaching, and others the assumed relative ease of simultaneously managing family commitments, as qualifying these types of jobs (*ippanshoku* and public service) as 'suitable for women'.

Their reasons for pursuing careers vary. Some seek 'success' and 'power and monetary reward' (like many of their male counterparts), while others pursue careers for more private and psychological satisfaction, such as 'self-enlightenment' and 'contribution to the society', the latter being predominant among female students (Ochi et al. 1992:137). This is partly due to the restrictions in the employment market that women face – making a virtue of necessity – and/or to the sex-specific expectations that give women an option of being out of the labour market (an option that men do not have).

Their reasons for choosing to be a full-time housewife also vary. First, traditional gender-specific socialisation subscribes them to it. Second, poor academic performance often compels a student to leave the competitive educational track with the justification that 'women's place is at home'. Third, the middle-class 'women's culture', which values consumption of expensive 'feminine' goods and services, leads women to see marriage to an elite husband as a strategy enabling them to enjoy such culture (Ochi et al. 1992:136). Indeed, the wealthier the family a female university student originates from, the more likely she is to aim for being a full-time housewife (Ochi et al. 1992:124). The poorer women's academic performance at school, the more 'feminine' they consider themselves to be, and these students also tend to opt for the full-time housewife path (Ochi et al. 1992:124).

Many female university students in the 1990s seek self-realisation through roles that have long been considered to be in the 'male' domain (careers), *as well as* roles typically considered 'female' (home). In order to resolve this conflict, they devise various strategies. The first is to integrate 'self-realisation' into the role of full-time housewife, by emphasising its creative features. The second is to allocate various stages of life to the two roles (e.g. quitting work while children are small, and later returning to work). The third is to pursue the kinds of careers that can be a 'supplement' to their family responsibilities (e.g. ballet teacher, writer, artist). The fourth is the 'super woman' approach, where women simultaneously pursue both family and career goals through sheer effort. The fifth is to first gain economic and social independence through their careers and then to marry. In this case women remove some of the functions and meanings traditionally attached to marriage and consider it purely as emotional bonding. The sixth is to integrate the traditional marriage norms into work patterns (e.g. co-authoring books, co-management of a shop) (Ochi et al. 1992:138).

These differences among girls and young women seem to derive from three factors: family, what school provides (e.g. curriculum, school missions) and the peer-group subcultures that they create at school. First, their mothers' employment histories and views on sex-specific roles have a strong influence on their plans for careers and on their views of gender-specific roles (Kameda 1977; Nakanishi 1993).

Second, the school matters as well. Nakanishi (1993) studied girls' high schools that took in girls of similar academic calibre and middle-class backgrounds but which advocated quite distinctive 'school charter or missions', and showed that the school that aimed for 'independent career women' produced a larger number of career-minded graduates than the school that aimed for 'traditional wife and mother' roles. Inter-school differences are also observed at tertiary level. Ochi et al. (1992:124) illustrated that the proportion of female university students who wished to become full-time housewives differed greatly across several universities that they researched.

Third, subcultures that girls themselves create contribute to the differentiation among them, by screening and mediating the messages that girls receive from family and school. Miyazaki's ethnographic study (1993) identifies four distinctive (and self-categorised) subcultural groups at a girls' high school: the Study Group, Comics Group, Ordinary Group and Yankee Group. These four groups drew clear mutual boundaries by criticising the stereotypical features of other groups.

Study Group girls were active participants in school activities and conformed to school rules and ideology. Comics Group girls were similar to Study Group girls, but differed in their common passion for comics, from which they had created their own unique 'culture'. Yankee Group girls did not believe in study and school rules, and enjoyed breaking rules and challenging teachers. They shortened their skirts, lowered their necklines, wore makeup and dyed their hair, which Study Group and Comics Group girls criticised as being 'promiscuous' and 'vulgar'. The Study Group and Comics Group valued 'proper' and 'decent' women instead. The Ordinary Group also broke school rules but in ways that teachers did not notice, and avoided direct confrontation with school authorities. Study Group and Comics Group girls were not active in socialising with friends outside school: they did not have part-time work or boyfriends. Many of the Yankee Group and Ordinary Group girls had part-time work and boyfriends, and spent much time with young people from outside the school at various haunts in town (e.g. *karaoke* bars, coffee shops). Having a steady boyfriend conferred status in these groups, but not in the Study Group and Comics Group.

Members of the four groups had different post-school plans. Study Group girls aimed for university entrance and showed a stronger desire for careers, while Ordinary Group girls planned to become office workers for a short time before marriage. These different views were reflected in the ways that the different groups saw schoolwork. Almost all the girls considered that schoolwork was not useful, but for different reasons. Study Group girls considered that it did not adequately prepare them for university entrance examinations, while Yankee Group and Ordinary Group girls thought it was irrelevant to their future. In fact, some of the latter girls considered that the only 'useful' subject at school was home economics.

Some of the above Study Group and Comics Group members would join the 18 per cent of the age-cohort girls who attend four-year universities. Given that they are more educated than the remaining 82 per cent of young women of the same age group, one might expect that these women all aim to use their education to pursue careers. This is not the case (Ochi et al. 1992; Price 1996). Price's ethnographic study of a private women's university (which she describes as 'a finishing school for middle-class girls') reveals how, even within the same institution, subcultural groups develop distinctive orientations regarding careers and femininity, and make different future plans. Girls are thus active and selective appropriators of what is being offered to them, and it is at least partially in this context that differentiation among women occurs at school.

In summary, we may say that the value and meaning of schooling differs between boys and girls. There are, in reality, differences in what boys and girls *can* obtain from schooling; that is, girls cannot translate their academic achievement into reward in post-school life in the same way that boys can. Such objective differences lead girls to hold different expectations of schooling and to make decisions about their educational participation accordingly. The differences derive from a combination of several factors: restrictions in the labour market for women (both in recruitment and in promotion), institutional arrangements (e.g. care for children and the elderly, working hours), parents' economic calculation of family resources, societal gender-specific expectations of family roles, and what occurs at school. Because of the compounded nature of the causes of differences, increased opportunities for career-track employment and promotion of women (enabled by the 1985 legislation) alone are unlikely to result in a dramatic transformation of gender-specific educational participation in the short term. Yet girls are not passive role players but actively contemplate how best, under the constraints they face, they can realise what they consider to be happiness in their lives. Consequently contemporary young women display diversity in their views on schooling, gender roles, post-school employment and family, and in the strategies that they devise to achieve what they aspire to.

Poverty and Schooling

Poverty in affluent Japan is visible neither to locals nor to outsiders (Yoshida 1995). Since the end of the war, as Japan has become increasingly affluent and, until the 1980s, more 'egalitarian' in terms of wealth distribution, the symbolic meaning that the public attaches to poverty has changed. Although inequalities in wealth distribution have widened from the 1980s (Japan, Keizai Kikaku Chō 1990), poverty in contemporary Japan is more likely to be understood as resulting from fair competition amongst individuals than it was half a century ago. Japan is now perceived as an open society where free competition amongst individuals determines what a person deserves to obtain as a reward, and where everyone is assumed to be given a chance to succeed. The assumption of the 'meritocratic' nature of Japanese schooling as a selection mechanism creates the myth of equal opportunities, and reinforces a view that the result is based on one's achievement (as opposed to inherited factors). The winners and losers that such a competition inevitably produces are thus justified.

A concrete level of poverty in Japan is difficult to delineate. Families who receive *seikatsuhogo* (the government living protection allowances for low-income families) and those with similar levels of income are said to constitute about one-third of 'working-class' families (Sugimura 1988:10). Poverty tends to concentrate in families with a single parent, returnees from mainland China, chronically ill or disabled members, or children in *yōgoshisetsu* (protective institutions for children). A disproportionately high percentage of elderly-only households, single-mother households and households with disabled and chronically ill members received the *seikatsuhogo* in 1985 (32.5, 14.4 and 43.6 per cent respectively) (Sugimura 1988:12). Amongst all middle-school graduates in the prefecture that Miyatake researched in 1988 (Miyatake 1990:20), 2.6 per cent came from *seikatsuhogo* families and 5.9 per cent from single-parent families. One can deduce from this that approximately 8 per cent of middle-school-age children suffered from poverty. In fact, poverty in families with the above tangible traits is relatively more visible. Other poor families are not so visible, since they seem to live like everybody else, although the insecurity of their employment and low income force them to resort to precarious loans to maintain the 'mass' consumption lifestyle of an affluent society, which often leads to further financial difficulties (Sugimura 1988:10).

Children of the poor do attend regular government schools, since the first nine years of schooling are compulsory. Their experience of schooling, however, differs from that of their middle-class counterparts, as outlined above. We will examine how children of the poor participate in, perceive, and benefit from, schooling.

Family Poverty and Children's Schooling

In schooling, family poverty is most evident in two ways: children's failure to go beyond compulsory education, and children in *yōgoshisetsu* (protective care institutions).

First, the retention rate to high schools among children from *seikatsuhogo* or single-parent families is significantly lower than the average. For instance, in Tokyo's *shitamachi* (an old quarter of a city where small shops and houses are crammed together) Adachi-ku, 70 per cent of children from *seikatsuhogo* families proceeded to full-time high schools, while Adachi-ku's average was 85 per cent (which is itself low relative to the national average of 94 per cent) (Otani 1990:50). Among Miyatake's (1990:20) middle-school graduates in the above-mentioned research, the retention rate of children from *seikatsuhogo* families was 78.5 per cent, and that of those from single-parent families was 85.5 per cent, in comparison to the prefectural average of 94.9 per cent (see Table 3.6). The available national-level figures are similar, although slightly out of date: the rate among children from *seikatsuhogo* families was 75 per cent, in comparison to the national average of 94 per cent in 1983 (19 per cent obtained employment while the remaining 6 per cent obtained neither a job nor further education) (Miyatake 1988:22). This phenomenon continues despite the fact that poverty alone is not expected to prevent children of *seikatsuhogo* families from attending high schools, because tuition fee exemption, welfare scholarships and allowances were established for that purpose in 1969 (Miyatake 1988:31–2). Parents' ignorance of such provisions seems prevalent. The second phenomenon, the institutionalisation of children in *yōgoshisetsu*, will be discussed in a subsequent section.

Studies (Miyatake 1988; Otani 1990; Kudomi 1990; Sugimura 1988; Umeda 1990) suggest a common educational scenario for children from poor families, which we briefly outline below.

A family's poverty does not derive from a loss of the household head, but the family often starts with financial vulnerability due to the husband's precarious employment conditions (e.g. day labourer,

Table 3.6 Relationship between retention rate to high school and poverty

	Retention rate to high schools
Children from *seikatsuhogo* families	78.5%
Children from single-parent families	85.5%
Prefectural average	94.9 %

Source: Miyatake (1990), p. 20

construction worker, waiter or unemployed). For instance, among the sole-mother households of Sugimura's study (1988:11), approximately 40 per cent of the women's ex-husbands were in so-called insecure employment (e.g. day labouring) and 40 per cent were unemployed. Parents in low-income families have lower-than-average levels of schooling, and are in unskilled, low-paid, insecure and often physically dangerous employment. A family's financial insecurity leads to conflicts within the family (often resulting from the father's alcoholism, gambling or affairs), and the mother's taking up a lucrative job in the night service and entertainment industry in order to support the family. By the time a subsequent marital separation occurs (where the mother is left with the children), the children have already suffered economically and emotionally, and have started having difficulties at school, leading to academic and interpersonal problems. These problems are not detected early by the mother, who is preoccupied with earning enough to support her children. At the end of middle school, the children have not achieved well enough academically to aim at entering high school, or have already abandoned such a path in the course of observing the family's plight.

These teenagers find jobs, through either referral from their middle school or a family connection, but the kinds of jobs they can obtain are unskilled, low-paid and physically demanding positions in the bottom end of the labour market. Although almost all those who enter employment immediately after middle school come from 'poor' families, they are unlikely to supplement the family finances through their own employment (Miyatake 1988:22). Many of them quit their first job within three months and become unemployed, a pattern repeated for several years. These teenagers become the so-called '*chūsotsu burabura zoku*' (unemployed and/or unemployable middle-school graduates) (Miyatake 1988:20; Otani 1990:50), who leave home and join delinquent teenager groups (Miyatake 1988:22–3). Alternatively, they remain in the same neighbourhood, marry and have children from a very early age, creating the next generation of low-income families, precisely due to their low level of schooling (Otani 1990:50).

The following case study traces a poor family of six children, which lost the household head, faced disintegration, and became unable to provide protective care for the children. The study draws on documentation from a local welfare agency (Miyatake 1990:19–32).

Case Study 3.1: Thirteen Years of a Single-Mother Family with Six Children – Kayo's Story

---

Prior to 1976 (When the welfare agency was contacted by the family)

Kayo (pseudonymous name) was born to a builder father and a mother who died while she was still very young. Kayo's uncle brought her up until she rejoined her father at nine. Kayo's father's alcoholism and the consequent poverty forced her to leave school at 11. At 14 she worked as a housemaid in Kyoto. At 19 she was working in a Tokyo bar. She married when she was 23, and bore seven children, a large number in comparison to the national average of 1.8 children per household at the time (1976) (Japan, Kōseishō 1995:14).[4] One of them, a premature baby boy who required hospitalisation, was adopted out to the couple who paid the medical bills. Since her husband, a day-labourer, had drinking problems and was a poor provider, Kayo worked at a bar to support her six children. Kayo's husband became violent and left the family home, following which the marriage was dissolved.

1976–88 (When the welfare agency monitored the family)

When the family started to receive *seikatsuhogo* in 1976, Kayo was 43 years old and her six children were aged 16, 12, 11, 9, 6 and 3. All of the family members were overweight due to poor diet. Kayo continued to receive treatment for anxiety neurosis. She initially worked as a handyperson at a bar from 4 pm to 11 pm, during which time her children were left unattended, but soon stopped working due to her medical condition and remained unemployed. In 1981 the family moved into government housing after having difficulty paying rent. Three years later the family moved again, believing that their flat was possessed by a spirit. Kayo subsequently suffered from insomnia and hepatitis, for which she received medical treatment. In 1988 she remained unemployed.

Kayo's eldest daughter was hospitalised with diabetes in 1976, subsequently refused to attend middle school and failed to complete compulsory education. She remained unemployed and continued to be hospitalised intermittently. Later she married a man whom she met in a religious group. She continued to suffer from diabetes and, three years after her marriage at the age of 22, became pregnant. However, her husband left her upon finding out that her diabetes would prevent her from bearing a child. She then returned home and had an abortion. A year later she started losing her eyesight and eventually became blind. In 1988 she was hospitalised for nephritis, accompanied by her mother.

The three elder sons were frequently absent from school, and all failed to complete middle-school education due to inadequate attendance. The eldest son was the first to leave home, after starting to work part time at a butcher's shop, and later for a carpenter. His own flat later became a venue for a motorcycle gang's parties and suffered from an attack by another group of motorcycle gang members. The three sons each had intermittent work in a timber factory, a car dismantling factory and a construction factory, interspersed with some periods of unemployment. The second son left home to live with a woman at the age of 21. In 1988 he remained in a car dismantling job and managed his own new family. The eldest son stopped working and spent Kayo's living allowance on himself. The third son was sick and unemployed.

The second daughter performed reasonably well at primary school. When she was a sixth-grader, she was hospitalised for low blood pressure. She then started a sexual relationship, which led her to an obsession with a 'spirit', and subsequently entered a mental hospital. After leaving the hospital she stayed with her elder sister (who by then had married). In the same year she stole valuables, began to experience illusions again and refused to go to school. Two years later she suffered from eczema, and failed to graduate from middle school, although she repeated a year. She started working part time at a lunchbox shop. In 1988 she lived with her boyfriend and eventually married at the age of 18.

The youngest child of the family, a son, was at nursery school in 1976. He was a cheerful third-grader. He later became reluctant to attend school, but managed to complete primary school with consistent encouragement from his teacher. Although he regularly attended middle school, he did not want to proceed to high school. In 1988 he was working at an acquaintance's construction firm, after completing middle school.

In the above case, poverty existed when the family was formed by marriage between two young people who both worked in unskilled jobs. The arrival of seven children and the husband's alcoholism placed emotional and physical pressure on the mother, who consequently suffered from chronic illness, making it difficult for her to look after the children. When the marriage broke down and the family started receiving *seikatsuhogo*, the family's living conditions had already contributed to chronic illness in three of the children. Their school attendance suffered and this impacted on their chances of achieving secure jobs.

It is important to note that none of the six children proceeded to high school. Indeed, five children did not even complete middle school due to inadequate attendance, and entered the 'adult world' via insecure and low-paid dead-end jobs that they found by word of mouth. This was despite the fact that adequate attendance alone would have enabled them to graduate from middle school. Two children started their own families while still very young and financially insecure. Only the youngest of the six children was able to complete compulsory education, but he chose to obtain employment, despite contrary advice from the school and welfare agency, since, the boy claimed, he was a poor academic performer. With none of the older siblings proceeding to high school, the youngest might have considered it natural to take the same path.

This case illuminates the importance of earlier intervention in the elder children's education, since their plights affected the younger members of the family. We concur with the study's author (Miyatake 1990), who argues that the welfare agency and case workers should conduct more intensive intervention, to ensure that children of such families receive formal education beyond compulsory schooling. If children completed high school with the appropriate orientation, they would not only be more mature when entering the adult world, but would also be able to make effective use of the school's resources, in particular, the school's official network with employers, to obtain permanent employment. The most important resources that high schools offer to these children are various employment-related services rather than academic instruction. For children without family resources, the more school resources they appropriate, the more likely they are to successfully enter the adult world (Okano 1995a). Perhaps the children in the above case were unaware of this role that high schools play.

Children in Yōgoshisetsu

Children are institutionalised in yōgoshisetsu (protective care institutions) from as early as birth when parents are unwilling to be responsible for, or are incapable of, taking care of their children. In 1987 the reasons for children entering yōgoshisetsu were as follows: the disappearance of parents (one or both; 26.3 per cent), parents' divorce (20.1 per cent), parents' long-term hospitalisation (11.5 per cent), and the death of parents (one or both; 7.5 per cent) (Kuroda and Takenaka 1990:60). The need to place children in protective care has always existed, but over the last 30 years the principal reasons have shifted from parents' death (23 per cent in 1952 and 7.5 per cent in 1987) to parents' divorce and disappearance (11 per cent in 1952 and 46 per cent in 1987) (Seishōnen Fukushi Sentā 1989:5–6).

The Centre for Youth Welfare (Seishōnen Fukushi Sentā) (1989:4–7) argues that the need for institutionalised protective care for children arises from problems of the wider social structure and relations, that is, from poverty in the widest sense of the term (which includes economic poverty, disintegration of human relationships, and personal inability in child rearing). Characteristics of the parents of children in yōgoshisetsu include poor educational attainment (compulsory education or less), and fathers in unskilled labour and mothers in the night service industry (Seishōnen Fukushi Sentā 1989:7–8). Family income levels are significantly lower than the average, with many families receiving *seikatsuhogo*. Economic poverty often leads to such phenomena as alcoholism, apathy, and gambling as a perceived means of escape (Seishōnen Fukushi Sentā 1989:8).

Many parents of these children also experienced poverty and related family problems in their own youth (Seishōnen Fukushi Sentā 1989:8). Institutionalised protective care of children is a measure taken to address these poverty problems, by taking care of the youngest and weakest member of the struggling family as a priority (Seishōnen Fukushi Sentā 1989:199). These measures are intended to intervene in the process whereby the poverty that the parents inherited from the previous generation is passed on to the next generation (Seishōnen Fukushi Sentā 1989:8). Given the extremely low retention rate of *yōgoshisetsu* children to full-time high school (varying from 73.3 per cent in Tottori prefecture to 25.9 per cent in Aichi prefecture in 1987) (Kuroda and Takenaka 1990:70), and the high rate of abandonment of first jobs, the end of middle schooling seems to be the decisive point in the reproduction of poverty and disturbed human development.

The term 'yō *yōgo kōrei jidō*' (literally, 'older children who require protective care') refers to youths over 15 who lack protective care. Many of them grew up in *yōgoshisetsu* and enter the workforce after middle school (often due to their inability to proceed to high school). They are forced to choose '*shūshoku dokuritsu*' ('independence through employment'), by leaving the *yōgoshisetsu* and abandoning protective care, the lack of which had sent them to these institutions in the first place (Seishōnen Fukushi Sentā 1989:17). This means that these youths are deprived of their rights to survival, development and a minimum standard of living (Seishōnen Fukushi Sentā 1989:16–17), a point that we will take up later in relation to children's rights. *Jidō Fukushihō* (Child Protection Law) considers persons under 18 years old to be 'children' (*jidō*), and states that national and local governments, as well as parents, are responsible for their care (Seishōnen Fukushi Sentā 1989:17).

These youths' progress to high schools has been helped by special scholarships since 1973, but their retention rate still remains under 40 per cent compared with a national average of over 90 per cent (Seishōnen Fukushi Sentā 1989:18). If they proceed to high schools, they can remain at *yōgoshisetsu*, and the proportion of such youths increased from 7.5 per cent in 1970 to 10.6 per cent in 1980 and 13.6 per cent in 1985. Still, every year about 2000 15-year-olds leave institutions to become 'independent', despite not being ready for it (Seishōnen Fukushi Sentā 1989:18).

These teenagers are the most at risk of experiencing poverty in the future. Having no 'home', they seek jobs that provide accommodation, and their lack of high-school qualifications (when over 90 per cent of their age group graduates from high school) forces them into low-paid unskilled jobs in small-sized companies (Seishōnen Fukushi Sentā 1989:25). In 1988, almost 28 per cent of those who obtained employment after completing middle school quit their first job within eight months (Seishōnen Fukushi Sentā 1989:27–8). Continuation in the first job depends on the individual youth's adaptation to the workplace and to working life in general, which is strongly influenced by protective support from the employer (Seishōnen Fukushi Sentā 1989:32). This demonstrates the necessity for 'social' support for these youths' entry into work and adulthood.

Severing the Poverty Cycle: High School Graduation

Many studies on poverty and schooling conclude that one of the most effective solutions for inhibiting the reproduction of *seikatsuhogo* families and poverty from one generation to the next is the completion of high schooling (Sugimura 1988; Miyatake 1990; Kuroda and Takenaka 1990; Otani 1990; Umeda 1990; Kudomi 1993). Miyatake (1990:28) reports that an increase in *seikatsuhogo* children's retention rates to high schools led to decreased delinquent activities in the neighbourhood, and provided the youths with better and more secure employment opportunities.

It should be noted at this point that high schooling for *seikatsuhogo* children (or children from poor families) has a function that is quite different from what the mainstream Japanese perceive it to be. For these disadvantaged students, high school is neither a site for intensive academic preparation and socialisation for entry into universities, nor a place for a competition in which one demonstrates his or her worth, as defined by certain criteria. Instead, high schools with 'appropriate' orientations are considered as means of preventing these young people from taking up insecure jobs and unemployment, early marriage and birth. In short, high schools are expected to keep these young people occupied until they become more mature and are qualified to achieve more secure employment. One could argue that such functions also represent an assistance to upward social mobility, as is expected of modern schools, but the functions we have been describing are quite different in nature.

Young People Making Sense of their Exclusion

Let us now examine how these young people view their own experience of dropping out of school. Do they know that their actions exclude them from more promising paths to the adult world that further schooling would have opened to them? Do they actively refuse the dominant achievement ideology? Why do they feel compelled to opt out?

Kudomi's project (1993) examined the schooling of children from poor families residing in a housing complex in a large city over a period of three years. 'Danchi A', the city's largest housing complex, has 26,000 residents, 70 per cent of whom reside in the government housing section. Danchi A was completed in 1977 by the city government, with accommodation capacity for 32,000 people. The city's Housing Department revealed that the low number of residents at the time of the research was due to many vacancies in the government housing section. Forty per cent of the government flats are allocated for those who satisfy 'stricter' entry requirements, for instance, *seikatsuhogo* families, solo-mother families, elderly families, families with chronic illness and disabled people, and recent returnees from mainland China.

The study (Kudomi 1993:107–45) revealed how young people themselves made sense of their own schooling, through interviews with 24 young people who, their parents claimed, had maladjustment problems at school. (The parents of 19 of them were also interviewed.) All of them had completed compulsory education and were under 25. Eight of them started refusing to go to school at primary or middle school; five did not go to high school, and five dropped out of high school.

Case Study 3.2: Dropping Out – Kane's Story

> Kane, a 17-year-old, lived with her mother and an elder sister, and worked a few hours daily as a checker [checkout operator]. Since her parents' divorce, the family had lived on *seikatsuhogo*. Kane quit school mid-way through her 11th grade because, she explained, she found it difficult to get up in the morning, was absent from school frequently and did not think that she could proceed to the 12th grade. She was neither behind in her schoolwork (because the level of her school was low, she claimed), nor did she dislike the school, although she did not like some teachers. She also had some friends there. Kane's homeroom teacher managed to allow her to proceed to the 11th grade despite insufficient first-year attendance, but told her to increase her attendance in order to proceed to the 12th grade. Her homeroom teacher regretted Kane's decision to leave school, saying 'It is a shame, since she was OK academically'. Kane's mother advised against her decision but did not insist. Her mother explained that she did not want her daughter to become delinquent as a result of her insistence, since there was no father in the house (Kudomi 1993:117–18).

Kane was uninterested in school and quit without thinking about the consequences of her action, despite the fact that she was achieving acceptable grades. The study argues teenagers like Kane neither are conscious that their opting out of schools might bring some negative consequence, nor understand that schools play an important role in forming their futures. For them school is a place they can choose to attend or not, depending on their mood, and since their moods happen to be negative at times, they simply leave (Kudomi 1993:109). These youths have not internalised the competitive ideology that school success will lead to upward social mobility as the motivating norm for themselves, although they may be aware that such an ideology is accepted by others.

This study identifies two distinctive types of youth who drop out of school. The first, like Kane, comprises those who have not found a lifestyle alternative to school that they consider appealing. After rejecting school, they live passively and somehow aimlessly, as if they are 'floating in the present', without searching for what they want (Kudomi 1993:123). The second type consists of those who live positively in the present, finding self-fulfilment and developing self-confidence through their employment experiences. They see no need for social mobility through school success, and intend to live through their present employment positions (Kudomi 1993:134–5). Kieko was one such case. She felt uncomfortable with the kinds of relationships that existed among her classmates, and did not see that the value of schooling outweighed the cost of enduring such relationships.

Case Study 3.3: Dropping Out – Kieko's Story

> Kieko, a 17-year old, lived with her mother and two brothers. Her parents had been divorced six years previously. She started refusing to go to school within a few months of her entry into middle school, where she had been a quiet student and had few friends. She felt she was 'being left behind by her classmates'. Her mother took her to the *jidōsōdansho* (a child counselling service), and then to a *yōgoshisetsu* (protective care institution), which Kieko described as 'having very strict regulations'. 'I was not allowed to be alone. Although I understand that such a rule is necessary for living in a group, I wanted to have more freedom. But I liked the way we all helped each other as a group.' In contrast, she commented, 'At school you were not recognised unless you talked continuously . . . If not, others labelled you as "dark"'. Because everyone was scared of being labelled as such, she kept talking. 'But no-one trusted anyone else. If you did something different from the others, you were labelled as "deviant". I had little in common with them.' She now works at a cake shop, and says that she enjoys communicating with customers. She serves customers with a smile, which she considers is natural for that type of work (Kudomi 1993:125–6).

What do we make of these young people's explanations of their dropping out of school? They do not consider schools as particularly important *for themselves*, and leave an institution which is expected to provide a wider range of life chances. Kudomi (1993:141) contends that neither type of youth actively refuses the dominant achievement ideology, but that they do not see the ideology as being applicable *to themselves*, or are simply reluctant to join the game. One could interpret this as meaning that they are not giving in to, or ignoring, or even challenging, the dominant achievement ideology; and that their existence suggests an incomplete permeation of the ideology. On the other hand, one might consider that these young people remain 'losers', since their actions (of not embracing the achievement ideology) justify their powerless social positions; and that as long as the power to define who are the 'failures' rests in the dominant group, these individual actions are not a substantial challenge to the dominant ideology. Recall Willis's study (1977) of the working-class 'lads' in Britain. Their refusal to comply with the school culture and their glorification of working-class culture eventually led them to the shopfloor like their fathers, an outcome that these lads were content with. Their refusal of, and challenge to, the school culture did not affect the legitimacy of the school culture at all.

Maintaining Family Privileges: An Elite Private School

The privileged's relationship with schooling differs from that experienced by the poor. Although schooling potentially provides opportunities to sever the cycle of poverty, we have seen that many children from poverty-stricken families have not made effective use of education. Because of this, schooling enables some to attribute the limited life chances of children from poor families, and the consequent continuation of poverty, to individual failure to utilise given educational opportunities. In contrast, children from privileged families generally use schooling effectively in order to maintain the privileges that they already possess. Some of them rely on selective private schools to do so. These schools also provide children from less privileged families with possibilities for social mobility.

Nada is an example of one such private elite school. We will draw on two case studies of the school: one conducted in the mid 1970s by Rohlen, an American anthropologist, and the other by a team of *Mainichi Shinbun* journalists in 1991.

Case Study 3.4: An Elite Private School – Nada High School

Nada High School is a private boys' school which has been one of the most successful in sending its graduates to the nation's top universities. In 1990 Nada students won 20 places out of 90 available in Tokyo University's medical course – the most difficult to enter, and therefore the most prestigious, in the country. Nada was followed by La Salle High in Kagoshima prefecture (seven places) and Tokyo Kaisei High (six places), both of which are also private schools (Mainichi Shinbun Kōbe Shikyoku [MSKS] 1991:51–3). In the same year, Nada students won 123 places at Tokyo University (MSKS 1991:53). Almost half of Nada's 220 graduates went on to the nation's top university.

Nada High is located in an eastern residential suburb of Kobe city, and receives students mainly from the nearby Kansai region. Those from other regions live away from home. A considerable number of students from Tokyo attempt Nada's entrance examination to see how they fare, although they are likely to settle on similar private schools in Tokyo where their families reside. Nada's school buildings are simple and similar to those of many government schools, and do not project an image of an institution for the nation's elites.

In fact Nada's origins are quite humble. The school was started in 1928 for boys from upper-middle-class families who had failed to secure a place in the then more prestigious government academic high schools in Kobe, and its graduates were destined for second-rate universities (Rohlen 1983:21–2). Nada came to win nationwide recognition for its academic excellence only in the 1960s, when it started sending a large number of its graduates to Tokyo University; it has maintained this prestige to date. Nada's rise was due to local government changes in school zoning in the 1950s, which prevented able students in nearby suburbs from attending Kobe's best government high schools (Rohlen 1983:21–2).

Students and Teachers

Contrary to popular perceptions, Nada boys experience a more liberal learning environment than is found in most government academic high schools.

School regulations are minimal. There have been no school uniforms and no rules regarding hairstyles and possessions since the 1970s, when students mobilised themselves to protest against such rules. The school advocates a policy of 'student independence and initiative' (MSKS 1991:82, 116–17). Students were allowed to leave the school grounds during lunch breaks until recently, when nearby residents complained that some Nada students disposed of cigarette butts into their gardens on the way back from the local shops (MSKS 1991:116–17). When the school finds students drinking, smoking, or cheating in tests, students receive *teigaku* (suspension from school) for three days, a punishment which normally occurs only three times a year (MSKS 1991:117).

Nada is a notably relaxed and lively place, blessed with bright and self-confident students (Rohlen 1983:26). The students are as diverse, healthy and athletic as those at other schools, rather than being anaemic and compulsive bookworms (Rohlen 1983:283). Approximately 60 to 80 per cent of Nada students are involved in one of the after-school extracurricular clubs (MSKS 1991:97–8; Rohlen 1983:282). Nada has 15 sports clubs and 22 non-sporting clubs. While the sports clubs' performance is mediocre, *go* and *shōgi* clubs are competitive at the top national levels (MSKS 1991:97–8). Students are notably efficient in their study skills, and their relative homogeneity (in terms of academic ability and family support) enables teachers to conduct lessons effectively. Despite large class sizes, of up to 55 in one class (Rohlen 1983:19), the pace of learning is fast. The continuity of secondary schooling (from middle to high school) allows Nada to complete the six-year curriculum within five years, so that the final year is spent on revision and preparation for the university entrance examinations (Rohlen 1983:25).

Nada's learning process is helped by experienced teachers: they are male, with an average age of about 50, and have been head-hunted from government academic high schools (MSKS 1991:84, 91). While the move from a government high school to Nada offers incentives such as intellectually challenging students, non-compulsory involvement in extra-curricular activities and higher social status (Rohlen 1983:25), teachers are placed under greater pressure to 'perform'. If students and their parents consider a teacher's performance inadequate, they can mobilise the PTA to replace him (MSKS 1991:164–6).

Those Who Are 'Behind'

Not all Nada students are self-confident and consider themselves to be 'successful'. Although the majority of Nada graduates are destined for the nation's top universities (with almost half going to Tokyo University), some students are 'behind' and manage to enter private universities only after several attempts. One student near the bottom of his grade was interviewed:

Interviewer: Why do you think you fell behind?

Student: I often fell asleep at home after sports club practice. I also rebelled against a Nada middle-school teacher. I got into a habit of going out – playing at game centres and drinking with friends.

Interviewer: Have you thought of leaving Nada for another school?

Student: Not really. Nada has an environment where those who devote themselves to something are acknowledged. I'm not good at academic work but did reasonably well in the club, so others recognise me for that. Naturally, teachers tell me to perform better academically – some teachers ignore poor-performing students altogether. But I've never thought of leaving school. I always attend classes.

Interviewer: What types of students do you think get behind?

Student: Well, the top 50 students (out of 220) are always up there. The next 100 students enter either medicine or Tokyo University. The next 50 boys somehow manage academic work, but students after that (i.e. the bottom 20 students) are far behind the rest. Most of these bottom students entered Nada Middle School – they thought that they would eventually catch up, and ended up diverting to non-academic activities. Those who enter Nada at the beginning of high school are very serious and diligent.

Interviewer: Have you felt a sense of failure (*zasetsukan*)?

Student: Well, yes. Our pride is high. Although everyone thinks that one can perform well if he works harder, he eventually gives up as he moves up the grades. But his parents won't give up their aspirations for him. They assume that their son will still go to Tokyo University . . . It is true that the school has an environment where even Waseda University (an elite private university) is considered somehow inadequate. (MSKS 1991:107–8)

At a Nada old boys' party, a man in his early thirties who works for a small company after graduating from a provincial national university lamented:

'See, the Nada old boys are all elite government bureaucrats, medical doctors or employees of first-rate companies. I cannot help sensing a smell of elite. This is hard for those who are "behind" like myself to cope with – in just the same way as when I was a Nada student.' (MSKS 1991:109)

Family Advantages and Destinations in Students' Adult Lives

Nada students' families are generally privileged in terms of the economic and cultural resources that they can make available to their sons. They are more privileged than their counterparts at the other four Kobe high schools that Rohlen (1983) studied, as measured by their lower average number of siblings, possession of study rooms, parents' occupations (professional and managerial) and high education levels, and the lower number of minority students. However, families need not be wealthy to pay Nada's tuition fees, which are within the reach of an ordinary family, and comparable with those of other private schools in the area (Rohlen 1983:23). In fact the tuition fees are relatively inexpensive for the value that students receive from Nada. Nada provides its students with a more intensive and effective preparation for the entrance examinations to the top universities (helped by the homogeneity of academic excellence, and committed teachers) than any of the other private preparatory schools (*yobikō*) that many high-school students attend after school.

More students from ethnic minority families now attend Nada than before. The number of third-generation Korean and Chinese at Nada increased from 18 to 23 over the last decade. A Korean from Osaka's Korean community, who has sent his two sons to Nada, commented:

'Although Koreans have now more employment opportunities, we still do not receive equal chances for promotion. These days some of us become lawyers, but I think that only medicine will give us a secure income and future. Maybe we Koreans are anxious to move up the social ladder.' (MSKS 1991:70)

A third-generation Chinese boy, whose father frequently travels overseas on business, entered Nada and then went on to Tokyo University with the aim of becoming a lawyer. Although the move from Kobe's ethnic Chinese middle school (*Chūka Dōbun Gakkō*) was not easy for him, his parents considered that the Chinese language and knowledge that he acquired at the Chinese ethnic school would benefit him in the long run (MSKS 1991:71).

Many of the Nada graduates achieve positions that are considered by the mainstream Japanese to be the most elite and prestigious. After going through the nation's top universities, they settle as elite government bureaucrats (especially in the Ministry of Finance and the Ministry of International Trade and Industry), lawyers and medical doctors, and create 'the establishment' of contemporary Japanese society (MSKS 1991:7). The Nada graduates maintain formal old boys' 'social clubs' and informal old boys' meetings and parties to maintain and utilise the solid social network derived from their Nada connection (MSKS 1991:12–23).

While the majority of Nada graduates follow a predictable route to the top universities and then to the elite occupations, a few choose lifestyles alternative to the Nada establishment routes. Mr Takeda, who resigned from a top-class company and now runs a small publishing firm after taking up several freelance jobs, comments that Nada graduates are technocrats, not power elites (MSKS 1991:35–6). Mr Fuji became involved in a 'new religion' after working as a medical doctor for several years (MSKS 1991:38–40). Mr Hata is a member of the Nada/Tokyo University elite who quit a job in Tokyo, moved to a small village in Kyoto and has taken up organic agriculture (MSKS 1991:41–3). Nonetheless, these men are still exceptions to the bulk of Nada graduates.

Elite private schools like Nada are few in number, and are an exception to the majority of private high schools that accommodate those who cannot make it to government schools. However, the students from that small number of private elite schools dominate the nation's top universities. For instance, in the five-year period from 1987 to 1991 only nine private elite schools (and five government schools) were among the top ten providers of new students to Tokyo University (MSKS 1991:61). In 1990 34.4 per cent of the entrants to Tokyo University came from only 15 elite high schools, and each of these schools sent over 50 students to the university (MSKS 1991:4). Given that in 1990 there were 5342 high schools throughout Japan (Japan, Sōmuchō Tōkeikyoku 1991), the predominance of this limited number of elite schools is extreme. It is important to remember that the (male) students who attend such elite private schools and the nation's top universities eventually dominate powerful positions and make decisions for society as a whole (Cutts 1997); and that these students are likely to possess families with resources that enable them to pursue this path. This situation is, of course, hardly peculiar to contemporary Japan.

An Alternative Form of School: Correspondence School

While Nada students are finishing a day at school and preparing themselves for extra tutoring classes, another group of students are starting their 'schooling' at home, working on assignments for correspondence high school programs. Students in correspondence programs are neither as homogeneous in academic excellence or family background, nor as ambitious as Nada students. These students are as diverse as one could imagine.

Correspondence high schools (*tsūshinsei kōkō*) were originally established to provide opportunities for post-compulsory schooling for those who could not afford full-time high-school education immediately after middle school. Recently the student population of correspondence programs has grown diverse, and includes teenagers who could not cope with, or chose to reject, mainstream day high schooling (Nagano Nishi Kōtōgakkō Tsūshinsei [NNKT] 1991:197). We would suggest that correspondence programs are one of the most flexible and 'accommodating' educational institutions for teenagers who bring diverse backgrounds to school, and that the role of correspondence programs in the 1990s and beyond deserves closer examination. Drawing on a collection of essays written by 34 recent graduates from the Nagano Nishi High School Correspondence Program (NNKT 1991), we will examine characteristics of the program and its students, and discuss the significance of correspondence programs in general.

Case Study 3.5: A Correspondence High School – The Nishi Program

The Nagano Nishi High School Correspondence Program (henceforth called the Nishi Program) offers a high-school diploma on completion of four years of study (NNKT 1991:197–207). Its outwardly distinctive features are that students do not come to school every day, and that the program runs a childcare centre. Since many students are in paid employment and have families, time management skills are essential.

The Program's academic study consists of three components. The first, submission of completed assignments (two-page question sheets for each of five or six subjects, twice a month), is equivalent to classes at day high schools. The assignments receive teachers' comments. The second component is 'interview lessons' (*mensetsu jugyō*) held on Sundays for those who work, and on Mondays for full-time housewives and those who work on Sundays, in order to assist independent study. Students can make up for missed interview lessons by arranging private interview lessons with teachers, or by studying via the Nippon Hōsō Kyoku (NHK) radio or television high-school program at the end of the academic year. Teachers visit those in hospital and provide missed interview lessons and/or examinations. The third component is study meetings (*gakushūkai*), held weekly in the evening at local community halls. Students in each area study for assignments under the supervision of one of the Program's teachers. Able students teach those who need help, and the seniors teach the juniors. These study groups organise social outings and activities as well. In order to take term examinations, students must have submitted final assignments one week prior to sitting the examinations. If a student fails in an examination, he or she can be granted second and third attempts.

The Nishi Program organises overnight summer schooling, which students are required to participate in at least once during their four-year enrolment. Participants are given credits for 'Special Activities' and Physical Education. Qualifying activities include excursions to historical places, hiking and other sports activities, which provide a chance to communicate with classmates and teachers.

The Program organises various events that regular schools provide, such as entry ceremonies, athletics meetings (which everyone is expected to attend), school festivals, three-day overnight school excursions, sports clubs (which participate in regional tournament matches), speech contests, *Dōwa* Education (lessons on the human rights of minorities), farewell parties for graduates, and graduation ceremonies. However, the nature of these events differs from those in regular schools because of the diversity of the Program's students; for instance, school excursions involve students' family members (spouse and children) and helpers for disabled students, and children at the Program's childcare centre participate in school festivals.

Four Types of Students

There are four distinctive types of students in the Nishi Program. The first comprises older people who are on the verge of retirement from paid work, and housewives in their forties or older. They want to realise their long-held wish to study at high school, without expecting an instrumental return for their schooling, in terms of enhanced employment prospects or promotion.

The second type consists of those in paid employment who wish to upgrade their academic qualifications and improve their promotion chances. By so doing, they want to recover self-esteem they have lost in humiliating experiences with colleagues at workplaces dominated by high-school graduates. Many of them have been employed since age 15, and have experienced an acute sense of inferiority about their lack of high-school qualifications. Having been away from academic study for over 20 years and now having their own families, such students find study demanding to organise.

The third group is young people with physical disabilities or chronic illness. They either choose, or are forced, to attend the correspondence program because regular day high schools often refuse to accept them, claiming that they lack adequate facilities and appropriate staff members. Those with a chronic illness, who often have to be hospitalised, find it difficult to satisfy the attendance requirement at day schools. Normal day schools often do not have the flexibility and understanding (among both students and teaching staff members) to accommodate such distinctive needs and backgrounds, as shown by the three cases below (individual student names are pseudonymous).

Fujie: Due to my chronic illness, I have been frequently hospitalised and found it difficult to attend day high school. After middle school, I entered the workforce and since then have changed jobs. When seeking jobs, I was disappointed to find that employers expect employees to be 'healthy' and to have graduated from high school. After completing the correspondence program, I now work as a clerk at a hospital. (NNKT 1991:92–8)

Hiroshi: I was born with cerebral palsy and cannot use my arms. I attended primary, middle and high schools for the disabled (*yōgogakkō*). However, due to the large number of seriously disabled students at these schools, half of the class hours were spent on rehabilitation activities, and I could not study academic subjects to the extent I wanted. So I decided to join the correspondence program. The teachers' help and availability of word processors enabled me to continue studying what I wanted. I now undertake university study by correspondence. (NNKT 1991:79–85)

Ryūichi: I have suffered from progressive muscular dystrophy since I was in grade four, but kept good academic marks at middle school, which I attended in a wheelchair. No regular high schools in the area were prepared to accept me, claiming that they were not adequately equipped to cater for my needs. (NNKT 1991:86–91)

The fourth group is teenagers who had not adapted to the 'regular' day schools and chose to attend the correspondence programs as an alternative. In fact this was the largest group in the Nishi Program in the 1980s. The essays in the NNKT collection reveal that many of these students suffered from bullying at regular school; lost trust in friends and teachers, as well as self-esteem; found it impossible to bring themselves to attend school; and eventually quit high school altogether. Some of them had attended high-ranking academic high schools, while others were disillusioned with the rough nature of low-ranking schools. We will discuss school refusal in more detail in Chapter 6.

Accommodating Different Needs

The correspondence program seems able to accommodate youth who could not adapt to the mainstream schooling. Young people who have lost confidence in themselves and no longer trust others tend to experience an empathy from, and develop friendships with, classmates, which enables them to eventually regain confidence. How does this happen?

First, the program's participants include those from outside mainstream schooling and employment. Coming from diverse backgrounds, they tend to be more willing to accommodate others' needs and backgrounds, and to be tolerant of, and sympathetic to, youths who dropped out of mainstream schooling. Second, since many 'adult' students have overcome various hardships in life (e.g. illness, poverty, lack of parents, physical disability), they are willing to help young people who have themselves suffered and have little trust in others. Third, since the school program is not geared to university entrance examinations, it can remain flexible. A few, however, choose to take up university study after obtaining a high-school diploma. Among the Nishi Program's graduates, Hiroshi studies law in a correspondence university program; Shinya is at a local university's education faculty; Shiori reads Japanese literature at a local junior college; and Junya studies economics at a day university. Fourth, since the correspondence program does not require daily attendance, students can independently manage their own study. Cooperation, rather than competition, among students is highly encouraged.

High-school correspondence programs originally catered predominantly for older people by providing flexible study arrangements through correspondence and occasional contact classes. They now attract young people who could not receive regular day high-school education due to physical disability and chronic illness. In addition, those who are either rejected by, or choose to reject, regular high schools participate in them after experiencing bullying and/or 'school refusal syndrome'.

Recently a new type of *juku,* called 'support schools', has been established by the education industry in order to accommodate those who attend correspondence high schools because of school refusal or dropping out of day high schools. By imposing few rules (e.g. attendance is not compulsory), starting lessons late in the morning, and providing a flexible environment, these 'support schools' create an alternative learning space. The daily classes review middle-school studies and supplement the students' independent correspondence high-school studies. The schools are expected to help students complete the correspondence school diploma, since a lack of the self-discipline and time management skills that independent study requires had been a significant cause for their failure to continue study through correspondence (*Asahi Shinbun* 17 March 1997).

We would suggest that regular day high schools are not adequately equipped to accommodate youths with 'differences'. This is demonstrated by the fact that correspondence programs are filled with those who were once marginalised by the majority, and/or hold diverse backgrounds and non-mainstream life histories. The correspondence programs create an environment where everyone, and what he or she brings to school, is treated with tolerance and understanding. The Nishi Program's case suggests that such an environment is conducive to learning processes, both academically and personally, for all students but in particular for the young who have lost confidence in mainstream schooling.

Rural Schooling: Agricultural High Schools

There have been changes in the clientele and school missions of some private schools (like Nada) and of correspondence schools over the post-war period. Nada has become the nation's top school for producing elites, while correspondence schools have begun to cater for young people who could not be accommodated in mainstream schooling. The status of agricultural high schools has similarly changed. Whereas these were once glorious institutions, sending out future leaders of the agricultural industry and local governments, they are now ranked in the lower strata of the high school hierarchy, and face difficulties in filling available places.

In this section, we will examine how youths from rural farming families experience agricultural schooling against a background of industry decline. Being vocational in nature, agricultural high schools share some features with the urban commerce and technical high schools that we illustrated earlier: they are lower-ranked than academic high schools, receive non-academic students, and aim to prepare their students for immediate employment. We have chosen to examine agricultural high schools here because detailed studies of urban commerce and technical high schools are available in English (Rohlen 1983; Okano 1993), and also because agricultural high schools reflect the state of rural communities.

The Decline of Rural Farming Communities

Post-war industrialisation led to a decline in the rural population as work opportunities in secondary and tertiary industries expanded. This process was reinforced by post-war agricultural policies, which encouraged small farmers to abandon the land, and large landowner farmers to become more efficient through 'modernisation' (the absorption of small farms and mechanisation). Consequently, the rural farming communities became depopulated, and small farmers have found it increasingly difficult to earn a living from agriculture alone.

The post-war expansion in the educational participation rate also impacted on rural communities, although initially at a lower level than the national trend (Matsuzawa 1994:6). In a small village in Akita prefecture, the boys' retention rate to high schools increased from 22 per cent in 1969 to 52 per cent in 1970, and reached 96 per cent in 1980 (Arai 1987:208). This trend had a profound impact on the lives of farming families in rural communities. First, rural families require greater financial resources for their children's high-school education. Since few high schools are within commuting distance, high-school education in rural communities costs substantially more than it does in urban areas. A case study of five villages in Kyūshū (Matsuzawa 1994:7) reveals that parents first try to send their children to schools within commuting distance. If this is impossible, they send their children to the nearest schools, or schools with dormitory facilities. A few parents are prepared to send their children to elite schools in the prefectural capital if they can secure places (Matsuzawa 1994:7–8). The need to support their children's high schooling has led some families to abandon farming and take up wage-earning jobs, or one family member (often the father) to take up seasonal labouring work to supplement the family's cash income (Matsuzawa 1994:7–8).

Second, once rural young people move to high school, they often do not return to their communities for employment (Matsuzawa 1994:10). The subsequent decline in the school-age population results in the amalgamation or closure of local schools. The number of schools designated as 'schools in depopulated areas' (*hekichigakkō*) decreased from 6000 primary schools and 2500 middle schools in 1960, to 3700 and 1300 respectively in 1990. Among these designated schools, the average enrolments were 50 at primary schools and 70 at middle schools (Matsuzawa 1994:10). In this context, the decline of rural farming communities is inevitable.

While the decline of rural farming has generally been viewed by the public as a consequence of post-war industrialisation, agricultural policies and expansion in educational participation, Nagasu (1984:67–8) explains the decline in terms of a conspiracy theory: that it is an intended outcome of the central government's 1961 agricultural modernisation policy. Nagasu (1984:67–8) argues that the government tried to decrease the number of farming families by advocating the creation of 'independent farming families' (*jiritsu nōka*), defined as farmers having over 3 ha of rice fields (the national average is 0.6 ha). The policy has made it difficult for many farming households to earn sufficient income to support themselves. The farming population decreased between 1960

(30 per cent of the working population, or 14 million) and 1980 (10 per cent, 5.4 million), although the extent of the decrease did not reach the target set by the government in 1960. Currently, only 10 per cent of farming households rely totally on income from farming, while over 70 per cent of the farming households earn more income from seasonal employment than from farming (Nagasu 1984:67–9).

The Decline of Agricultural High Schools

Farming has thus become an economically unprofitable occupation in comparison to increased employment options in the secondary and tertiary sectors of industry. In an Ibaraki prefecture town where 72 per cent of households are farmers, half of them had nobody to take over the farm (Nagasu 1984:65). Nationally, from around 1975, fewer than 10 per cent of the graduates from agricultural high schools have taken up farming. At 13 agricultural high schools in Ibaraki prefecture, about 60 per cent of farm management students came from farming families (Nagasu 1984:65), but only a small number of them intended to take over the family business. As a result of this trend, agricultural high schools have become the least popular schools, and therefore the easiest in which to secure a place, and are now at the bottom of the high-school hierarchy (in descending order: academic, commerce, technical and agricultural).

Some agricultural high schools have devised ways to encourage young people to step into family farming. In 1983 they introduced an entry-by-recommendation system, whereby the school accepts applicants who promise to take over the family farm by placing less emphasis on their prior academic achievement. These schools often require a written oath from the student and his or her parents. Another measure is to provide scholarships to those who were admitted to the schools through the entry-by-recommendation system. Such scholarships are expected to discourage the young from opting out of farming at the end of high schooling (Nagasu 1984:75).

Many agricultural high schools receive fewer applicants than the number of places offered (Taga 1988a:224; Nagasu 1984:26). Students have derogatory attitudes towards agricultural high schools, labelling them 'potato school' or 'fertiliser school' (Nagasu 1984:17–18); and some are ashamed of the 'agricultural' part of the school name (Nagasu 1984:39). Some teachers confess that agricultural high schools receive dropouts who could not secure a place at any other high school (Nagasu 1984:21). Another teacher said, 'The problems of agricultural high schools are that students are apathetic, suffer from poor academic performance and delinquent activities, and drop out of school. We teachers are too occupied to cope with these problems, and our morale is low' (Nagasu 1984:21). Knowing this, some farming parents encourage their sons to attend academic high school and then the Faculty of Agriculture at university, before returning to the farm (Nagasu 1984:66).

Below we illustrate two distinctive types of agricultural high school. The first is one that suffers from low morale, poor academic achievement and other problems associated with 'unpopular' schools. The majority of agricultural high schools or agricultural courses in comprehensive high schools fit into this category. The second is one of 36 'elite' government agricultural high schools, many of whose graduates do return to farming.

Case Study 3.6: An Ordinary Agricultural High School – Akagi High

Akagi Agricultural and Forestry High is located amid greenery in a small provincial city in Gunma prefecture. The school grounds are large, and include greenhouses, farmland and an 80 ha forest. The school has five courses: agriculture, horticulture, animal husbandry, green-zone civil engineering (*ryokuchi doboku*), and home science (*seikatsu*) (Taga 1988a:55). The author of this study worked as a social studies teacher at Akagi High for five years in the 1980s. When the school was established, about 85 years ago, it sent out graduates who went on to occupy powerful positions in society. Recently the school has been no exception to other agricultural high schools across the country: it fails to receive sufficient applicants to fill its places.

Student Culture

For Akagi High students, the school is a place where they make friends and 'have a good time'. Their main interests are their own appearances and speeding on motorbikes.

'Having a good time' includes vandalism. Students damage desks and chairs and draw graffiti on school property. Classroom curtains are dirty, since the boys use the curtains as towels after going to the toilets, forcing the school to buy new curtains every year. They eat lunch (which they bring from home) in the class during the morning break. By the afternoon, the classrooms are full of rubbish, which soon accumulates near the 'weaker' boys, giving teachers a clue about the power dynamics of the class (Taga 1988a:15–17).

Students show great interest in their appearance. Boys always carry combs and gaze at themselves in the mirror in the school corridor. Mirrors in front of each sink in the men's toilets are commonly stolen. Even during lessons, they comb their hair, stare at small portable mirrors and brush their school uniforms (Taga 1988a:17–18).

Both boys and girls are concerned with their facial appearance and hair. They shave their eyebrows into narrow lines, and curl their eyelashes. Some put glittering powder on their cheeks; others maintain long fingernails, have them manicured and wear conspicuous rings. Some boys have pieced ears and wear rings that are matched with their girlfriends'. Many wear what they call 'technocut' hairstyles, where hairlines above the ears are kept extremely short or stripe patterns are created at the back of the head. Others let only a handful of hair grow longer, which they tie with a colourful string. A student claimed, 'I had thought that my mother and homeroom teacher would get so angry at my appearance that they would let me quit school. I really want to quit school'. Unfortunately, the student's mother made him shave his head in the boys' hairstyle prescribed by many middle schools, and returned him to school. Boys and girls have their hair permed, dyed or bleached, although fully aware that the school prohibits this. When warned by teachers, they insist that their hair is 'natural' by producing a letter from their parents and a childhood photo of themselves. Whatever they do, they are skilful in deviating from the school rules 'gradually', so that teachers are less likely to notice changes. It is a game for students: they are often found out and are forced to comply with the rules (Taga 1988a:22–5).

About 80 per cent of Akagi High boys favour a particular type of appearance, preferring wide trousers with a particular design near the ankles. They wear military-style black school jackets either too long or too short; some boys going to the trouble of shortening their jackets, while others are proud of the very colourful (unofficial) dragon pattern lining of school jackets. Some replace the Akagi High bottoms with something else, wear sharply pointed shoes, and walk in a particular manner, always in a group (Taga 1988a:25–7). They do not carry school bags, leaving all their textbooks and notes at school (since they do not study at home); and scorn heavy school bags. A recent vogue has been sacks (e.g. a Snoopy bag, a red vinyl kindergarten bag, a small quilting sack). Imagine a young man of 180 cm stature coming to school with a small red sack sporting 'kitty' cat patterns and containing just a pack of cigarettes and a lighter. Boys also like female pink umbrellas (Taga 1988a:28–9).

Another important element of the student culture is speeding on motorbikes and in cars. Many students welcome occasional visits by riders into the school ground when lessons are in progress. The school had maintained a policy of 'Three Nos to Bikes' (no motorbike licence, don't buy a bike and don't ride a bike) in accordance with the prefectural policy. Students are not allowed to ride motorbikes unless they reside in areas where public transport is unavailable. Students are required to obtain school permission before they apply for a driving licence (legally they must be at least 18 years old); but many go without permission, are found out by the school authorities and receive 'home detention' for a while (Taga 1988a:240–2). Perhaps the school's prohibition makes motorbikes more appealing.

Schoolwork

Studies assume a low priority among students. For the majority of Akagi High students, the school is not a site where they endeavour to acquire academic qualifications or useful knowledge in order to obtain an advantage for their post-school lives.

The contents of MOE textbooks are too difficult for Akagi students, who hardly manage to read these texts. Many Akagi teachers do not complete even a half of the texts, and feel that the MOE should provide a wider range of textbooks. Students cannot read all the *tōyō kanji* (approximately

2000 Chinese characters, which are to be mastered during compulsory schooling); have not understood basic mathematical concepts; and try to endure 50 minute lessons without understanding what is being taught, although quieter students still take notes (Taga 1988a:236).

The number of students who fail in exams is considerable. Students receive a 'fail' for an exam when receiving under 30 per cent, and for a subject when receiving one mark out of five at the end of each term. With 'fails' in over four subjects, a student is required to repeat the same year (*ryūnen*). Many of the repeaters eventually drop out of school in the following years (Taga 1988b:90), a tendency also present in the two urban vocational high schools that Okano (1993) studied. In order to avoid this, homeroom teachers of students 'at risk' lobby subject teachers in the staffroom in order to get their students 'passes' (Taga 1988a:228–9).

Dropping Out of School

Akagi High's dropout rate is relatively high. Out of 280 entrants, over 40 students normally leave school before graduation (Taga 1988a:224), making the school's dropout rate approximately 14 per cent. Although there are no nationwide figures, Okano's study in a city of 1.5 million provides an indication of the trends. The average dropout rate over the three-year period of high schooling was 2.7 per cent in 1990 (Okano 1993:65); and that for one of the city's technical high schools was 17.5 per cent (Okano 1993:74).

Poor academic performance and 'delinquent behaviour' are the two major reasons for dropping out of school. The two are in fact related. 'Deviant behaviour' (e.g. violence against classmates and teachers) is first punished by *kinshin,* where students are required to stay at home over a specified length of time under parental supervision. Akagi High has somebody on *kinshin* every day. This is very frequent in comparison to Nada (the private elite school), where suspension from school occurs only three times a year. When a student has a series of *kinshin,* his or her homeroom teacher persuades the student to apply to leave school. Quitting school is euphemistically called '*hōkō tenkan*' ('a voluntary change of direction'), and cannot be forced on students unless they commit a criminal offence or violence against teachers. Some girls at Akagi get involved in sexual relationships, often with older men, and marry much earlier than the average, often just like their mothers (Taga 1988a:196–7).

Although teachers can threaten the students with dismissal, students seem to assume that high school is a continuation of middle school, and that whatever they do (even breaking the law and committing violence), the school will let them graduate (Taga 1988a:163). When they are about to quit the school, students often request the school to arrange a transfer to evening high school. In most cases the school agrees (Taga 1988a:151).

Some teachers question the effectiveness of *kinshin,* given that the students' 'problematic' behaviour derives, at least partly, from family troubles (which they see as resulting from poverty in an affluent society); for example, parents with no wish to work, alcoholic fathers and domestic violence. They consider it better for the students to be at school rather than keeping them at home as punishment (Taga 1988a:221). Other teachers are simply indifferent to students' behaviour, pretending not to notice glue sniffing and card playing during classes (Taga 1988a:34). Taga quotes the case of one of her students:

Rika's father recently opened an all-night bar and made her work as a bar hostess. When Rika's manner gradually changed and she stopped coming to school, Taga asked the father and daughter to come to the school, where the father complained, 'Well, I am proud of my daughter . . . my customers have formed a fan club for my daughter. Could you bring an ashtray? Maybe people like you teachers don't understand my feeling. My daughter is mine. It is up to me how I use this child for whichever work. Even if it is an all-night job, it is her parents who are using her. It has to be OK'. Taga responded, 'Whether she is your own child or somebody else's, it is illegal for the underage to work all night. She is physically weak. She fainted twice at school. It is not good for her health' (Taga 1988a:190–1).

Students' Perceptions of the School

Students regard Akagi High as an inferior school. They remove the school badge from their uniforms so that people cannot recognise them as Akagi High students. Many of them dislike the 'Agricultural and Forestry' part of the school name. Before a school overnight excursion, students asked that the school flag be printed as simply Akagi High (Taga 1988a:50). Taga quotes an early conversation with her students:

'Ms Taga, this is not your previous elite school. This is Akagi High. You need to change your ideas about teaching. There is no way that we understand such difficult questions!' (Taga 1988a:45)

Although some children who intend to carry on the family farm often choose an academic high school, others do come to Akagi High because they want to acquire the practical skills they need. Such students are often academically good performers with stable personalities. They often find lessons at Akagi too easy, and can achieve top positions without much effort, which discourages motivation to excel. Additionally, they suffer from the stereotypical labelling of Akagi High (Taga 1988a:47–8).

Case Study 3.7: An Elite Agricultural High School – Shizu High

Almost 100 per cent of Shizu Agricultural Management High's (*Nōgyō Keiei Kōkō*) male graduates enter agriculture, including those who do so via university education. There are 36 such schools among 436 agricultural high schools in Japan (Nagasu 1984:86). Shizu High was established in 1964, and maintains 24 ha for practical sessions, as well as a range of modern agricultural machinery.

Shizu High's 'success' is due to two factors. One is its admission procedure, which ensures that the new entrants are the future successors of 'independent farmers' (those owning large farms), and the other is the stipulation that students reside in the dormitory. The school's selection criteria are detailed. The appropriate entrant should: (1) be a successor (usually the first son) of a full-time farming family (*sengyō nōka*); (2) be the child of farmers who, the local agricultural committee (*Nōgyō iinkai*) confirms, are capable of modern agricultural practice; (3) have performed well at school; (4) commit themselves to a rigid three-year period of dormitory residence; and (5) in the case of a girl, be from a full-time farming family, and intend to take over the family farm or to become a full-time farm housewife (Nagasu 1984:88–9). The school meets each applicant and his or her parents in order to confirm that the applicant satisfies the above criteria (Nagasu 1984:89). The school also requires new entrants' parents to submit a written oath to the effect that their son or daughter is to work in agriculture after graduation.

The curriculum is based on modern agricultural methods, whereby a farm produces a limited range of products efficiently through large-scale mechanisation. The school maintains close contact with the parents, and provides workshops for them, through the students. Students use their parents' farming practices as case studies for their projects, for which their parents are encouraged to provide records of their farm management.

Shizu High seems to educate future successors of the 'elite' farmers (i.e. those endowed with resources). The selection process for new entrants ensures that students will have a solid base for modern large-scale agriculture (as practised in the United States), and that they will have confidence in their future. Nagasu (1984:113–14) argues that Shizu High effectively implements the government's agricultural policy, whether deliberately or otherwise, to promote the productivity of 'modern', large-scale, labour-efficient agriculture among the well-resourced farmers, while encouraging small farmers to leave agriculture.

We have observed two distinctive types of agricultural high schools, one that fits the stereotypical picture of a declining agricultural high school, and the other an elite high school for future 'modern' farmers. What does 'school' mean to the respective groups of students? For Akagi High students, schooling is neither a stage where they demonstrate merit that they can utilise for their post-school lives, nor a means by which they climb the social ladder. Many Akagi students do get pleasure from their schooling experience, however transitory it may be, by circumventing the school's numerous rules through ingenious strategies. One could argue that these students willingly reject the dominant achievement ideology and are proud of it. On the other hand, one could also suggest that they are, first, excluded from the arenas where they might have been able to participate in schooling governed by the dominant achievement ideology; and that their exclusion has led them to resort to other ways of making sense of their schooling experiences. For Shizu High students, the school is a place with clearly defined long-term purposes, not a 'fun' place as their Akagi High counterparts find their school to be. The school provides them with the knowledge and skills that are necessary for their already-decided future occupation through well-structured education and rigid training. The above comparison demonstrates that agricultural high schools can function to divide prospective farmers.

Summary

In this chapter we have examined how schooling is experienced differently by children from varying social groups, namely the middle class, girls, the poor, the privileged, correspondence school students, and rural youth from farming families. We have identified the diverse relationships that children from these social groups develop with their schools, and the differential benefits that they obtain from participating in schooling. We have thus illuminated the diverse and often contentious roles which modern schools play in contemporary Japanese society.

We will return to this part of the discussion at the end of the following chapter. There we will integrate the experiences of the so-called minority students (ethnic Koreans, *buraku* children, and newcomer children) that the following chapter examines, in order to develop a full discussion of students' experiences of schooling.

Further Reading

Fukuzawa, Rebecca E. (1994). The path to adulthood according to Japanese middle schools. *Journal of Japanese Studies*, 20(1), 61–86.

Lewis, Catherine (1995). *Educating Hearts and Minds: Reflections on Japanese preschool and elementary education.* Cambridge: Cambridge University Press.

Okano, Kaori (1993). *School to Work Transition in Japan: An ethnographic study.* Clevedon, Avon and Philadelphia: Multilingual Matters.

Rohlen, Thomas (1983). *Japan's High Schools.* Berkeley: University of California Press.

Sato, Nancy (1993). Teaching and learning in Japanese elementary schools: A context for understanding. *Peabody Journal of Education* (Japanese Teacher Education Part II), 68(4), 111–47.

Notes

1 Surveys of primary and secondary schools were conducted in July 1995, while those on tertiary education were undertaken in May 1993. See especially (Japan, Monbushō 1995a:7–29) and (Japan, Monbushō 1994:6–25).

2 Article 75 of the School Education Law (*Gakkō Kyōikuhō*) defines special education homeroom classes.

3 For example, Takeuchi (1995) provides an excellent study of the meritocracy in Japan (but based on a male-only sample).

4 The average number of children per household was 1.78 in 1994 (Japan, Kōseishō 1995:14).

CHAPTER 4

Students' Experiences of Schooling, Part 2: Minorities

Contemporary Japanese society includes several distinctive minority groups, although the government has been reluctant to acknowledge the fact officially. 'Minority' here refers to a culturally distinctive social group that has been defined as 'different' from the mainstream and is often marginalised by the powerful in the society. These minority groups are: long-time residents of Korean and Chinese (including Taiwanese) descent, Ainu people, Okinawans, recently arrived 'guest workers' from the third world, and descendants of the feudal outcaste population (*buraku* people). All except the *buraku* people are popularly considered to be 'ethnically distinctive' from the 'Japanese', at least in their origins. However, what constitutes 'ethnicity' and the nature of ethnic boundaries remain open for sociological debate, as do the minority groups mentioned above. The boundaries of these groups are unclear, due to intermarriages and forced assimilation over the years (which has led to a loss of ethnic languages and cultural mores to a large extent); and also because the boundaries can be drawn arbitrarily, either by the groups in question or by the authorities, in order to suit a particular need at a given time. Exploring the ethnicity and boundaries of these minority groups offers us an opportunity to re-examine the boundaries of 'the Japanese people' and what constitutes 'Japanese' ethnicity (if it is identifiable at all).

In this chapter we will examine in detail the schooling of people from three minority groups, namely third-generation Koreans, *buraku* people and the children of 'newcomers' (guest workers from third-world countries). Koreans and *buraku* people are long-lasting minority groups, while 'newcomers' have appeared only since the mid 1980s. Before doing so, we will briefly discuss the other groups, the Ainu and the Okinawans.

The exact numbers of these groups are difficult to estimate since they all hold Japanese citizenship. The Ainu, an indigenous people, once lived extensively across northern mainland Japan, but fled to the northernmost island of Hokkaidō when the Japanese pioneered north-ward. Following the feudal government's initiatives, the Meiji government's modernisation program vigorously sought development by expropriating both Ainu land and labour (Hirota 1990:449; Kaizawa 1993). In 1986 the population of the Ainu in Hokkaidō was 24,381, a slight increase from 1979 (Hokkaidō-chō 1988:3).

Okinawa is a group of small islands located between Kyūshū, the most southerly of Japan's main islands, and Taiwan. Okinawa prefecture's population in 1992 was 1.2 million (Japan, Sōmuchō Tōkeikyoku 1994:37). The Okinawans had maintained their own kingdoms and culture before Okinawa's official annexation in the nineteenth century (Hirota 1990:449). From the end of the Second World War until 1972 the islands were governed by the United States (Miyagi 1992). Government policy has aimed to assimilate both Ainu and Okinawans into the mainland Japanese through modern schooling (Tanaka 1964:77–99, 106–30).

Modern schooling has been utilised to assimilate ethnic Koreans and *buraku* people as well, although in recent years not as overtly as before. More importantly, schooling has had other unintended outcomes for children of these minority groups, as we shall see in what follows. While the urgent issues faced by the three groups differ, their experiences of schooling reveal rarely disclosed aspects of Japanese schooling.

A Lasting Ethnic Minority: Third-generation Koreans

Koreans form the largest ethnic minority group in contemporary Japan. In 1994 Korean nationals numbered 688,144 (Japan, Sōmuchō Tōkeikyoku 1994:55); when naturalised ethnic Koreans and Japanese nationals with a Korean parent are included, the number is said to approach 1.2 million (Zenkoku Zainichi Chōsenjin Kyōiku Kenkyūkai Kyōto [ZZCKKK] 1993:7). Below we will examine how Korean youths experience schooling and grow up in Japan. After emphasising the diversity of Koreans, our focus will shift to third-generation Korean youth.

Diversity of the Koreans in Japan

The Koreans in contemporary Japan constitute a diverse ethnic minority. Within this minority group, the most important boundary lies between 'newcomers' and 'oldtimers'. The 'newcomers' are those who were born and mostly educated in South Korea, and came to Japan for economic reasons. They do not intend to reside in Japan permanently, and many of them are illegal workers due to the difficulties involved in obtaining work visas in Japan. The 'oldtimers' are the descendants of Koreans who have resided in Japan since the time of Japan's colonisation of the Korean Peninsula (1910–45). Newcomer Koreans naturally differ from oldtimer Koreans. Newcomers are younger, more self-confident, and more aggressive; and have achieved greater success in their businesses than their oldtimer counterparts (Hoffman 1992).

Among the long-term resident Koreans, further divisions exist. Some have taken up Japanese citizenship; the number of ex-Koreans who were naturalised in the period 1952–90 is estimated to be 156,000 (Youn 1992:133). Differences are observed in terms of generation, affiliation with North and South Korean organisations, regions of residence and social class. There are university-educated young Koreans from middle-class backgrounds, who are self-confident and proud of their ethnic identity, and who take leadership roles to improve the situation of the Korean community and who challenge the dominant Japanese definition of Koreans.

The presence of the oldtimer Koreans in contemporary Japan is a direct result of Japan's colonisation of the Korean Peninsula from 1910 to 1945. The original Koreans fled to Japanese cities in pursuit of employment after being dispossessed of their farming lands by the Japanese colonial authorities, or, from 1937, were shipped to Japan as forced labour to fill an acute shortage of workers in the war economy (Lee and De Vos 1981, Part 1; Mitchell 1967; Lee 1980:340–435). The Korean population in Japan at the end of the war was almost 2.3 million, about three-quarters of whom returned to Korea within a year (Tanaka 1991:57; Lee 1980:181, 185; Youn 1992:131). Those who had lost land and property in their homeland stayed on longer in Japan, but soon faced the division of Korea in 1948 and the outbreak of the Korean War, which made their repatriation difficult. Under Japanese colonisation, Koreans were Japanese subjects, but in 1952 when Japan regained sovereignty, Koreans living in Japan suddenly and unilaterally became foreign nationals.

There remains a legacy of the colonial period when the dominant Japanese *defined* Koreans as an inferior and second-class group of people, and deliberately discouraged the maintenance of their language and ethnic culture. Koreans, as well as Japanese, are said to have internalised this dominant definition: they hold a negative identity of themselves and their culture (Wagatsuma 1981). While facing symbolic prejudice and discrimination in employment, marriage and interpersonal relations, in common with the other three involuntary minority groups (the Ainu, Okinawans and *buraku* people), most Koreans face the added disadvantage of not possessing Japanese citizenship.

Over 90 per cent of Korean long-term residents possess Japanese names in addition to their real names, and use the former in daily life

(Kanagawa prefecture 1984 survey, quoted in Youn 1992:148). The majority of second- and third-generation Koreans do not have functional Korean language skills (Lim 1993:64). Changes are observable across generations. Marriages between Japanese and Koreans have increased: in 1989, in 81 per cent of Korean marriages the partners were Japanese (Tanaka 1991:156). Among those Koreans naturalised in 1987, over three-quarters were in their twenties and thirties (Youn 1992:135–6).

Korean Participation in Schooling and Employment

Since the late 1970s, over 80 per cent of school-age Koreans have been enrolled in Japanese schools (Miyawaki 1985:1). The majority of the remainder were enrolled in North Korean-affiliated schools, leaving only one per cent attending South Korean-affiliated schools (Rohlen 1981:186; Lee 1980:248). Although enrolments in Korean schools have been in decline since the late 1970s (Lee 1980:147,162–4), the presence of Koreans in Japanese cities can still be felt most vividly when one sees commuting girl students wearing the *chogori* (Korean ethnic dress) school uniforms of their North Korean schools.

In Japanese school grounds, Korean students are not discernible, even to average Japanese people, although many urban schools would have some Korean students. For instance, in 1992 some 2.7 per cent of students of Kyoto metropolitan primary and middle schools were Koreans (ZZCKKK 1993:16). Japanese schools do not actively take the presence of Koreans into consideration, treating Korean children *in the same way* as the Japanese children. This does not help Korean students to obtain the same benefits from school as the Japanese students. In fact, it does quite the opposite. Japanese students behave as if all their classmates were Japanese, sometimes with or without knowledge of the presence of Korean classmates. They may make insensitive and derogatory remarks in the presence of Korean students, either intentionally or otherwise. Korean children thus learn, through primary schooling processes, that being Korean is negative, and decide to hide their Korean identity.

Given the limited resources that they possess, one might expect that Koreans would see success in schooling as being important for their future employment. Yet while some Koreans are very successful, overall Korean young people have benefited less from mainstream schooling than their Japanese counterparts. Nationwide data on Korean students' academic performance and post-school destinations are absent (Nakajima 1994:33). A 1976 Hyōgo prefecture survey revealed that in comparison with their cohort (93.7 per cent), proportionately fewer Korean students (88.2 per cent) proceeded beyond compulsory schooling (Rohlen 1981:194–7).

If they do go on to high school, they are more likely to attend schools with relatively low entry requirements. Similarly, proportionately fewer Koreans than Japanese undertake university study (Rohlen 1981:194–7). In Kyoto 84.9 per cent of Korean students (in comparison to the city average of 92.5 per cent) went beyond compulsory schooling in 1978; and in 1990 the respective figures were 89.7 and 95.3 per cent (Nakajima 1994:33). These statistics suggest that the gap between Korean and Japanese students still exists but has decreased over the last decade.

Korean students of high-school age are aware of their nationality. Until recently, Korean nationals were legally required to be fingerprinted and to hold an alien registration card from the age of 16 (C. Lee 1981). (This requirement is to cease as a result of the 1991 Japan–Korea agreement [Youn 1992:22].) To what extent Korean students are open about their ethnic origin depends on the culture of the individual school. On turning 16, many high-schoolers are excited about obtaining motorcycle licences, but this also causes trauma for Korean students since such licences must show their real Korean names (ZZCKKK 1993:26). Some high schools actively encourage their Korean students to apply for the scholarship offered by a Korean association (*chōsen shōgakkai*), which also provides various opportunities to study Korean ethnicity and social status in contemporary Japan (ZZCKKK 1993:28).

High schools with relatively large proportions of Korean students have Korean Cultural Study Clubs (*chōbunken*). The club provides a place where Korean students can share their experience of being Korean, and learn about the Korean language, culture and history, and human rights, under the leadership of a teacher committed to equality issues. As Okano (1993) observed during fieldwork, only a few Korean students (always seniors) joined the club, since joining meant 'coming out'. Nonetheless, the clubs' influence on individual members is enormous: such clubs helped young Koreans to come to terms with their Korean identity and to use their real (Korean) names in public. The process of 'coming out' involves courage and determination on the part of those concerned (ZZCKKK 1993, 1994, 1995).

Admission to universities is based on competitive entrance examinations, and such examinations are open to anyone who graduates from a Japanese high school. Those who participate in the North Korean school system can proceed to the North Korean University in Tokyo, but are not eligible for many of the Japanese universities. No national universities accept graduates from North Korean schools for their entrance examinations, while 11 local government universities and about 112 private universities approve their eligibility (ZZCKKK 1993:33). North Korean school graduates who wish to enter national universities circumvent this restriction by taking correspondence high-school courses while studying at North Korean high schools (ZZCKKK 1993:33). A very small number of private Japanese universities have set quotas for students who are recommended by either North Korean or South Korean high schools (ZZCKKK 1993:33–4). The limited number of places at Japanese universities to which Korean ethnic school graduates have access contrasts with the favourable treatment that returnee Japanese children (i.e. children of Japanese expatriates who have been posted overseas) face: both national and private universities have set quotas for these students (Goodman 1990).

It is public knowledge that Koreans face barriers in the employment market, although their extent is difficult to quantify. Koreans have been denied access to employment with the public service, which requires that applicants be Japanese nationals. Although such restrictions have been abolished by some city-, town- and village-level governments, national, prefectural and municipal (cities of over one million) governments have been reluctant to follow suit. It was only in 1996 that the Kawasaki municipal government led the way. Osaka municipality, Kobe municipality, Yokohama municipality, Kanagawa prefecture and Kochi prefecture followed in 1997, although foreign nationals are still ineligible for some positions (*Asahi Shinbun* 26 March 1997, 24 April 1997; *Asahi Shinbun Evening* 2 May 1997). In response to the Osaka municipal government's move to grant foreign nationals eligibility to apply for the government service, an organisation of South Korean residents in Japan hosted a series of seminars for foreign residents, covering preparation for the selection examinations. The organisation believes that the inclusion of foreign national residents in the government service will give their views more prominence in local administration (*Asahi Shinbun* 29 April 1997).

Osaka prefecture eliminated its restrictions in respect of public school teaching in 1973, a decision followed by several other local governments in the 1980s (H. Tanaka 1991:134–8). In the 1970s several court cases against prestigious employers who refused Korean applicants on the basis of foreign nationality were resolved in favour of the plaintiffs (Tanaka 1991:120–3). In spite of improvements brought about by these cases, Koreans have yet to achieve equal access to the employment market. Disillusionment is experienced by all young Koreans seeking a place in the workforce, but is felt more keenly by better-educated Koreans who have formed high expectations for their adult life (Lee 1980:45).

A survey of Korean residents in Kanagawa prefecture revealed that 38.6 per cent of them experienced some kind of discrimination when obtaining employment (Kanehara 1986:31–2). Among Koreans the proportion of self-employment is relatively large, and they are more likely to obtain jobs through family social networks (Nakajima 1994:33). Koreans in general are not able to capitalise on a successful academic career in

Japanese schooling to obtain employment to the same extent as the mainstream Japanese, but with professional qualifications they are more likely to succeed in converting their education into employment (Nakajima 1994:33). Although Korean high-schoolers face barriers when entering the workforce, they are more protected from blatant discrimination and bias than those who do not attend high school, since the recruitment process for high-schoolers is regulated by a school-based institutional arrangement called the Job Referral System (JRS) (Okano 1997).

Below are autobiographies by two young third-generation Korean women who have experienced quite different forms of schooling. Suja received North Korean ethnic education from kindergarten through to high school, and is now studying at a Japanese university (Kim 1994: 25–35). Sachiko is one of the majority of third-generation Koreans who received 12 years of education at Japanese government schools. She now also studies at a Japanese university, and recently started 'discovering' her own ethnic identity (Yamashita 1994:14–8).

Case Study 4.1: Twelve Years of North Korean Ethnic Schooling – Suja's Story

> I was born in 1973 and am now 21 years old and studying at a Japanese university. Before that I attended North Korean schools for 12 years.
>
> I recall realising that I was Korean sometime after I started North Korean kindergarten. At that time I used the Korean language for father, mother, grandmother and aunts, while using Japanese terms for my siblings. I remember wearing the kindergarten uniform of pink *chogori*, black *chima* and smock. Our teacher was referred to by a Korean term, and my Korean vocabulary increased. My classmates' Korean names, which were difficult to pronounce at the beginning, became familiar. The primary school uniform was like those at Japanese schools. My classmates were those from kindergarten. We learned Korean language, and other subjects in the Korean language, as well as Japanese language. We learned a lot about the Korean Peninsula, while the geography and history of Japan were taught as a part of the world history subjects. When I was a fifth-grader and going home with my elder sister, boys of our age threw stones and said to us 'Go home'. I did not know then what to make of this. My sister cried, 'Do you know why we are here in Japan?'. I cannot forget this conversation and the pain from the stones. It was somehow strange that students of the kindergarten, primary and middle schools studied on the same site. Since there was only one class (of fewer than 30 students, and the numbers have been decreasing since then) in each grade, everyone knew each other by the time we were in middle school.
>
> At middle school, we wore the *chima chogori* uniform. I used to think it troublesome, since we had to sew the *chogori*'s collar on every three days and iron the *chima* daily. When we moved house, I stopped seeing old friends. In the new town I found it hard to make friends with my contemporaries, but

made a good friend at school. This friendship made me consider my future seriously, and then I started wanting to enter university.

The North Korean high school that I attended had a larger number of classes and new faces. I joined a sports club. The adjustment to the high school took me a while, since I found human relationships in the club more difficult than I had expected. Besides, one hour of commuting to school was tiring, and class requirements were demanding.

I completed North Korean high school and 12 years of ethnic education without (I now feel) deeply contemplating my Korean ethnic identity as such, perhaps because I was so occupied with busy daily routines. There were, however, three occasions that affected my sense of ethnic identity. One was when I met my mother's elder brother on our school's one-month visit to North Korea. He is the only relative of mine who returned there after the war, since all my other relatives live in South Korea. Although he looked different from his photo, I recognised him immediately. He shed tears on seeing me. It may be difficult for us living in a capitalist society to understand the realities of a socialist society, but I felt that wherever one lives he or she is the same human being. The second occasion was when I started carrying a foreigner registration card on my 16th birthday. The third was when I discussed with my homeroom teacher my Korean name before entering a Japanese university: whether to continue using my Korean name or adopt a Japanese one. After all, I wrote my name in Chinese characters with both Japanese and Korean pronunciations on the official document submitted to the university.

At university I introduced myself by my Korean name to new friends, who then used the Korean name. I was nervous, but excited that I was making friends with Japanese contemporaries for the first time. I was exhausted every day after joining a sports club, but enjoyed the company of my seniors and contemporaries in the club. In classes I noticed a few *zainich*i Koreans (literally 'foreign residents in Japan', but in particular 'oldtimer' Korean and Chinese residents), including a *zainichi* Korean man who used Japanese pronunciation of his Korean name. A *zainichi* woman then approached me on a train platform and we gradually formed a friendship. I found that the majority of the *zainichi* Koreans that I met at university had grown up in a 'Japanese' environment different from that I had experienced. I had been aware that only 10 per cent of the *zainichi* Koreans had lived like me, and now think that the percentage was similar among the *zainichi* Koreans that I got to know at university.

At university I joined the university's Korean Cultural Study Club, although I became busy with two clubs' activities. I was greatly moved when I learned ethnic dancing from Korean overseas students and performed it at the university's student festival. I felt as if I were confirming my identity as a *zainichi* Korean. Around that time, my friend and I went to the US to experience homestays with American families. One of my host father's friends was an ex-serviceman in South Korea, and talked of the beauty and hospitality that he had experienced there. I talked about my grandmother's home town in South Korea. In New York we found a Korean section, and I was delighted that I could communicate with Korean Americans in the Korean language.

My contact with South Koreans had a strange influence on me. After frequenting a Korean grocery shop near the university, I became good friends with the son who minded the shop. We used to watch videos of South Korean news and other television programs. He and his family were surprised to receive a postcard written in Korean from me. When talking to his family members, I found his father's stories fascinating. My subsequent encounters with other South Koreans made me aware of the varying existences of Koreans, and I wondered why I feel so different towards them despite the fact that we belong to the same ethnic group. This made me feel sad.

I spent the second half of my third year at university in Melbourne, Australia. I liked Melbourne since many racial and ethnic groups coexist with the assumption that they are different. I could express myself more freely there. I remember an Italian that I met at a party. He had been in Australia for thirty years since he was seven, but still said that he was Italian wherever he resided. I thought then that many different people live in the world and that I am just one of them; and that I would be proud, and face the reality, of the fact that I am *zainichi* Korean in future. (Kim 1994:25–35)

Case Study 4.2: Twelve Years of Japanese Schooling – Sachiko's Story

I am now a student at a Japanese university, after attending Japanese government schools from kindergarten through to high school. All these years I could never reveal my *zainichi* Korean background.

It was in my first year at university when I first revealed my ethnic identity to a friend. It was a courageous act for me. Whenever the word 'Korea' came up in a casual conversation with friends, I became tense and nervous, and desperately pretended that I was not affected. When Social Studies classes referred to 'Korea', I pretended that it had nothing to do with me. Deep in my mind, however, I was always worried that somebody might uncover my secret, thinking how I would react if found out. While I wanted to hide that identity throughout my life if possible, I also felt a sense of guilt that I had this secret.

When we moved to my mother's home town in the fifth grade, I started attending a new primary school, where I started making friends. One day on our way back from school, two of the friends asked various questions to check if I was Korean, as if they had planned it. I could not answer these questions. On knowing that my identity was known to them, I started hating school. At middle school I hated 'human rights' education classes, since they reinforced a sense of inferiority that I had already developed. When our teacher lectured enthusiastically on *zainichi* Koreans, I pretended to be indifferent, but felt that some of my classmates knew my background and were attentive to my responses to these classes. I continued to deny my background. It was around that time that I decided I would never reveal my identity.

Looking back, I spent enormous energy in order to hide my *zainichi* background. I tried to project myself as a 'typical' Japanese. When filling in the high-school application form, I made sure that I was alone in the staff-room so that nobody could see me writing my real Korean name. I never displayed my graduation certificate having my real name. Although invited by my friends, I ensured that I attended a driving school alone to avoid my friends noticing my Korean background. My parents kept telling me not to worry about it, but the fact that I was *zainichi* imposed a huge anxiety and burden on me.

My university has a relatively larger number of *zainichi* Korean students than the average, and I have encountered some of them. The club that I joined had a *zainichi* Korean senior. Her use of her Korean name did not seem to affect her relationships with club members. Never having seen such a situation, I found it strange and confusing but I was also envious. I wondered then how others would react if I too were to reveal my identity, but the thought was frightening. I was then sharing a room in a women's dormitory at the university. Our conversation turned to the *zainichi* senior. My roommate said, 'Do you know that XYZ is *zainichi*?'. I was tense and nervous, but managed to grab the opportunity to reveal my *zainichi* background. She was not surprised and said, 'It is not fair', upon discovering that *zainichi* are denied the right to vote, and positions in the public service. I was so glad that I revealed my identity to her and was relieved that not everyone rejected *zainichi* people. Although I was not prepared to reveal my identity to everyone, this was the beginning of my long journey.

One and a half years have passed since this revelation to my roommate. My uncle took me to an event for *zainichi* Koreans. I was reluctant to go at first, since I was worried that somebody that I knew might see us there. I ended up seeing one of my *zainichi* classmates to whom I subsequently revealed my *zainichi* status. When I returned home, I was anxious that she might reveal my identity to other classmates. I did not want them to know, since I recalled one of them saying 'I definitely want to marry a Japanese, although people say that *zainichi* are the same as us'. After thinking it over, I decided to reveal my identity myself, since I thought that it would make me feel better. My friends acted as if my revelation made no difference, which I was relieved about; but their later attempts to avoid the topic sometimes made me feel uncomfortable. I then continued my revelation to specific individuals. I spent four months in the US as a part of the university's curriculum. When practising 'self-introductions' (introducing one's nationality) in the pre-departure intensive English language lessons, I became speechless. When asked why, I managed to whisper that it was because I was Korean. I was so afraid of everyone's response that I could not raise my face and look at them.

Having revealed my identity to one individual did not make it easy to do the same to everybody. I could not stop worrying about the consequences of my revelation to an individual: he or she might reveal my secret to others behind my back. Only when I was convinced that I could trust a particular individual, I revealed my Korean background. However, when I look back to the time when I could not talk to anybody about it, I feel that I have come a long way. It may be a small step for me but I feel that the accumulation of these small steps has slowly led to my liberation. Now when somebody asks me 'You are *zainichi*, aren't you?', I can honestly respond positively, although sometimes with embarrassment. (Yamashita 1994:14–18)

Both Suja and Sachiko were students at Japanese universities when they wrote the above autobiographies. Prior to that they had experienced different kinds of schooling, which seems to have affected their personal development and sense of ethnic identity. Suja acquired the language and a knowledge of Korea, as well as a Korean peer group, in the protective environment of 12 years of North Korean ethnic schooling, which, as she acknowledges, might have insulated her from the realities of mainstream Japanese society. She claims that she was not made conscious of her 'ethnic background' through schooling, except for three occasions that occurred outside the school grounds or in preparation for her exit from the ethnic school. When mixing with mainstream Japanese at university, she saw no need to hide her *zainichi* Korean identity. Ethnic education seems to have given Suja a sense of confidence in herself, although she does not seem to have realised this until encountering Korean youths who had undergone mainstream schooling.

Ironically, it was Sachiko, who experienced mainstream Japanese schooling, that was acutely conscious of her Korean background. Having little knowledge and language of Korea and few Korean friends, Sachiko perceived her 'Korean background' in a negative light, in the way that the majority of Japanese do. She was in constant fear of her *zainichi* identity being discovered by her peers, and maintained a sense of guilt that she had been lying. Having encountered a Korean senior at university who was open about her ethnic identity, she now strives to have a new relationship with her Korean background. What did Sachiko obtain from the mainstream Japanese schooling that Suja missed out on at North Korean schools? The mainstream Japanese schooling theoretically gave her 'the same' opportunities for further education as the majority children, whereas graduates of the North Korean school system are still ineligible for many universities (including national ones). Some Korean youths, like the two Korean boys at Nada (see p. 96), do make effective use of the opportunities offered by mainstream schooling to move up the social ladder. However, if one considers the cost, in terms of personal development, for many Korean youth, of attending mainstream schools, the choice between ethnic or mainstream schooling must be a difficult one for students and parents.

Suja and Sachiko are privileged third-generation Koreans who are able to receive a university education. In this regard, they can be considered 'successful' in their experience of schooling. Many more Korean youths enter the workforce directly from high school, and face the realities of the adult world sooner than Suja and Sachiko. As mentioned earlier, high schools, through institutional mechanisms, try to protect Korean students from blatant discrimination by sending them to 'Korean-friendly' mainstream companies, which offer 'desirable' working conditions. Some Korean students make effective use of such initiatives by their schools, and land so-called 'desirable' jobs (as defined by the dominant society). Others, however, choose jobs in the Korean community (e.g. jobs in companies run by Koreans, and where Korean workers are predominant), because they value the comfort of the workplace and the Korean subcultural community bond, rather than moving up in the mainstream society (Okano 1997).

A Lasting Caste Minority: *Buraku* Children

There are said to be about 6000 *buraku* communities, representing some three million *buraku* people, in contemporary Japan (Takagi 1991:281). After briefly illustrating national trends in *buraku* children's education, we will examine their experience of schooling at a microlevel, drawing on the most recent case study available in Japanese. In so doing, we will explore how *buraku* children fail to benefit from schooling to the same extent as the majority children.

In the previous chapter, we touched on the past policies and practice of schooling for *buraku* children. The realities of *buraku* people's lives have been illustrated in anthropological studies, although these are now somewhat dated (Sakai and De Vos 1966; Donoghue 1966; Cornell 1966; Shimahara 1971). The 1969 Special Measures for Regional Improvement Law Project (*Tokubetsu Chiiki Kaihatsu Sochi-hō*; for details refer to Buraku Kaihō Kenkyūsho 1983:188–9) has brought positive changes in *buraku* children's education, through the provision of scholarships and *Dōwa* Education (a variety of programs that aim to redress the discrimination that *buraku* people face) (Hawkins 1983; Shimahara 1984, 1991a; Hirasawa 1983; Ikeda 1985:249).

Nationwide trends are apparent in *buraku* children's education. First, *buraku* students' retention rates to post-compulsory education and to tertiary education have approached the national averages, but differences still exist (68 per cent for *buraku* children and 95 per cent nationally to post-compulsory education, and 20 and 31 per cent respectively to tertiary education) (Nabeshima 1993:214, 212). Second, a higher percentage of *buraku* children attend lower-ranked high schools. Third, *buraku* students' high-school dropout rate is higher than the average. Fourth, the absolute level of *buraku* children's school performance has improved, but still lags behind relative to the national average. Fifth, a greater disparity exists among *buraku* children's school performance than among their non-*buraku* counterparts.

The case reported below depicts a rural *buraku* fishing village in the 1980s, which has seen fewer local improvements than typical urban *buraku* communities. We draw on three papers published concerning the same community (Ikeda 1985, 1987; Nishida 1990).

Case Study 4.3: A *Buraku* Community – Hana

Hana is a *buraku* community in a rural coastal town called Tama on Shikoku Island. (Hana and Tama are pseudonymous names.) Tama's population was approximately 5000 in 1980. Hana includes 379 households and 1055 people in a densely populated area, constituting one-fifth of Tama's population. Tama's population has been decreasing, but Hana's has remained stable.

Fishing is Hana's major occupation. Since one-third of Hana's households and half of Hana's employed people make their living from fishing, outsiders have long associated Hana with fishermen. Many (20 per cent) also live on *seikatsuhogo* (welfare payments). Although Hana fishermen were once employees of boat-owners elsewhere, changes in the post-war Fishery Act enabled them to form a fishermen's cooperative, to acquire fishing rights in nearby waters and to organise group fishing. In Hana, a relatively large number of people work in physical jobs other than fishing (e.g. construction, day labouring and truck driving) and receive daily wages or commissions (instead of monthly income). Their dependence on physical work in precarious working conditions makes their livelihood vulnerable to external and often uncontrollable factors, which has an indirect influence on their children's socialisation, a point we will take up later.

Hana people have long suffered from *buraku*-based discrimination and poverty. As late as 1968, 60 per cent of households lived on *seikatsuhogo*; fishing was seasonally conducted only half of the year, which forced people to take up casual employment in cities; and housing conditions were deplorable (Nishida 1990:126). Since 1970 various measures (*Dōwa taisakujigyō*) have been implemented to improve housing conditions and fishing methods, which have raised Hana's living standard. Outsiders' covert discriminatory consciousness still persists, however, such as in the case of marriage. As of 1987, Hana people had not formed a political or social organisation in order to promote their welfare, and local schools had not commenced educational programs on *buraku* problems (*Dōwa Education*) (Ikeda 1987:53).

Hana is a closely knit community where children's grandparents, uncles, aunts and cousins all reside nearby. Hana's language use is distinct from that of neighbouring communities, due to a close social network and to its long separation from the rest of the town (Nishida 1990:127–30). Children can readily observe their fathers at work. Hana's particular regional culture (*chiiki bunka*) includes a glorification of physical labour and strength, manliness, roughness and laughter (Ikeda 1985:251; Nishida 1990:128). Nishida illustrates this point with a quotation:

'You may be brainy, but we learn with our bodies. Imagine that we are on the sea and strong winds come. If you are thinking, "What shall we do?", you will be too late to save the boat. That's why we use rough language, like "Hey, do this or that"'. (Nishida 1990:128)

Schooling in Hana

Hana children numerically dominate local schools. Their proportion in local schools has increased over the years, constituting on average 75 per

cent (Ikeda 1985:253). At the local middle school, Hana children constituted 48 per cent in 1968, 68 per cent in 1978 and 85 per cent in
1987 (Nishida 1990:134). This is due to demographic and social reasons.
First, the size of Hana's population has been stable in contrast to the
decrease that has occurred in surrounding communities. Second, non-
Hana parents send their children elsewhere, to avoid the local schools
dominated by Hana children (Nishida 1990:134, 142). In 1987, for
instance, the four students who moved out of the local school were non-
Hana high achievers.

Hana children's school performance has been consistently poor, in
particular after fourth grade. In sixth grade, the maths performance of
two-thirds of Hana children fell in the bottom one-third of the class. Hana
children's retention rate to high schools has always lagged behind that of
other children, but has shown some improvement over time. It was
41.4 per cent in 1973 (as compared to 87.5 per cent among non-Hana
students), reached 72 per cent in 1977 (when *Dōwa* special measures were
vigorously undertaken), but remained at 60 to 70 per cent from then until
1983 (Ikeda 1985: 255). Most Hana children attend a branch high school
in a local town, which was converted from an evening high school in 1970.
Locals consider it to be a 'school for dropouts' (Ikeda 1985:254–6; Nishida
1990:131–3).

It is not true that Hana parents do not value schooling. In fact they want
the best education possible for their children, in particular because they
themselves had less than compulsory schooling. They encourage their
children to do well at school, but confide that 'I can't help with homework
once kids reach third or fourth grade', 'I have no choice but to rely on
study assistance from the teachers', or 'I want to help with my kids'
homework, but I can't. When kids start their homework, I am too
embarrassed to stay with them at home, so I make up errands, to go out'.
Their parents' inability to provide 'concrete' assistance for Hana children's
schooling is a factor in the children's lower-than-average school
performance (Ikeda 1985:253–4).

Besides a lack of individual parental help, there are collective factors
that contribute to the Hana children's poor school performance. First,
Hana children perceive their families to be poor, and maintain a deep
sense of their own poverty, although Hana's living conditions have
improved considerably through various *Dōwa* measures. The insecure
nature of their family incomes is partly due to the kinds of occupations
Hana adults undertake. Continuing derogatory perceptions on the part
of neighbouring communities of Hana's lifestyles, language and consumption patterns also enhance the children's feelings of inferiority
(Ikeda 1985:256).

Second, Hana children's daily experiences of the immediate realities of
the community contribute to a view that school qualifications are
ineffective for their own adult lives (Ikeda 1985:256–8). Although their
parents may emphasise the value of schooling, what they see is their close
adults surviving without schooling. A father commented:

'You don't need a brain for fishing. The most important thing is your
body. Without physical strength, you can't fish. With weak arms like yours,
you won't be able to work. Courage is also important. Without guts you
can't be a fisherman. There are times when we dive into the rough sea and
tie our net. If you are afraid of waves, you can't fish . . .' (Ikeda 1985:257)

Hana children rarely encounter role models of adults who have built their careers on successful school performance. Theoretically this option is open to everybody, but whether an individual subjectively feels that such an option is available to himself or herself is another matter, since people adjust their aspirations to what they consider to be possible for them (Okano 1995a). In the community, children see that success in middle school does not often lead to success in later life, as evidenced by university graduates who return to Hana jobless and by the large numbers of high-schoolers who subsequently fail to graduate. Hana people with whom children have contact through their family social networks thus provide few models that demonstrate the value of school qualifications. Their aspirations at the time of middle school are unrealistic options such as professional baseball player, cowboy, and car racer, which require few academic qualifications (Ikeda 1985:257; Nishida 1990:135). The children's own comments reveal their realistic understanding of the value of high schooling for their employment prospects:

'Even if I graduate from high school, I will perhaps end up being a supermarket sales person or a carrier for a transport company. So, it's better to quit school and work now. I can earn some money and do whatever I like.' (Ikeda 1985:264)

'Are we really able to get a job at a decent company? Even if I can, it will be no good. Because I don't like working while sitting down all the time. I will perhaps choose a job which uses my body.' (Ikeda 1985:264)

Third, Hana children's experience of schooling makes them feel that schools are inappropriate and alienating (Ikeda 1985:258). Recall that they are already behind academically by fourth grade and thereafter endure incomprehensible lessons. They do have occasion to taste a sense of satisfaction, but form low self-esteem due to poor academic performance throughout schooling. This further alienates them from schooling and what schools represent.

Fourth, the content of schooling and the school's responses to what Hana children bring to school are problematic (Nishida 1990:136). Teachers attribute Hana children's school performance to 'the narrow range of their experience' and to 'the distinctive community culture being backward'. Teachers view the local subculture as 'a backward alien culture', which requires 'correction'. This is reflected in the school's attempt to discourage distinctive Hana language use (Nishida 1990:136–7). Some parents do support such attempts. One parent (who is the vice-president of the local PTA) said:

'It is no good using a language that is not acceptable elsewhere. Our living standards have improved, and outsiders now see us in different ways. Only if our language changes, the place will change.' (Nishida 1990:137)

These school attempts have been unsuccessful. The language (and many other aspects of the local subculture) is rooted so deeply in their daily material lives and in the local subculture that the changes encouraged by schools are not easily welcomed. The relatively closely knit nature of the Hana community enables adults to pass on the Hana subculture to their children. Adults may see what schools try to impose as untrustworthy and threatening, given that many of them have sad memories of their own schooling (such stories abound). A gap between the Hana subculture and the school culture is observable in child-rearing practices. Hana fathers maintain 'manly' education and use physical punishment, rather than explaining why some actions are undesirable. A headmaster of the local school commented:

'. . . when a teacher visits a child's home to consult with his parents about the child's misbehaviour, the father immediately yells or physically goes at the child without letting the child say anything. So children say that teachers visit their homes in order to let their fathers slap them.' (Nishida 1990:138)

Performing poorly at school, Hana children seek to 'prove' themselves and to gain self-esteem through non-conformist activities (e.g. making fun of and rebelling against teachers, vandalising school buildings and equipment, truancy, smoking and glue sniffing) (Ikeda 1985:259). More frequently observed forms of resistance against academic learning are passive actions to refuse learning (e.g. being inattentive in classes, and reading comics under desks). The local middle school has suffered from a prevalence of such 'problematic' actions, which have endlessly occupied teachers (Nishida 1990:133). However, not all Hana community children engage in such 'problematic' activities, as we discuss below.

Intragroup Diversity Among Hana Children

The fact that a small, closely knit *buraku* community provides common material experiences and subcultural norms to its residents does not preclude some children from managing (against all odds) to achieve social mobility through effective use of schooling. Hana is no exception. Hana children's academic achievement displays a polarisation (Nishida 1990:141) consistent with the overall patterns of *buraku* children's school performance. The percentage of high achiever *buraku* children is similar to the national average, but there are a significantly high proportion of low achievers and relatively small number of middle-range performers in relation to the national average (Ikeda 1987:60).

High achievers are able to make an 'appropriate' and effective use of 'school culture' and 'local culture' (e.g. language use, behavioural patterns) according to context. We would suggest that this is similar to a British working-class child attending an independent school on scholarship. High-achieving Hana children's parents tend to have worked in urban centres first and returned to Hana to work in fields other than fishing, to cooperate for school activities, and to want their children to obtain stable jobs. While these parents underwent alienating schooling themselves and still maintain ambivalent feelings towards schools, they are prepared to do whatever is necessary for their children's 'success' (Nishida 1990:141–2).

In contrast, low-achieving students abandon learning activities, are rebellious towards school authorities, and spend out-of-school time with unemployed youths (Nishida 1990:142). They tend to come from troubled or the most disadvantaged families in Hana (Nishida 1990:133). Many of them obtain employment in urban centres, but quit work within several months, return home, and remain unemployed, playing with motorbikes and glue sniffing.

Peer-group influence is an important factor. Ikeda's study (1985:260–4) showed that Hana children's peer group formation strongly reflected their academic achievement and post-school destinations. Two high-achieving

Hana students from fishing families, who eventually went to the top-ranking high school, had little contact with the other low-achieving Hana students who went to the bottom-ranked high school or to employment. The latter group distinguishes themselves from the two boys, saying:

'X never plays with us, did you notice? They can do well in school work. He wears ordinary school uniforms unlike us. Their hairstyles are not trendy. They are liked by teachers, you know.' (Ikeda 1985:265)

All non-Hana boys in the school went to high schools in a larger city nearby, resulting in the numerical dominance of Hana students in the local branch high school.

The dominant social groups in Hana comprise low-achieving Hana boys who attend the local high school, high-school dropouts, those who did not take up further education, and unemployed youth who have returned from elsewhere. They are the major players in maintaining a distinctive local subculture (Ikeda 1985:263), in particular, the local 'male sub-culture', which emphasises physical strength and roughness (Nishida 1990:142). They spend much time together at one of their homes, and are aware of every small event in Hana. Their lifestyles can be characterised by their appearance (clothes and hairstyles), motorbikes, music, glue sniffing and smoking, and ritualistic behavioural patterns and distinctive language use (Ikeda 1985:264–8). These shared elements of the male youth culture which differentiate them from 'others', are a medium of interaction among themselves and reinforce a sense of solidarity. These elements also express an independence from adult generations, and from the urban-centred youth cultures (Ikeda 1985:267).

The Children's Awareness of Being buraku

Hana children are often unaware of the existence of buraku-based discrimination against them until they enter middle school (Ikeda 1985:268; Nishida 1990:140). In fact, unless they leave Hana for employment or further education, they do not experience direct discrimination as such.[1] Hana children are, however, aware of the outsiders' perception of Hana that it has 'bad language use', 'many scary residents', 'a bad reputation' (Nishida 1990:140) and is 'rough' (Ikeda 1985:269). A child commented:

'I get angry when somebody moves to the other side of the street in order to avoid me when they notice me approaching. I have done nothing wrong to them. That makes me so angry that I feel like hitting them. Anybody would feel that way, don't you think?' (Ikeda 1985:269)

Adults are acutely aware of outsiders' perceptions of Hana:

'You know that Hana people speak roughly. We may get into fights, but we all have honest hearts. Outsiders may say pleasing things, but we don't know what they are thinking about.' (Nishida 1990:140)

In the past Hana people faced overt discrimination from teachers, schools and elsewhere. For instance, only Hana children were scolded even if other children were also involved; and teachers refused to come to Hana's festival banquet (Nishida 1990:139). In recent years, rather than showing such blatant discrimination, outsiders try to avoid close relationships with Hana people by, for example, sending their own children to other schools (Ikeda 1985:270).

Unintended Effects of Schooling on Buraku *Children*

One could argue (like De Vos and Wagatsuma 1966) that *buraku* children internalise the external labelling about themselves and form a negative self-image, even if they are unaware of the true origin and nature of *buraku*. We would suggest that their experiences of schooling, where they learn to 'fail', reinforce such a view of themselves. Hana's case provides examples aplenty to demonstrate this.

Schools in Hana are among the few places where children come into direct contact with the dominant culture (e.g. achievement ideology, the myth of equality of opportunity, 'correct' language usage, abstract thinking, 'important' knowledge), and where that culture is institutionally disseminated. These children are naturally exposed to the dominant culture through mass media, but the nature of its contact is not immediate. The dominant culture that schools attempt to teach is alien to many Hana children (Ikeda 1987:64; Nishida 1990:142). Their direct life experiences incline them to undervalue it at best, or make it look irrelevant or even oppressive at worst. Consequently, children find themselves in a kind of cultural clash in that what they value at home and what the school values are dissimilar; or what is valued at home is undermined by school, as illustrated by the school's attempt to 'rectify' Hana language use (without much success). *Buraku* children often 'fail' in performing the tasks that the school assigns and considers important. Since 'failure' at school often leads to social failure in the dominant adult world, the view that they are somehow inadequate and inferior is reinforced.

Children instead seek other ways to express themselves, to assert themselves and to maintain self-esteem, through various forms of 'delinquent' activities. As far as boys are concerned, such subcultural activities are congruent with the local adult macho male subculture. This subculture is rooted in particular features of adult work (i.e. fishing and labouring), such as an emphasis on physical strength, 'guts' to take risks, and intuition, rather than the abstract knowledge or reasoning that schools value. Young men, then, are in a suitable position to carry on the distinctive local culture, whose nature is at least partly responsible for their 'failure' at school in the first place.

We must emphasise that the foregoing discussion does not preclude the possibility of social mobility through an effective use of schooling. This was demonstrated by a few Hana children who learned to manipulate two distinctive cultures (the local subculture and the dominant culture) according to context, and climbed the school ladder despite their disadvantages. Such cases would be seen more frequently in urban centres.

While the school performance of Hana students conforms to the national trends of *buraku* children, as mentioned at the outset of this section, variations in *buraku* children's school performance do occur across communities, reflecting different communities' situations and individual schools' initiatives (Ikeda 1987: 60–1). A *buraku* community's situation depends partly on its degree of *buraku* mobilisation (such as those led by the Buraku Liberation League, *Buraku Kaihō Dōmei*) and on the local government's political commitment to *buraku* liberation, both of which can bring varying degrees of improvement in living conditions and in social integration with the non-*buraku* population. In urban centres *buraku* people are more likely to remain anonymous due to the sheer size of the total population, high population turnover, the dominance of nuclear families, and diverse employment opportunities, all of which reduce the residential segregation of *buraku* people. Urban local governments also tend to take more initiatives for the *buraku* cause. On the other hand, it would be more difficult for urban *buraku* communities to maintain the kind of closely knit subculture and solidarity that the rural Hana community hands down from one generation to the next.

Political intervention can affect the opportunity structure and the social and economic conditions of *buraku* people, as can be seen in the impact of the 1968 Law. The changes in material conditions had some impact on children's educational performance (although its extent was not what *buraku* people had wished for). These changes, in turn, are likely to influence the ways in which *buraku* people perceive themselves and their options, and how the majority perceives *buraku* people. Hana children's relationships with schools, and what they gain from schooling, reveal the contentious roles that modern schools can play.

A New Diversity: Children of Newcomers

Contemporary Japan is a more multi-ethnic society than ever before, with an increasing number of foreign guest workers having arrived since the mid-1980s (Sekine 1990; Karthaus-Tanaka 1990). In 1992 the total number of foreign residents registered to reside for over 90 days in Japan exceeded 1.28 million (Japan, Sōmuchō Tōkeikyoku 1994:55). The 'newcomers' voluntarily came to Japan from third-world countries in pursuit of economic benefits unattainable in their homelands; the strong Japanese currency and the shortage of labour made Japan an attractive place. They have worked at construction sites, on factory floors and, in the case of young women, in the entertainment industries. Due to the demanding nature of the work, such workplaces were not attracting Japanese workers. Many of the newcomers are illegal workers.

With these workers came their families, including school-age children. These children were sent to local schools. For the first time Japanese schools faced a considerable number of children distinctively different from their Japanese counterparts. Various school-level episodes of 'problems' were reported in the media; for example, *Nihon Keizai*

Shinbun's article entitled 'Children of foreign guest workers: Increased troubles at school' (*Nihon Keizai Shinbun* 27 January 1992, p. 30). There have always been foreign children in Japan, but expatriate parents (only skilled expatriates had been allowed to work in Japan) traditionally sent their children to American-style international schools. Japanese schools had long assumed that their students were 'Japanese', and assimilated those who are 'a little different' such as third-generation Koreans. The arrival of newcomer children posed a challenge to the assumed practice of such schooling.

In September 1991, 1973 primary and middle schools, representing 5463 students, required special Japanese language classes (Ministry of Education April 1992, quoted in Tanaka 1993:78). These schools concentrated in Tokyo (350), Kanagawa (261), Shizuoka (158), Aichi (271) and Osaka (134). Thirty-five per cent of these children were speakers of Portuguese, 30 per cent Chinese, and 11 per cent Spanish (MOE April 1992, quoted in Tanaka 1993:79).

There are four groups of newcomer children. The first comprises the grandchildren of Japanese orphans who recently returned from China. These orphans were left behind in China (Japan's former colonial territories) by their Japanese parents who fled back to Japan at the end of the war, and were brought up by Chinese people as 'Chinese'. In the 1980s some of them decided to return to Japan with their children and grandchildren in order to start a new life (Mino 1993:55; Kawamura 1993). Their children (second-generation returnees) have little knowledge of Japanese language and cultural mores. The third generation is now of school age.

The second group consists of second- and third-generation descendants of the Japanese who emigrated to South America in the first half of this century. They were granted the privilege of working in Japan, regardless of the level and kind of employment skills they held, by the revised Immigration Act in 1989. The revised Act was intended to control illegal guest workers, making it almost impossible for unskilled foreigners to gain work-permit visas. (The other major aspects of the revised Act were the categorisation of all resident visas into work or non-work permits, and the introduction of penalties for employers of illegal workers.) (Tanaka 1993:68; Karthaus-Tanaka 1990:10; Shimada 1994: 61–8). As a result, the number of Brazilians and Peruvians working in Japan jumped from 2865 to 145,614 in the 1987–91 period (Tanaka 1993:68); this group now constitutes the majority of legal foreign workers. They mainly reside in Aichi, Shizuoka and Kanagawa prefectures, where they work in automobile factories (Tanaka 1993:68).

The third group is illegal foreign workers. Many foreign workers of non-Japanese descent work illegally – one estimate claims that about

300,000 foreigners work illegally in unskilled employment (Henshū-bu, Gekkan Fukushi 1995:34; Tanaka 1993:71). These workers have no access to social welfare and medical insurance services, in spite of their often physically dangerous employment. In 1992 their major countries of origin were Thailand, South Korea, the Philippines, Malaysia, Iran and China (Tanaka 1993:72). The occupations of those who were arrested for overstaying (approximately 33,000 in 1991) included bar hostesses, construction workers and factory workers (Tanaka 1993: 72). Among 1988 female illegal foreign workers, 88 per cent were hostesses and barmaids, while among the males, 43 per cent were construction workers and 39 per cent were production workers (Sekine 1990:4–5).

The fourth group of newcomers comprises approximately 8000 Indo-Chinese refugees who have settled in Japan. Some have taken up Japanese citizenship, but over half of the refugees who arrived in Japan have subsequently left for the US, Canada and Australia (Sekine 1990:10).

Below we present case studies of three schools that accommodate newcomer children. We will see what changes the newcomer children have brought to the schools, and how individual schools and teachers have responded.

Case Study 4.4: Newcomers at Nursery School – Nana

Nana Nursery School (pseudonymous name) accepts guest workers' children, reflecting the changes in its neighbourhood. The author of this study teaches a class of 21 four-year-olds, including five children of Filipino, Korean and Bangladeshi parents (Komiya 1993). Komiya reports on Asheq (pseudonymous name), a Bangladeshi boy who came to Nana in that year (1992).

Asheq had attended another government nursery school before moving to Nana. The landlord of their previous flat forced Asheq's family to leave, because, the father said, they were foreigners; they then found another flat and decided to send Asheq to nearby Nana.

This was not the first time that Nana had accepted foreign children. Nana contacted a welfare office, as well as Asheq's previous nursery school, so that it could prepare for him. At his parents' request, Nana's teachers discussed Asheq's Islamic diet in relation to the school lunch. Various necessary items (e.g. bags for pyjamas, quilts for afternoon naps) were offered to Asheq by the previous year's students.

The Nana children accepted Asheq quite smoothly. Asheq was small and could not speak Japanese. Other children thought that Asheq was younger than themselves, and were willing to help him. Asheq seemed somewhat adapted to nursery school life, accepting and thanking other children for their help. However, he found it difficult to join group activities. Although he tried hard, he did not understand the rules of games, got bored and left the group. This was perhaps because he did not understand the language and interaction rules of the nursery-school yard. Asheq found few of his own favourite activities, often walked behind the other children, and demanded more attention and one-to-one interaction with teachers. He did not understand the nursery-school routines or the timetable, and was often absorbed in other activities when lunchtime came. As the time went by, however, he learned to develop friendships, despite the language barriers, and adapted to the Nana routine while learning the language.

Komiya (1993) makes an optimistic observation that young children learn to interact with each other through mutual exploration, and to accept each other much sooner than adults.

Case Study 4.5: Newcomers at Primary School – Saka

Saka Primary School (pseudonymous name), in the *shitamachi* part of metropolitan Tokyo, is a medium-sized government school with an enrolment of 667 students (Kawamura 1993). Saka includes children from Tokyo government rehabilitation housing, which accommodates the orphans who have recently returned from China and their second- and third-generation relatives, amongst others. In 1993 Saka enrolled 24 grandchildren of returnees from China, 2 Filipinos and 24 Korean children. The author, Kawamura, has been the coordinator of Saka's committee for returnee children from China.

Saka's returnee children's grandmothers have a knowledge of the Japanese language, and some of them participate in school activities for their grandchildren. Almost all of the second-generation returnees entered Japan without government assistance, received social security living assistance and rehabilitation accommodation on their arrival, and started sending their school-age children (the third generation) to Saka. They took Japanese language classes and training at government institutes, and commenced working long hours. At school their children (the third generation) learn Japanese language and cultural mores and typically within several years start to feel a cultural gap with their parents.

The children are placed in grades according to their age, following the local government policy. Their adaptation to Saka depends on their age and their prior experience of schooling in China. The younger the children, the sooner they learn the language and come to experience a cultural gap with their parents. Most children adopt Japanese names at school.

In the first week at Saka, children learn the minimum necessary basics of school life, and then study Japanese language from three Chinese-speaking instructors in special language classes. These classes are held for two hours daily in the first term, and then six hours weekly for the next six months. These teachers also conduct *seikatsushidō* (lifestyle guidance, e.g. instruction about school life, taking baths, hair hygiene, greetings, non-violent behaviour, use of educational equipment) in consultation with homeroom teachers. Despite being only sessional staff, the teachers are willing to help Saka in relation to meetings, translating, and individual consultations. Besides these special classes, children attend normal classes. They also receive a few hours of after-school private lessons to supplement the normal classes from two teachers assigned for this purpose. Although the children receive assistance with language and class work, they still find it difficult to catch up with the mainstream students and have not performed well in assessment tests.

Saka School and its teachers, lacking prompt guidance from above, have managed newcomer children in ways that they believe to be effective. Senior teachers have taken leadership, and subject head teachers have devised ways to accommodate the children's distinctive needs. School nurses have taken initiatives in helping those children whose parents speak no Japanese (e.g. taking them to a health institute to receive vaccinations, and providing other necessary guidance about hygiene). Saka formed a committee for returnee children from China, which consists of one teacher from each grade, specialist Japanese language teachers, specialist teachers concerned with the children's welfare, and the principal and deputy principal. Saka also holds annual meetings with the community, including the staff of the rehabilitation housing where many of these children reside.

Besides the school's organisational arrangements to manage newcomer children, Kawamura explores how best teachers can assist in turning the simple coexistence of children into 'happy coexistence'. First, what are teachers' roles in influencing these children's cultural identities? Kawamura believes that the children will learn 'double' cultures if their parents conscientiously maintain their culture. However, Saka children's parents are too occupied with daily survival to consider their children's cultural identities. As a teacher, Kawamura feels a need to help the mainstream Japanese children learn to accept friends who are different and to make fruitful relationships with them. She noticed that some Japanese children are frightened of 'different' classmates and make utterances which innocently hurt the newcomer children. How best can classroom management make use of the plural cultures that the newcomer children bring to the school? Simply being present in the same classroom does not automatically lead children to mutual understanding. Kawamura found a great potential in the third-generation Korean children at Saka, since they know the Japanese language while maintaining Korean cultural habits and customs to a certain degree.

Case Study 4.6: Newcomers at Middle School – Kama

Kama is a government middle school in Shikoku, which in recent years has accepted over 10 returnee students from China every year, and the current enrolment is 15 (Mino 1993). Kama calls these students '*kikokushijo*' (literally 'returnee children'). The term *kikokushijo* was originally used to refer to children of Japanese expatriates but now has acquired the additional meaning of 'returnee children' from China. The author, Mino, is a teacher at Kama.

Like other schools, Kama initially had no special arrangements to facilitate these students' entry, being left to fend for itself by the local education board, but since then some developments have taken place. Currently, a sessional teacher runs Japanese language classes that these students attend in addition to the normal school curriculum, in a classroom assigned for that purpose. In 1993 the teachers' union's negotiations with the prefectural and city education boards resulted in two further developments: the education board's provision of extra funding enabling Kama to receive help from Chinese overseas students at the local university, and the assignment of a Chinese speaking teacher to Kama.

Kama's major problem has been bullying, which is faced by most of the returnee students shortly after their entry into the school. Some of them withdraw into themselves, while others start displaying delinquent behaviour. In response, Mino organised a 'study evening' in a meeting room of the local government housing complex where many of these students reside, in the hope that they would learn academic skills and develop a group consciousness and solidarity so that they could discuss their problems among themselves.

Keio was one such boy that Mino encountered in his eighth grade homeroom class at Kama. Keio was nine when he arrived in Japan from China's north-eastern region in 1987. He was immediately placed into the third grade at a local primary school, which then offered no language classes for these children. Keio underwent bullying by his classmates, both intentionally and otherwise; stopped studying in his fifth grade; and started behaving rebelliously towards his teacher. By the time he was an eighth-grader at Kama, Keio was rough and alienated from school. Keio did not participate in the 'study evening', and often went out with one of his seniors, dyed his hair and rode motorbikes. Mino tried to help Keio make friends with his classmates, and encouraged Keio to talk about the China that he knew, but he remained withdrawn. Keio was then caught when he and his friends threatened and stole money from students of another school. When Mino became enraged and slapped his face in the staffroom, Keio revealed how he had suffered from bullying. Later Keio was asked to talk to the class about his experience as a returnee student in Japan. He started opening up and got involved in school and class activities, and began attending the 'study evenings'. Below is a part of the essay he wrote at the end of that year.

'I always think about my future. I am anxious about being able to enter a high school. Everyone studies the basics from grade one. I was different. I came to Japan from China and immediately started the third grade here. I did not know any Japanese language. But my teacher was very kind and patiently taught me. I thank that teacher. But I was fooled by the classmates, perhaps because my language was different. Since I hated defeat, I became violent. I cried and pleaded with my mother that we return to China. . . . I then began to go out with older people and to wear trendy clothes. I smoked and rode motorbikes. I became violent when I got angry . . . If God determines my future, I cannot do anything. But, if I can do something, I would like to have a normal and happy life with my friends.' (Mino 1993)

Mino is deeply concerned with these children's life after middle school, since high-school qualifications are essential if they are to escape from poverty. Although every returnee child dreams of attending high school, the option remains difficult for many of them.

Responses at the Individual School Level

The cases above show that individual teachers and schools have taken initiatives in devising what they believed to be the best ways to manage changes brought by the presence of newcomer children, although none of them had prior training for, and experience with, such situations. Their responses might have been haphazard but were based on the everyday realities of schooling that they faced. A number of teachers have written essays based on their own experiences (e.g. those collected in *Kyōiku Hyōron* December 1993, and *Kyōiku* 43(2) 1993). All of them were unsure of the merits of their actions, and were somewhat frustrated with themselves, but they greatly appreciated the positive effects that these children have brought to their Japanese counterparts. (Naturally these teachers, who wrote essays for publication in professional journals, may be more enthusiastic and self-conscious than an average classroom teacher.) Individual teachers' concerns and initiatives were taken up by their schools and/or unions, who then requested that educational administration authorities consider specific measures to cater for the needs of newcomer children. Only in 1993 did the Ministry of Education start to provide extra teachers specifically to teach Japanese as a second language; but as the numbers were inadequate, local education boards still send out extra teachers to needy schools, set up classes for Japanese language and cultural adaptation, and send out instructors with the children's mother tongue (Enokii 1993:25).

To date, newcomer children's opportunities for post-compulsory education have been limited. They have found it extremely difficult to compete with Japanese children in securing places at high schools through the normal 'merit'-based entrance examinations. Although Tokyo metropolitan high schools have a quota for returnee children from China, once at high school they struggle to keep up with the rest of the class (Ozawa and Sanuki 1993:14). Tokyo Metropolitan University sets a small quota for these children as well, and allows applicants to take Chinese language in the entrance examination (Ozawa and Sanuki 1993:14). No such arrangements have been made for other newcomer children.

This situation contrasts with the relatively extensive measures devised for Japanese children who return, after several years, following a family's posting overseas. The 'problems' of Japanese returnee children have been much more widely discussed both in the media and amongst educationalists (Kobayashi 1989). Expatriate Japanese parents are able to use the social networks of their powerful employers (multinational companies) in order to lobby policy makers to devise measures so that their children are not disadvantaged in their academic careers and beyond (Goodman 1990). Many urban schools offer special classes for these children, and a considerable number of high schools and well-known universities (including national universities) set a quota for them.

In 1991, 92,948 foreign students attended Japanese schools, while 24,727 enrolled in schools for foreign children. (These numbers included oldtimer Koreans.) In the same year 13,313 returnee children attended Japanese schools; 576 of these were the grandchildren of returnee orphans from China (Tanaka 1993:76). Schooling for the children of newcomers and oldtimers has received much less attention than that for the children of Japanese expatriate returnees. Perhaps newcomers have not been powerful enough to make their voices heard either in the media or to policy makers, leaving it to individual school teachers to act on their behalf. Possibly this is due to a belief that Japanese nationals have a priority right and 'duty' to receive education, and that government schooling is designed first for Japanese nationals.

Children's Rights and the State

Apart from individual teachers' and schools' daily responses to continuous changes at the microlevel of schooling practices, the flux of newcomers' children raises larger questions regarding children's rights to education, and the relationship between schooling and the state.

The Japanese Constitution provides no clear definition of the status of foreign workers, and their entitlements to the basic human rights guaranteed by it (Shimada 1994:161). The dominant interpretation contends that the right to receive education (article 26) applies only to Japanese citizens (Shimada 1994:161–2). However, a significant gap exists between the dominant legal interpretation and the reality of local schools. As the above case studies show, children of foreign workers are already attending local schools; individual schools and teachers are currently providing a range of services to them; and they are requesting local education authorities to provide extra resources to address the situation.

Education authorities have long understood that only Japanese nationals have a duty to participate in schooling until the end of compulsory schooling on constitutional grounds, although no specific reference is made to restricting non-Japanese nationals from the same education (Miyajima 1993:19; Enokii 1993:25). Based on this understanding, local governments used to send out *'shūgaku tsūchi'* (notification to attend school) to all school-age Japanese nationals only (excluding oldtimer third-generation Korean residents). The 1991 Japan–South Korea Agreement ruled that local governments send *'shūgaku an'nai'* (information on attending school) to school-age children of all registered (i.e. legally resident) foreign nationals residing in Japan, which outlines the availability of local schools and the procedures to be taken to enrol children (Miyajima 1993:19; Enokii 1993:25). Kawasaki city's ethnic schools objected to this, arguing that the invitation mentioned only Japanese schools and did not include other options such as ethnic schools and International Schools (Miyajima 1993:19).

As for the school-age children of illegal newcomers, no legal document states specifically that school-age children of illegal foreign residents are to be denied entry into Japanese schools (Miyajima 1993:20). Miyajima (1993:20) reports that most local education boards decline to admit illegal newcomer school-age children to local schools, while Nomoto (1994:38) reports that such responses depend on individual local governments, some of which are willing to enrol these children.

In this context, two recent international conventions on human rights are important. They are the Convention on Children's Rights (*Kodomo no Kenri Jōyaku*) (1989), ratified by the Japanese government, and the Convention on the Protection of the Rights of all Migrant Workers and their Families (*Subeteno Ijū Rōdōsha to sono Kazoku no Kenri Hogo ni kansuru Jōyaku*) (1990) adopted by the United Nations (Nomoto 1994:38–39; Sasagawa 1993:20–1).

The former Convention confirms that the children of foreign guest workers are entitled to education, including that concerning their respective mother languages and cultures, to enable them to maintain their cultural identities. The Convention covers all children under 18 years of age, regardless of the nationalities and legal status of their parents and themselves. Furthermore, Article 30 assures the rights of children of minority groups to their own culture, religions and the use of their own languages (Nomoto 1994:39; Sasagawa 1993:21).

The latter Convention ensures that all guest workers and their families (including children) are entitled to what it considers minimum forms of human rights, and then lists further entitlements granted to legally registered guest workers and their families. In relation to education, all children, regardless of their families' legal residential status, possess a basic right to education on an equal basis with the nationals of the country concerned (Nomoto 1994:39). In addition, the children of legal guest workers have rights to more educational services specified by the Convention (Nomoto 1994:39). This Convention differs slightly from the Convention on Children's Rights, in that it grants different entitlements to children depending on their parents' legal residential status.

Given that no Japanese domestic Act exists regarding the rights of foreign children to education, these conventions provide useful guidelines when considering how Japanese schools may respond to the influx of guest workers and their families. In the light of the guidelines in the two conventions, the present situation for these children is far from satisfactory.

The Assumptions Being Challenged

One could attribute the 'problems' of newcomer children to them as young individuals, an approach which might appeal to the general public at the 'common-sense' level. We would suggest, however, that these 'problems' lie in the taken-for-granted assumptions that have long characterised Japanese schools. These assumptions are that Japanese government schools are designed to provide education only for Japanese nationals; that the majority of the students are Japanese who have knowledge of the language and culture; and that if they are not, such children are expected to attend 'special' schools that cater for their 'different' needs. It seems that these very assumptions are now being challenged.

The influx of newcomer children has also illuminated the nature of schooling, which creates winners and losers through competitive selection based on what is believed to be objective 'merit', which provides differential benefits to children with different family backgrounds, and which thus justifies such differential outcomes. Typically the children of lower-income, single-parent, and other minority groups (in particular *buraku* and oldtimer Koreans) as a group perform relatively poorly in their academic careers, and, consequently, beyond schooling. Now the newcomer children are creating *additional* strata below these groups at the bottom of the academic achievement hierarchy, resulting in more stratified (or unequal) social relations (Ozawa and Sanuki 1993:12–13). One teacher commented that the presence of newcomer children pushed the existing low achievers up the class rankings (Enokii 1993:27). It may be time that schools adopted a 'gentler' approach towards the socially powerless. It will also be a challenge facing Japanese schools to guide children in accepting and appreciating mutual group and individual differences. This perhaps is an unexpected effect on Japanese schooling of the globalisation of capitalist economies and labour markets, which shifts capital, commodities, information and labour across nation-state boundaries in pursuit of the maximum profit (Mouer and Sugimoto 1995). It is a trend which has the potential to create positive educational outcomes.

Summary

In this chapter we have examined the schooling experienced by children from three minority groups: third-generation Koreans, *buraku* people and newcomers' children. We hope that our examination has brought readers closer to these children's experiences of schooling. Urgent issues faced by the three groups differ. For third-generation Koreans, the place of schooling remains controversial: there is a tension between maintaining (and feeling comfortable with) ethnic identity and pursuing success in the dominant Japanese society. The nature of *buraku* children's relationship with schools remains dependent on the community's relationship with the dominant culture, and the individual school's attempts to become closer to the *buraku* community. This partly explains the internal differences (often urban versus rural) in the *buraku* children's experiences of schools. As for children of newcomers, as yet we cannot fully evaluate their experiences of schooling. They are still at the stage of overcoming practical barriers such as language, although teachers already warn that the prospect of high schooling for these children is grim unless definite measures are taken now. These children find their local circumstances and subcultures incongruous to those that predominate mainstream schooling (which can even undervalue what they bring to school from home), and subsequently make their own sense of their schooling and of themselves. The relationships that they thus develop with schools, and the consequences of such relationships, highlight the diverse and sometimes unexpected functions that schools perform.

Modern schools are normatively expected to disseminate knowledge and culture to help every child realise his or her full potential. They teach certain sets of 'official' knowledge and the dominant ideology to every child across the nation-state in both rural and urban areas, regardless of family background; and are thus assumed to provide 'the same' schooling and opportunities to everybody. Schools theoretically do perform this task. Indeed, post-Meiji modern schools are said to have been effective mechanisms for selecting the 'talented' from every corner of the country. Those selected were then sent to the urban centres for further education, which would enable them to take up powerful positions (Amano 1990).

In the last two chapters we have tried to demonstrate that the reality of schooling as provided by institutions does not conform to such expectations; and that even when 'the same schooling' is provided, children from various social groups (girls, the poor, the male elites, correspondence high school students, rural youth, third-generation Koreans, *buraku* people and children of newcomers) make different uses (or no use at all) of schooling. How does this occur?

First, children are not equally predisposed to 'learn' the school culture and knowledge. Children from certain family and regional backgrounds (often the urban middle class) possess resources that are more congruent with the school culture than others, and are willing and able to learn what schools offer and to make effective use of educational opportunities. Children who possess a culture that is very different from the school culture find themselves disadvantaged. As we have seen, the poor and *buraku* children do not often have 'successful' immediate adult role models, and their parents are uninformed or under-resourced to make the most of schooling. The odds are stacked against these children, although this does not mean that none of them can succeed in the system.

Second, the meaning and value of schooling vary for different social groups (although the dominant Japanese may find this difficult to acknowledge). Because of this, many in the above social groups make decisions regarding their own participation in schooling (levels and kinds) by considering factors other than their academic achievements. This may not result in 'meritocratic' educational participation.

The different meanings and values that various social groups attach to schooling are firstly due to the fact that the assumed link between schooling and employment or social status in the adult society is not the same for everyone. Girls, third-generation Koreans, the disabled and *buraku* people, for instance, face a 'job ceiling' and a 'promotion ceiling'; and are fully aware that they cannot convert their educational qualifications into employment relevant to their qualifications in the same ways that others can. Rural youth from farming families are aware that a good performance at agricultural high school will not enhance the prosperity of the family farms that they may take over, due to the declining nature of the industry.

The second contributing factor is students' direct experience of schooling, which influences how they perceive its value and meaning. Teenage correspondence school students, for instance, found that mainstream schooling did not cater for their distinctive needs (e.g. due to disability or chronic illness). For third-generation Korean students, mainstream schooling not only undervalued their ethnic culture, but also instilled the dominant (negative) view of Koreans in general. Newcomer children and parents were eager to benefit from mainstream schooling, which they found does not fully accommodate non-Japanese students' needs. Girls were expected to manage two contradictory messages from school, namely the achievement ideology and sex-specific roles.

The third factor in the perceived meaning and value of schooling comprises the distinctive subcultures that different social groups have developed through their members' shared material experiences and traditional values (in the case of girls and ethnic groups). We have seen that the Hana *buraku* community maintains a macho male subculture based on the physical nature of work, and a culture of 'indifference' to mainstream schooling and what it offers. The latter attitude is also shared by the poor and by rural youths from farming families. These groups' indifference to schooling and its assumed benefits might be considered a challenge to the dominant achievement ideology, in the sense that it is not universally accepted. Having said that, as long as the dominant group maintains the power to define winners and losers by its criteria, such challenges will remain insignificant.

Challenges to the assumptions that have long underpinned Japanese schooling are in order. The recent arrivals of newcomer children and the rise of feminism have affected educational practice at the school level. The assumption that equal opportunities mean providing the same education to everyone has now been undermined, and a new approach to address equality and diversity is called for.

Further Reading

Lee, Changsoo and De Vos, George (eds) (1981). *Koreans in Japan: Ethnic conflict and accommodation.* Berkeley: University of California Press.

Okano, Kaori (1997). Third-generation Koreans' entry into the workforce in Japan. *Anthropology and Education Quarterly,* 28(4):524–49.

Shimahara, Nobuo (1991). Social mobility and education: Burakumin in Japan. In Gibson, Margaret A. and Ogbu, John (eds) (1991), *Minority Status and Schooling* (pp. 327–53). New York: Garland Publishing.

Notes

1 It is important to note that Hana children do not experience overt and direct discrimination unless they cross or go near the boundaries between them and the mainstream society (by leaving Hana for employment or further education). This case is similar to that of Suja, the third-generation Korean youth who experienced the separate North Korean system of education, protected from the outside world. It is then understandable if such students choose to obtain the kinds of employment (or unemployment) that allow them to remain in their communities. They have made rational decisions, having calculated the pros and cons of their options, and decided that the emotional bonding and comfort provided by their local communities and peers are more important to them than moving up in the mainstream society (Okano 1995b).

CHAPTER 5

Teachers' Experiences of Schooling

Teachers form the front line of the schooling process, facing children in classrooms daily. Having illustrated in the previous two chapters how children experience the schooling process in different ways, we now turn our focus to the teachers, who experience the same schooling process from 'the other side'.

Essentially, teachers are expected to guarantee the children's right to receive education, but the roles that teachers play in the schooling process are complex. These roles require individual teachers to possess a professional capacity to organise their curriculum based on their academic studies, and to disseminate it in the most effective way, in accordance with the developmental stage of each child. Such capacities are not given but are acquired through pre-service and in-service teacher education programs, as well as through the actual practice of teaching. They are also influenced by the status accorded to teachers, their working conditions, and teachers' rights both as citizens and as workers.

Our aims in this chapter are threefold: to examine the institutional systems that produce and constrain individual teachers; to illustrate how teachers experience schooling under such constraints at the school level; and to present the diversity of teachers that sustains Japanese schools under the centralised school system. Teachers are examined as educational professionals, workers, and 'ordinary people' who have private lives and concerns. Teachers' union activities in the past will not be covered here since they were discussed in the context of the history of modern schooling in Chapter 2. Neither will the reforms to teacher education and certification in the 1980s and 1990s, which will be included in the discussion of education reforms in the following chapter.

We begin this chapter by setting out the institutional frameworks that concern teachers (i.e. teacher education, certification, appointment,

141

salaries, school transfer, promotion and in-service education), and by illustrating the realities of teachers' busy lives. Second, we will discuss teachers' rights in relation to children's rights; third, we will present three examples of the practices that, Japanese teachers consider, demonstrate the ideal practical capacity of teachers. Fourth, we will examine teachers' professional associations and unions. Our focus will then shift to the culture of teaching, and the life histories of three teachers. Throughout this chapter, our emphasis will be on the experiences and perspectives of 'ordinary teachers', rather than those of principals.

The Institutions of Teaching and the Realities

Approximately 1.1 million teachers currently teach at primary and secondary schools in Japan. These teachers cater for students who, overall, achieve an impressive attendance rate (at least in number): almost 100 per cent for compulsory schooling (6- to 15-year-olds) and 96 per cent at upper secondary schools (16- to 18-year-olds). While the teaching profession grew along with the development of modern schooling, its nature underwent a drastic change after the end of the Second World War.

Teachers Under the Imperial Constitution of Japan

A teaching profession was quickly established as modern schools were built after the passing of the 1872 Education Law (*Gakusei*). The national system of primary schools required a large number of primary-school teachers. In the 1880s the government established normal schools (*shihangakkō*). Many of the initial entrants to, and teachers at, normal schools were of feudal *samurai*-class origin. From 1890 onwards, the majority of normal-school students came from farming families. As the Meiji imperial state developed, teachers became a part of the state's bureaucracy across the country; and were expected to cultivate 'fidelity to the emperor and patriotism' among the young, in accordance with the Imperial Rescript on Education (*Kyōiku Chokugo*).

Legislation regarding teachers gradually established normal schools, and the systems of teacher certification, appointment, working conditions and work regulations in the 1880s. To be a government school teacher normally required graduation from a normal school, although one could gain teaching qualifications through an academic examin-ation. There was also a regulation whereby the qualification was not to be granted to those with 'undesirable behaviours'. The basis of the pre-war teacher certification mechanisms was finalised by the 1890 Teacher

Certification Act. The Act established the principle of teacher certificates, but was not complete in that it allowed certain exceptions; for instance, the teacher certificate was not required for pre-war middle-school teachers. The authority to appoint teachers has remained the responsibility of prefectural governors since 1890.

Teachers held the status of an imperial civil servant, and were to carry out their duties accordingly. For instance, the Service Regulations for Civil Servants (1887) set out that government primary-school teachers 'be loyal to the emperor and his government, follow its laws and orders and carry out their duties'. The Regulations for Primary School Principals and Teachers (1891) required primary teachers to defend the Imperial Rescript on Education. Subsequent Acts maintained these basic features, strengthened principals' supervisory authorities, and restricted freedom of speech, thought, meeting and membership of organisations.

Serving the Whole Community: Post-war Teachers

The post-war legislation brought fundamental changes to the right-and-obligation relationship between citizens and the state regarding education. It required teachers to serve the public as a whole, not the emperor. The Allied Occupation force demanded that teachers who promoted militarism and ultranationalism be expelled. Some teachers volunteered to leave teaching, feeling responsible for the fact that education had been an ideological force to mobilise the innocent young into the war. Others remained in teaching with a renewed determination to contribute to peace and democracy through schooling that was independent of politics.

The Fundamental Education Law (*Kyōiku Kihonhō*) states that 'teachers shall be servants of the whole community, and shall be conscious of their mission and endeavour to discharge their duties'. The requirement that teachers 'serve the whole community' not only corresponds with the requirements on general civil servants (as prescribed by the Japanese Constitution); it also confirms that education is provided for all citizens and that schools are public institutions (the Fundamental Education Law, article 10). The notion that teachers serve the whole community has been widely debated in relation to the premise that schools maintain a 'public' nature. The MOE, for instance, emphasised that a teacher's mission is to follow the directions of the Fundamental Education Law, and that 'given that general public employees also serve the whole community, teachers should possess a distinctive mission as educators, in addition to serving the whole community' (Japan, Monbushō, Kyōiku Hōrei Kenkyūkai 1947). Arikura and Amagi (1958) interpreted this to mean that 'teachers work for the benefit of all citizens, not just for the benefit of minorities, a political party or a social class'. The notion that teachers serve the whole community requires teachers to organise educational activities as educational professionals in order to realise every citizen's right to receive education. In order to achieve this, the post-war systems of teacher certification, appointment, tasks and in-service training were established.

Teacher Education and Certification

The post-war teacher education system was based on two principles: 'teacher education at university' and 'an open system of granting teacher certificates'. These aimed to overcome the closed nature of the pre-war system, whereby teacher certificates were granted almost exclusively by normal schools, and to enlarge the number of opportunities for obtaining teacher certification.

The 'teacher education at university' principle meant that the basic qualification for teaching was university graduation. This requirement was to improve the quality of teachers and enhance their professionalism. It was expected that, as a result, teachers radically different from their pre-war counterparts would emerge from among the graduates educated at 'new' universities. The 'open system of granting teacher certificates' gave eligibility to a graduate from any university as long as they could satisfy the above requirements. Besides completing the required academic studies at university, applicants must satisfy conditions set by legislation regarding education and government employees, in order to become certificated to teach in kindergartens, primary schools, middle schools, high schools and special education schools; these conditions included the lack of a criminal record and non-membership of any organisation that aims to overthrow the present government through violence. The system of teacher education became fully 'open' from 1949, when a new system of universities was established and the Teacher Certification Law was passed. From 1953 the government required students to complete specified subjects in the teacher education course that are approved by the Minister of Education. Although this was a modification to the original system, since almost all universities and junior colleges had received approval for their teacher education courses, the two principles are largely followed in practice (Tsuchiya 1984).

More recently, diversity and flexibility have been introduced to teacher education. From 1970, one could gain teaching certificates by examination (for primary teaching; martial arts, nursing, and interior design at high school; and special education). The 1988 reform of teacher education saw the introduction of a one-year postgraduate course for

Table 5.1 Highest academic qualifications of teachers

	Masters degree %	4-year undergaduate degree %	2-year undergraduate diploma %	Others %
Primary schools	1.0	80.7	17.8	0.5
Middle schools	2.5	88.3	8.9	0.2
High schools	7.8	89.3	2.0	0.8

Source: Japan, Monbushō (1997:92, 110, 128)

teaching and a 'special certificate' granted by local education boards, as will be examined in Chapter 6.

Amongst all university graduates of March 1994, approximately 16.5 per cent (69,239) obtained teaching certificates. The percentage of graduates who obtained teaching certificates was stable at around 25 per cent over the period 1976 to 1983, but has since declined: it was 20 per cent in 1991 and 17 per cent in 1994 (Kawakami 1997b:2–4). The trend reflects a decrease in the number of newly appointed teachers, due to the decreasing number of school-age children.

Almost all teachers have received tertiary education of some kind (see Table 5.1). Amongst primary-school teachers in 1995, approximately 82 per cent had received four years or more of tertiary education. The corresponding figure for middle-school teachers in the same year was approximately 91 per cent. Amongst high-school teachers (including those at vocational high schools) almost all (97 per cent) had at least a 4-year undergraduate degree (Japan, Monbushō 1997:92, 110, 128).

Initial Appointment

Prefectural education boards (in the prefecture where each university is located) grant teaching certificates to those who complete the university course. The prefectural education boards then appoint government school teachers from among those with teaching certificates issued by that or another prefecture. Private schools appoint their own teachers independently. Universities, both public and private, exercise their autonomy to select their staff members.

For government school teachers, the right to select rests with the superintendent of education, and the prefectural education board appoints those recommended by the superintendent. This process of appointment differs from that for general civil employees.[1] The difference is significant, and illuminates distinct characteristics of the teaching profession. First, having two different institutions authorised to 'select' and to 'appoint' was intended to maintain 'an appropriate and fair process of selection of teachers', to 'eradicate the state's control' and to 'secure the autonomy of teachers' (Japan, Monbushō, Kyōiku Hōrei Kenkyūkai 1949). Second, while employment of general civil employees is based on 'competitive examination (*kyōsō shiken*)' (National Public Service Personnel Law, article 36, and Local Public Service Personnel Law, article 17), the basis for appointing teachers is 'selection' (*senkō*), not a competitive examination. 'Selection' by definition refers to an assessment of professional capacity, and differs from a competitive examination, which aims at 'evaluating applicants' relative professional capacity' (National Personnel Authority Rules [*Jinjiin Kisoku*] 8–12, article 30).

Whether or not the current practice of teacher selection examinations conforms to the above-mentioned notion of 'selection' has been widely debated. Concerns have been expressed regarding the closed nature of the process of selection, and cases of discrimination based on applicants' beliefs. For instance, the employing authorities have long avoided appointing foreign national teachers (including Japan-born Korean residents), with the justification that teachers exercise 'public power', despite the fact that teacher certificates have been granted to them. The issue of appointing foreign national teachers in government schools was brought to public attention again more recently. As of 1998, about one-third of the 47 prefectural and 10 metropolitan governments have removed the requirement that teachers be Japanese nationals, and some of them already employ foreign nationals as teachers. However, none of these foreign national teachers have been granted the status of 'ordinary teacher' (*kyōyu*) enjoyed by Japanese national teachers. A foreign national can only be appointed as a 'full-time teacher' (*jōkin kōshi*), a position that does not allow the appointee to serve as a homeroom teacher and that receives a lower salary. This arrangement has been challenged by critics, and it remains to be seen how it will be affected by the recent relaxation of the nationality requirement for a limited range of positions in several prefectural and metropolitan governments (e.g. Osaka and Kawasaki).

Due to the supply of, and demand for, new teachers, the examinations to select teacher candidates have been, in reality, competitive. The number of newly appointed teachers reached a peak (42,000) in 1980, and has declined since then. In 1994 newly appointed teachers in primary and secondary schools numbered 12,251, representing only 17.3 per cent of those who had obtained teaching certificates in that year. Teaching is a competitive profession for graduates to enter. For example, the number of qualified graduates who applied for places at primary schools in 1994 was 4.8 times the number of available positions. The equivalent figures for middle schools and high schools were 8.0 and 7.2 times respectively (Kawakami 1997b:2–4).

Salary Structure, Transfer and Promotion

Individual teachers' professional paths are strongly influenced by the salary structure, school transfer system and the process of promotion.

The salary system achieved its present form in 1954. Teachers' salaries were streamed into three categories: universities, high schools, and middle and primary schools. The salary structure for Japanese teachers offers every teacher an annual increment until he or she retires at the age of 60, unlike those in many Anglophone societies. Each category (universities, high schools, middle and primary schools, and technical colleges) contains several divisions (e.g. principals, vice-principals, ordinary teachers, non-academic technical staff members), each of which is further stratified into steps. For high-school staff members, for example, the division of ordinary high-school teacher contains 40 steps, and the division of principal 15 steps. An ordinary high-school teacher can thus receive an annual increment of salary (about US$600 to US$1000, Shimizu 1996:164) for 40 years, even if he or she does not take any position of responsibility. Teachers with 20 years' experience, for instance, would earn twice as much as novice teachers. This is likely to encourage teachers to remain in teaching on a long-term basis.

A different salary structure applies to principals and vice-principals. Positions of responsibility other than principal and vice-principal do exist, such as that of dean, who oversees a particular grade (*gakunen shunin*); these positions provide additional remuneration at a specified percentage of the teacher's salary. Salary levels are higher at universities and high schools than at middle and primary schools, and this has been considered problematic by many. Differences also exist across regions, since prefectures are left to determine salaries with reference to the National Personnel Authority, which advises the salary levels of national government school teachers. Often urban prefectures offer higher wages than regional prefectures. The rate of salary increase for teachers has been smaller than that for employees of private enterprises.

Teachers are regularly transferred from one school to another every several years, within the area governed by an education board. In 1994 approximately 16.5 per cent of teachers were transferred (Shimizu 1996:169). Both teachers and education boards consider three years an appropriate period for a novice teacher to stay at the first school; and five years at any one school for other teachers (Satō et al. 1991:155). The life histories of three teachers that we present later show that the period at a given school can range from three to over ten years. The majority of teachers perceive school transfers positively, in terms of individual teachers' professional development (50 per cent) and in terms of the school's educational activities (36 per cent) (Satō et al 1991:150–1). Transfer exposes teachers to diverse types of schools, where they discover or confirm their strengths and weaknesses as teachers and find their own identities, as we will discuss later.

In Japan teachers are appointed as principals and vice-principals at a much later stage of their teaching careers than in Anglo-Western countries. In 1994 the average age of appointment to vice-principal was 48 years, and to principal 53.3 years old (Shimizu 1996:170). Over the last decade, the average ages of appointment decreased. More female teachers assumed these positions, particularly at primary school.

Opportunities for promotions are limited. The only recognised positions of responsibility had been principal and vice-principal until the mid-1970s, when the MOE introduced so-called *shunin* (medium-level management positions to be remunerated). This move angered the union, which argued that *shunin* positions would divide teachers (whom it believed to be all equal) and would be unconducive to good teaching. Since the enforced implementation of this policy, teachers in some prefectures have pooled the allowances from *shunin* teachers and offered them to disadvantaged students as scholarships. *Shunin* generally include *kyōmu shunin* (the head of general instruction, who oversees the operation of the whole school through yearly scheduling of school events and timetabling), *gakunen shunin* (the dean of each grade), and *seitoshidō shunin* (the head of student guidance) at primary schools. In addition to the above, middle schools and high schools normally have *kyōka shunin* (the head of each subject department) and *shinroshidō shunin* (the departmental head of guidance for further education or employment). There is also a school-wide position called *hoken shuji* (teacher in charge of student health and hygiene), but this is often not remunerated. *Shunin* remuneration is approximately 4 per cent of the annual salary of a teacher who holds such a position.

Positions of responsibility are not publicly advertised. The covert nature of the appointment process attracts criticism from some corners. A *shunin* is appointed by the principal of the school, after the principal's recommendation is authorised by the education board. A vice-principal's appointment is also initiated by the principal of the school, who first recommends a teacher to the education board, which advises the teacher concerned to take the vice-principals' examination. If successful in the examination, the new vice-principal is then appointed by the education board. Candidates for vice-principals are expected to have successfully performed various *shunin* positions since their mid-thirties. As for a principal's appointment, the education board advises selected vice-principals to take the principal's examination, and then promotes successful candidates to principals. In the above cases, when a principal (or education board, in the case of a principal's appointment) first approaches a teacher considered appropriate for such a position and asks if they are interested in it, the teacher can choose not to accept this invitation. In fact, some choose to remain 'ordinary' classroom teachers instead of pursuing promotion, for various reasons, as the life histories presented below will reveal.

Union involvement is generally detrimental to an individual teacher's chances of receiving promotion. Union membership must be relinquished once a teacher is appointed vice-principal. Those who aim to pursue the promotion track leave the union in their thirties or forties, sometimes urged to do so by their principals, who are willing to recommend them for promotion. In some prefectures, however, past active involvement in union activities can work in favour of promotion (Yagyū 1992:68). Given that teacher union membership and power have declined in the last decade, the influence of past union involvement on one's promotion prospects is likely to change.

A significant proportion of teachers do not aim to pursue the career track to principal. Nor do they believe that those who become principals are the most deserving of that position. There is some cynicism about pursuing the career track, and this is a reflection of the long history of the relationship between the union and the MOE, which until very recently was antagonistic.

In-service Education

In-service education of teachers can be categorised into (1) voluntary education which individual schools, organisations, groups or individual teachers conduct; and (2) workshops that administrative bodies (local and national) provide. The former type continuously occurs in schools, while the latter is often organised on monthly or yearly schedules and participating teachers are exempted from teaching duties during such education. The administration-initiated in-service education is currently being reorganised in a more systematic way.[2]

The nature of in-service training of teachers is considered to differ from that for general public employees. While the latter aims to improve work 'efficiency', in-service training for teachers goes beyond that and is legally guaranteed as an important component of their professional tasks. This is because teachers are expected to constantly improve their professional knowledge in order to assist children's development and to have the freedom and independence to select the education that they consider to be the most appropriate to their own teaching. The Law

Lesson attended by other teachers and students' parents as observers.

'Could you tell us your educational philosophy?'

'Aah . . .' (She has never thought about it.)

'Well . . . personal formation through education . . . yes, yes, since it is balance that is important . . .'

'Children should be encouraged to sing, dance and act, and so forth.'

'Teacher, you mean cognitive development, moral development and physical development?'

Source: Asahi Shinbun 2 April 1996 © Hisaichi Ishii

of Special Regulations concerning Educational Public Service Personnel (LSREPSP, article 19) states that 'public educational personnel *must* constantly be engaged in study for their work', and that the employing authorities '*must* plan, and provide resources for, in-service education' (emphasis ours). Long-lasting debate has centred on the degree to which principals can exercise their authority to approve their teachers' participation in in-service education.[3]

In-service education for teachers underwent a major change in 1988. Newly employed teachers were required to undertake in-service education ('internship', *shoninsha kenshū*) for one year. Employing authorities have an obligation to provide 'practical' training through 'hands-on' experience under supervision. The introduction of the internship has caused wide debate, which will be discussed in more detail in Chapter 6.

Workloads

Teachers work long hours. Japanese schools alternate between a six-day week and a five-day week over a fortnight. The government is now hoping that a five-day week will eventuate by 2003. While students have a forty-day summer vacation, a fourteen-day winter vacation and another fourteen days of spring vacation, their teachers often work during these periods.

Classroom teaching time is 26.5 hours a week for primary-school teachers, 19.7 hours for middle-school teachers, and 16.8 hours for high-school teachers (Zenkyō 1993:45). In addition, primary-school teachers supervise recesses, lunchtimes and school cleaning sessions. Middle-school and high-school teachers are involved in supervision of after-school club activities, and in offering counselling and supplementary lessons for entrance examinations to higher-level schools. Teachers feel overworked and want the government to increase teacher numbers (Zenkyō 1993:45).

Two separately conducted surveys present similar pictures of teachers' busy lives: one was of 853 middle-school teachers in 1991 (Fukaya 1992) and the other covered 1350 primary-, middle- and high-school teachers in 1992 (Zenkyō 1993). Teachers spent an average of 10 hours 36 minutes a day at school, arriving at school at 7:49 am and leaving at 6:25 pm; and even during the forty-day summer holiday, 44 per cent of teachers spent less than 10 days free at home (Fukaya 1992:62–3). More experienced teachers spent fewer hours at school because they were less likely to be involved in sports club supervision and were more efficient with their routine work (Fukaya 1992:62–3). Zenkyō's data were similar: teachers averaged 55 hours a week at work, 11 hours more than the required 44 working hours (Zenkyō 1993:26). This was in addition to time spent commuting, preparing lessons and marking assignments at home. Teachers' recreation time was consequently squeezed. On weekdays, over 54 per cent of teachers had less than two hours of recreation time, in comparison to 41 per cent for the average working person. Female teachers had even less time to themselves (Kudomi 1995:13–14).

Figure 5.1 is an example of a female primary-school teacher's weekday. She recorded these activities on a set date in response to the above-mentioned 1992 Zenkyō survey (Zenkyō 1993). She was 46 years old and married with two children.

The teacher added a comment after recording this diary: 'In reality my day consists of many small tasks completed simultaneously over a short time. For example, during the 20-minute break (between third and fourth periods), I read the class diary and talked a while with some pupils in the classroom; and then went down to the staffroom where I confirmed a few things with my colleagues while having a cup of coffee. After that I called the pupils on the student council on the school broadcasting system, and gave them a few handouts; and then rushed to the next class after hastily making photocopies of teaching materials . . . I feel that I do many things simultaneously.' (Zenkyō 1993:25)

Many teachers feel that they are overworked or on the verge of 'burn-out'; some even fear '*karōshi*' (death from overwork). In the above-mentioned Zenkyō survey, 58 per cent of teachers had been desperate enough to consider quitting teaching, and the majority cited overwork and overwork-caused health problems as the reason (Zenkyō 1993:43). Teachers on average take seven days of annual leave, and quote as reasons for their reluctance in taking their entitlements work to be done and concern with the inconvenience that it might cause to other teachers (Zenkyō 1993:42).

Despite heavy workloads, the teaching profession seems to be an appealing option to a considerable number of graduates. Not only is entry into teaching competitive, but teachers tend to remain in the profession. The average length of service of teachers in 1995 was 17 years for primary schools, 15.7 years for middle schools and 17.3 years for high schools (Japan, Monbushō 1997:10). The average ages of teachers in the same year were 40.5, 39.7 and 42.4 years respectively (Japan, Monbushō 1997:9).

The attraction of teaching as a career seems to derive from a combination of various factors, which appeal to different teachers to differing extents. No doubt the salary structure, whereby teachers receive an annual increment until retirement, encourages many to stay. They have the job security of a government employee and are paid at a slightly higher

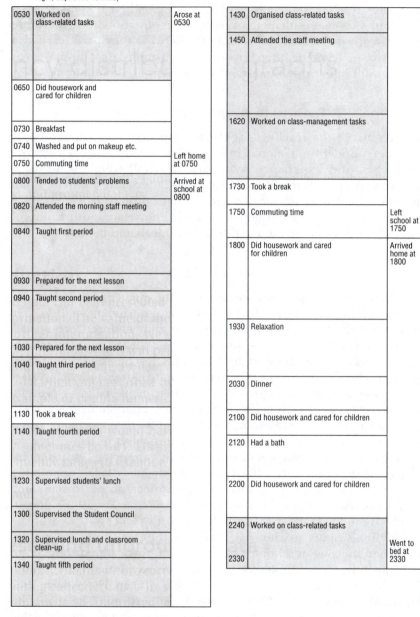

Figure 5.1 A female teacher's day
Source: Zenkyō (1993:25). Adapted with permission of All Japan Teachers and Staff Union.

level than those in other equivalent government services. For female graduates, teaching remains one of the few areas where they enjoy 'equal pay' and various entitlements related to motherhood. Furthermore, teachers are more likely to be able to use what they have learned at university in teaching than in other occupations. In country areas, teachers still enjoy a traditional level of respect from community members.

Teachers' Rights and Children's Rights

The nature of the teachers' rights that Japanese educationalists and teachers consider fundamental influences the ways in which teachers see themselves and experience schooling. The following discussion of teachers' rights will therefore help us to understand teachers' union activities, the culture of teaching and teachers' professional life paths. It is assumed that teachers' rights are closely interrelated with children's rights. We will examine these rights both as ideals and in reality.

Children's Rights

Children's human rights and welfare form the essence of the Children's Charter (*Jidōkenshō*) issued by the Japanese government in 1951. The nature of children's rights is unique in that children are socially powerless to voice their views, and that their realisation is subject to an understanding of children's rights by parents, teachers and the public in general. The United Nations Convention on Children's Rights (*Kodomo no Kenri Jōyaku*), signed by the Japanese government in 1989, adopts the view that every child be recognised as an independent human being who possesses and exercises his or her rights. To grow up as a person in his or her own right, a child needs to acquire a certain set of knowledge and abilities through development in a specially 'protected' environment. Children are, for instance, to be protected in families, local communities and the society at large, and to have guaranteed access to schooling. Various parties in the society thus need to have relationships that are conducive to the realisation of children's rights (Tsuchiya 1990).

Children's rights are, however, at risk in the face of physical punishment and bullying at school. The realities of physical punishment and bullying in Japanese schools were revealed in several surveys (e.g. Nihon Bengoshi Rengōkai 1985; Japan, Hōmushō, Jinken Yōgo-kyoku 1985; Japan, Monbushō, Shotō Chūtō Kyōiku-kyoku, Chūgakkō-ka 1986), and included cases in which children's human rights were blatantly violated, as will be examined in more detail in Chapter 6. What may be considered as 'violence' in the public arena is often committed at school under the labels 'cane of affection' and 'educational consideration'.

While larger societal causes for a prevalence of physical punishment exist, factors at the school level also contribute to it. Some teachers resort to physical punishment out of desperation, unable to maintain classroom 'order' without it. Some use physical punishment, genuinely believing that it has pedagogical merit despite being aware of its illegality. Others may mistakenly believe that the exercise of moderate physical punishment is legitimate. Some parents may want teachers to provide strict guidance by means of a 'cane of affection'. Above all, the school authority's response to its own cases of severe physical punishment is often not forthright, leading to an inadequate awareness of human rights at school. Authoritarian administration at the school level can be a significant cause leading teachers to attempt to maintain school rules and order through physical punishment. For example, some schools maintain strict rules in the name of anti-delinquency measures and improving students' academic performance, without questioning whether this might contradict the underlying assumption of respect for children's rights.

Teachers' Rights to Educate Children

Ideally, teachers would possess professional freedom and the authority to conduct their tasks. However, this does not mean that teachers can do anything with the children in their charge, since the teacher's right to educate children is subject to the inherent nature of education (autonomous, scientific and pro-human rights), and, externally, to parents' rights to educate their own children. This inherent nature of education affects teachers' right to educate children in the following ways. Due to the autonomous nature of education, teachers are expected to teach without surrendering to inappropriate external control. The scientific nature of education requires teachers to select and arrange the curriculum from knowledge based on empirical research, and the pro-human rights aspect of education requires teachers to provide the kind of education that respects fundamental human rights.

Teachers' rights to educate children endow them with a set of responsibilities. First, they are responsible for ensuring children's rights to receive education. This involves designing scientific and systematic curricula, adopting teaching methods appropriate to children's develop-mental stages and providing guidance for a collective living and safe learning environment. Second, teachers are responsible for accom-modating parents' rights to educate their own children, based on professional judgement that considers the interests of all children. While parents entrust teachers with a part of their rights to educate their own children, they hold the right to select the kind of education and culture to be taught to them, and to express their views on teachers' educational philosophy and guidance methods, curricula and school administration. Parents are not able to exclude their children from receiving education, however. Third, teachers as a professional group are responsible for being involved in, and commenting on, school administration in order to maintain the autonomy of education. This would ensure that the administration takes account of the teachers' right to educate children and provides resources that would ensure children's right to receive education.

In reality, not all teachers' educational activities remain harmonious with the children's right to receive education or parents' right to educate their own children. For example, some teachers exercise physical punishment and conduct authoritarian forms of teaching that violate children's human rights. The teachers' right to educate children and the parents' right to educate their own children often conflict in cases of physical punishment, school rules, and confidential reports to be sent to higher schools. Where contradictions and conflicts of interest exist among parties, the teachers' right is often compromised.

Why do some schools face contradictions between the teachers' rights and the children's rights, which are essentially not supposed to be in conflict with each other? These contradictions seem to derive, at least partly, from undesirable relationships between the administration and teachers. Such relationships distort democratic interpersonal relationships at school (including those between teachers and students), and create an environment not conducive to the realisation of children's rights. Satisfactory relationships between the administration and teachers are thus important for ensuring the children's rights. One cannot expect teachers to ensure children's rights, when they themselves do not enjoy what they consider to be their own freedoms and rights. To teach about human rights, for instance, teachers must understand their significance, and be willing to 'practise' them.

The Civil Rights and Labour Rights of Teachers

Teachers in government schools have often felt that their civil rights and basic labour rights have been compromised. While both national and local government employees' political activities are restricted by legislation in the name of assumed political neutrality and impartial administration, such restrictions are even stricter for educational employees and national government employees (the LSREPSP and the National Personnel Authority Rules 1417).

'Political activities' (in relation to local government employees) include: (1) forming political organisations, or participating in them as an executive or a canvasser; (2) canvassing votes (and signatures and donations) and displaying written documents for the purpose of supporting/rejecting a particular person or an incident in an election; and (3) enticing public employees in relation to the above. For local government employees, such political activities are prohibited within the area under the local government of the employee. For national government employees and teachers, this applies to the whole country. Such restrictions placed on teachers' civil rights in government schools do not conform to international standards, for instance, the 'Advice on Teachers' Status' (*Kyōshi no Chii ni kansuru Kankoku*, 1966) issued by the International Labor Organisation (ILO) and UNESCO. Teachers' civil rights are fundamental human rights, which are indispensable in the conduct of their professional duties for all (not just a particular group or individual), and in the cultivation of the political knowledge needed by all citizens.

Restrictions are also placed on teachers' basic labour rights. Current public employee legislation restricts the right to bargain collectively (the National Public Service Personnel Law [NPSPL], article 108.5.2, and the Local Public Service Personnel Law [LPSPL], article 55.2); prohibits the right to strike (NPSPL, article 98.2; LPSPL, article 37); and punishes conspiracy and enticement in relation to these actions (NPSPL article 110.17; LPSPL article 61.4). In lieu of these rights, the government in 1948 established the National Personnel Authority (*Jinjiin*), which mediates between public employees and their employers, so that despite these restrictions, public employees still have a means of negotiating with their employers. Court cases have been fought as to whether the current legislation is constitutional, but their verdicts have been mixed, as shown in the Tokyo Metropolitan Teachers' Union's case which we discussed in Chapter 2.

The Practice of Guiding Child Development

The so-called practical capacity of teachers has been widely discussed by those who blame teachers for serious 'problems' at school. Parents and the public have expressed grassroots-level concern with the state of schooling, and their expectations of the crucial role that teachers play in the resolution of these problems. At a national policy level the Ad-Hoc Council on Education in 1984 advocated an 'improvement in the quality of teachers', and attempted to 'upgrade' it (see the discussion in Chapter 6). Just what constitutes the 'practical capacity' of teachers is difficult to define.

Below we shall examine the essential nature of the practical capacity of teachers by illustrating three concrete examples of practice which, many teachers agree, demonstrate such capacity. In so doing, we hope to delineate the capacities that Japanese teachers strive for as their ideals.

Ideally, professional teachers are equipped with scientific knowledge and skills regarding child development. Their task is to promote children's development (both cognitive and personal) through learning activities, by selecting a curriculum that is appropriate to the developmental stage of the individual child, and by guiding their systematic learning. To achieve this, teachers require an academic understanding of child development as well as a practical capacity. A teacher's practical capacity is acquired through first-hand attempts to resolve day-to-day issues while interacting with the children in his or her charge. This practical capacity is considered to be based upon a commitment and endless effort to comprehend the true feelings of children, to encourage children to experience a sense of joy and pride in learning, and to achieve meaningful coordination with parents and the community in the education of children. The three cases below represent each of these ingredients.

Case Study 5.1: Understanding the True Feelings of Children – Ms Niwa's Practice

Teachers try to overcome serious distortions in human development in children through their commitment to comprehending the children's true feelings. One example of such efforts is the Citizens' Education Congress of Nakatsugawa city in Gifu prefecture. Participating teachers, parents and citizens acknowledged 'distortions' in the development of some children, and explained such distortions as a sign of the children's difficulty in gaining independence. Based on this premise, they organised learning activities to promote dialogue between adults and children. The Congress reasoned that 'growing up in affluence, children find it difficult to gain independence, and want adults to understand their difficulties. Teachers need to respond by making efforts to understand the children's desires. They also need to make their wishes understood to the children, and to join them in exploring the path to independence together.'

This is easier said than done. One teacher, Ms Noriko Niwa, reported on her teaching through having children write essays about immediate experiences (*seikatsu tsuzurikata*) (Seikatsu Tsuzurikata Ena no Ko Henshū Iinkai 1982). Her teaching motto was 'to make every child experience a joy in extending himself or herself in cooperation with classmates'. Ms Niwa did not force children to write. Instead, she emphasised the importance of children experiencing a life that they would spontaneously consider deserved writing about, and patiently waited for their initiatives in writing. Prime importance was attached to 'the truth' that children experience in their immediate lives, and their inner freedom. Children were urged to cherish their development with classmates. Below is one of the essays resulting from her teaching. The author is a fifth-grader.

. . . This happened when I was a second-grader. I have not yet told my family about this. On our way home from school, my friend Kumi said to me, 'Miyuki, let's steal money from our homes.' I did not realise how vicious the act of stealing was. I went home and got 200 yen from the money box in my mother's shop. Kumi did not bring any money, saying she could not find any. With the money we bought lollies. Since then almost every day I stole 500 yen or 300 yen from home, and spent it with Kumi. When I said to Kumi, 'Since it's always me, you should bring money as well', she brought 100 yen only once. I might have thought that my family was wealthy, since other kids used to tell me 'Your family has a shop and a *tatami* mat workshop, and must be rich'. We once bought a comic magazine with the money stolen from home. We divided supplements to the magazine between us. We decided that Kumi would say to her parents that she got them from me, and that I would say to my parents that I got them from Kumi.

This is not all. When the school announced 'One hundred yen has been found. The person who lost a hundred yen, please come and collect it', Chiyo said to me, 'Let's go and get it', although she had not lost it. I followed her. We bought sweets with the money. There is more. When Satomi was arrogant, Chiyo and I threw away her shoes in the toilet, and said 'We wonder who did it'. One day a shopkeeper did not appear for a while after we called him. While we were waiting for him, we put chewing gum in our pockets, and candies and chocolate in our bags. Soon, I found myself committing more serious offences. We went to a shop without money and put sweets into our pockets before calling out to the shopkeeper. When the shopkeeper came out, we left, saying 'You don't have what we want. We will come back later'. Whenever a shopkeeper appeared immediately, we looked around, and said the same thing.

Finally my mother found that I had been stealing her money. 'I have been wondering what's been happening. You have been doing this, haven't you?'. Since it was so sudden, I could not lie to her. My mother told me to tell her everything. I told her about Kumi and me stealing money from home, but did not dare reveal our stealing sweets from shops. My mother's face became teary and frightening, and she tied my hands tightly with rope, took me upstairs, and made me sit there. I cried, telling myself that I would never steal again. When my mother released me before dinner, my hands were red. Kumi said, 'Your mother was strict, wasn't she? My mother did nothing'. It was perhaps because Kumi told her mother that it was I who bought her sweets with the money that I stole. I hated Kumi. I thought I would not play with her. Now I regret what I did. I wonder why I did such silly things. I could not bring myself to confess to my mother other things that I did, since I thought the police would arrest me. I am writing this to you, Ms Niwa, since I believe that you will understand how I feel. I want you to know that I have now learned an important lesson. If I do a wrong thing, I can deceive others but not myself, and I suffer from it. I was sick in my heart. I want you to tell other kids who may be sick like me what I went through. I am so pleased that I could write this before becoming an adult. This is my most important achievement this semester. My family is struggling. I now think that it is hard work for my parents to run both a *tatami* workshop and a cafe. So, I regret what I did, although I was young then. I am glad that I could write this. (Seikatsu Tsuzurikata Ena no Ko Henshū Iinkai 1982:143–8)

This fifth-grader girl explained that she had extended herself by the act of writing of her most painful experience. That is, she learned to overcome what was troubling her and to find joy in doing so. This act was based on her trust that her teacher would not make a judgement about her past actions and would understand her. Such a pedagogical relationship between a teacher and a child was developed because the teacher closely observed the child, valued the truth in her immediate life, and consciously wanted to cultivate humane dispositions in the student through her teaching.

Case Study 5.2: Teaching Children to Enjoy Learning – Mr Nakamoto's Practice

Some children struggle with schoolwork. There are high-school students who have difficulties with the English alphabet and basic arithmetic. Primary, middle and high schools have undertaken various measures to recover the basic academic skills, and are still exploring other teaching methods appropriate to different developmental stages.

An attempt to teach differential and integral calculus to students who hate mathematics deserves mention here. Nakamoto (1979), a mathematics teacher at a private girls' high school, at first found it impossible to teach differential and integral calculus to students who had come to dislike mathematics as a result of poor performance at primary and middle schools. He used to teach closely to the textbook in a conventional way, getting students to memorise the differential formulae and conduct mechanical calculations. Nakamoto reflected on those days: 'It made me feel hopelessly in vain. I suspect that the students were not moved. They understood neither the essence of differential calculus nor its power' (Nakamoto 1979:11).

Nakamoto then sought to devise lessons that would be understandable and enjoyable. For instance, he invited students to make *origami* paper boxes which would be of maximum capacity. Students learned to use differential calculus as an instrument to achieve this task, and were encouraged by the result. In introducing integral calculus, he had students spin tops of various shapes. They learned the essence of a function through analogy to a 'black box', where a regular change takes place between its entrance and exit. Students delighted in discovering that the curve of a coin became a straight line when observed through a microscope, and learned that a curved line consists of an infinite number of straight lines.

Observing his students' responses, Nakamoto came to suspect that students' dislike of mathematics derived from their lack of understanding of basic mathematics, and started to review the meaning of simple multiplication and division. Nakamoto then taught step by step what he considered to be the minimum basics required to grasp differential calculus: average variation rate, limiting values, differential coefficients, derived functions, how to draw the graph of a quadratic function, and the maximum and minimum values of a quadratic function. He writes:

I think that every high-school student can understand the notion of differential and integral calculus even when their mastery of other basics in mathematics is problematic. In fact, while learning differential and integral calculus, students can recover the basics in mathematics. (Nakamoto 1979:170) ... Differential and integral calculus reflect Descartes's method 'when you have a problem, divide it', and are among the concrete forms of analysis and integration of modern natural science. By studying differential and integral calculus as a method of recognition, students learn that studying can be interesting and enriching. I believe that differential and integral calculus deserve to be taught to high-school students as cultural heritage. (Nakamoto 1979:135)

Students commented positively on his teaching. 'At the beginning I felt as if we were learning primary-school maths, although I had not understood these basics. I feel that I studied mathematics for the first time at high school.' 'I had understood maths but never enjoyed it. Activities using *origami* and "black boxes" made us wonder what he was up to. Now I understand the basics.' (Nakamoto 1979:272).

Through his practice, Nakamoto believes that every student can become motivated to learn if he or she understands the basics and receives the kind of teaching that enables him or her to 'experience' the joy of studying. He argues:

When a school functions as was originally designed (to educate children), students' voices tell us that they have potential to grow up healthily. Students can experience that kind of engaging and enjoyable learning through studying differential and integral calculus (an area of mathematics which has been considered so difficult that many rather want to avoid it). I don't agree with a recent move to offer 'easy maths' to poor academic achievers. (Nakamoto 1979:232–3)

Schools in Japan are considered to be relatively closed to parents and the local community, in that their views are not well reflected in the running of schools. This is partly because parents and the community do not have a formal channel for participation in their children's schooling. This is regrettable, since cooperation among the three parties would assist in making schooling more relevant to children's immediate lives at home and in the community.

Teachers have long stressed that a decline in a child's motivation to study and behavioural problems are closely related to his or her family life. Individual teachers often take initiatives to connect with parents, for example, by sending out class bulletins, but few schools have institutionalised concrete measures to involve parents and the community in the schooling process. Given that children represent the future of the society, as well as that of individual families, parents and citizens hold expectations of them as the next generation of the community. A teacher's practical capacity includes acknowledging these varying expectations on the part of parents and the community, and devising actions to coordinate their participation in schooling. Such attempts will assist in overcoming the present 'desolate state of education' (as it is described in the media), and in making schools responsible to parents and the wider community. We now examine one such example.

**Case Study 5.3: Involving Parents and the Community –
F Primary School's Practice**

F Primary School in Hyōgo prefecture created and implemented a school-based policy to offer the kind of teaching that involved parents and the community (Morigaki 1979; 1982). F Primary teachers first made systematic observations of the development of individual children, reported their observations to parents and the community, and conducted a parental survey on their wishes regarding schooling (academic and extracurricular). The result of the survey formed the basis for the policy, which was presented to parents and the community members for further discussion.[4]

The policy resulted in concrete actions. The school conducted regular academic drills to monitor students' progress in Chinese characters and arithmetic so that every student achieved the basics; designed a school report to parents which emphasised the students' progress towards stated goals rather than their achievement relative to other students; published an annual collection of every student's essays; taught students to keep a diary; and involved parents in students' learning activities. Parents made it a rule to read books to their children for 20 minutes every day. The community organised physical training activities.

In contrast to typical classes based on textbooks, F Primary students received education based on more immediate experience of the community. When studying Japan's modernisation, students studied traditional industries and learned about the experiences of farmers and factory girls in the local community from their grandparents. A 70-year-old local man, Mr Oki, was invited to the sixth-graders' lesson on the Japanese Constitution every year, and spoke about his experience of the Second World War.

Mr Oki first brought his war medals to the classroom and talked about how hard he worked for the country. He then closed his eyes and recited fully the Rescript on Education. Children asked, 'What is this sutra?', 'When did you memorise this?' Mr Oki explained, 'This is called the Rescript on Education. Unless we could recite this fully, we were not allowed to proceed to fifth grade'. Responding to a child's question as to whether he understood its meaning at the time, Mr Oki responded, 'Even if we did not understand its meaning, we had to recite it to proceed to fifth grade. The Meiji Constitution advocated the War, and we had to show respect and follow any order from above. We could not even look at the Emperor's face. You are so fortunate to live with the post-war Constitution' (Morigaki 1982:186).

Through such dialogues, children learned the history that their grandparents and relatives had lived through, in addition to the textbook history, and understood their immediate relatives' genuine wish for peace and happiness. Teachers and parents also learned from these lessons. A parent stated:

I have learned enormously with my children from their grandparents' life stories. I was moved by the hardship that they overcame, and have renewed respect for them. I am also glad to communicate with other parents, children and community members through learning activities at school. I feel that the good coordination of school and community has brought enjoyable educational experiences to all children. (Hyōgo-ken Kyōiku Sentā, 1984:55)

The teachers' attempts to involve parents and community members in schooling assumed that teachers alone cannot overcome distortions in child development. By bringing the experiences of local people and the ideas of parents into classrooms, these learning activities provided teachers with opportunities to heighten their practical capacities. Teachers could thus play a major role in establishing meaningful relationships with parents and the community, and ensure that parents and community members shared responsibility for the children's education.

The modes of teaching that we have illustrated above (provided by Ms Niwa, Mr Nakamoto and the teachers at F Primary School) are considered by many Japanese teachers to demonstrate excellent practical capacity for teaching. They also represent the kind of education (in terms of both curriculum and method) that would ensure the realisation of children's right to receive an education.

Professional Associations and Unions

Teachers are both professional educators and workers, and participate in professional organisations and unions. On the one hand, teachers collectively study, and voice their views on, educational and social issues that they consider relevant to the future of their students. On the other hand, they collectively demand a certain standard of working conditions, so that they can perform their professional tasks and maintain their own private lives in a satisfactory way.

There are three types of teacher organisations. These are unions, professional associations, which do not represent themselves as unions, and associations for studying a particular field of education. Five major teachers' unions currently exist. The largest is *Nikkyōso*, which we have already touched on in previous sections of this book. The second is *Zenkyō*, which was formed by those who left *Nikkyōso* when the latter changed its platform and started to adopt a cooperative stance towards the MOE in 1989. While *Nikkyōso* still maintains an affiliation with major political parties, *Zenkyō* does not. A union of high-school teachers (*Nikkōkyō-uha*) was formed in 1950 by teachers in *Nikkyōso* who were dissatisfied with the latter's focus on primary and middle schools; it

Table 5.2 Union membership of teachers, October 1996

	Nikkyōso %	Zenkyō %	Nikkōkyō-uha %	Zen'nichi-kyōren %	Zenkankyō %	Others %	Total %
Primary school	37.2	7.4	–	3.6	0.6	10.3	59.1
Middle school	40.0	6.9	–	3.4	0.7	7.2	58.3
High school	22.8	16.7	5.6	0.1	–	4.8	50.1
Schools for the deaf and the blind	19.2	15.5	3.8	0.1	0.1	5.9	44.6
Schools for the handicapped	18.6	13.3	3.0	0.2	0.1	4.8	39.9
Kindergarten	9.3	1.8	–	0.5	–	25.2	36.8
Teachers at all levels	33.0	9.6	1.4	2.5	0.4	8.3	55.3

Source: Kawakami (1997a:11)

adopts political neutrality and moderate strategies. Other unions are a national federation of teachers (*Zen'nichikyōren*), which claims to be a semi-union association but avoids involvement in activities of a political nature; and an organisation of teachers who hold management positions (mainly vice-principals) *(Zenkankyō)*.[5] Membership levels are difficult to determine accurately, since the MOE and unions present divergent estimates. For example, *Nikkyōso*'s self-claimed membership is 450,000, while the MOE's figure is 380,000. Table 5.2 shows the pattern of union membership provided by the MOE's 1996 survey.

Non-union professional associations include the National Association of Principals (primary, middle and high schools), the National Association of Deputy-Principals, and the Japan Association of Teachers (which displays an inclination to the right). Besides the above organisations, teachers often join teachers' associations for study in particular fields of education. They include associations of teachers of specific subjects (e.g. English, history, physical education) and of teachers with specific school-level responsibilities (e.g. student guidance, guidance for further education and employment, school nurses, human rights). These associations tend to focus on studying, and sharing the findings of, practical aspects of teaching and guidance, often through their own journals. Approximately 50 such associations are currently registered.

It has been through union activities, rather than other types of associations, that teachers have most vocally and effectively expressed their views on educational and social issues, pursued their educational philosophies, and influenced the practice of schooling to date. They have also won better working conditions and the protection of their civil rights through unions. Past union activities and their significance were discussed in Chapter 2. Greater detail is provided by Duke (1973), Thurston (1973) and Ota (1989).

While we emphasise the significance of what teachers' union activities have achieved, these activities have not been free from criticism. This has come from two directions: the government on the one hand, and parents, the public and teachers themselves on the other. The government has disapproved of the unions' demand for various 'entitlements as workers', because it officially held the view that 'teaching is a sacred profession (and teachers therefore do not carry the status of a "worker")', and because it regarded the unions as inconvenient obstacles to implementing its own policies.

Parents, the public and some teachers have directed their criticisms to three aspects. First, it has been claimed that some union teachers use their job-related entitlements 'unprofessionally', for example, taking their annual leave of 20 days at the end of the year when they have no 'professionally appropriate' reason for doing so. (The fact that this practice is perceived as 'unprofessional' reveals an interesting expectation of teachers and workers generally.) Second, excessive and rigid adherence to the union's official positions has, in some cases, adversely affected school management. There have been cases where teachers have refused to accept, and work with, a newly appointed principal, claiming that principals act as managers to control teachers. Another example is the union's (unreasonable or inflexible) insistence that the staff meeting is the supreme decision-making body within a school; and its demand for principals to accept its decisions even when principals are legally required to perform certain duties that may conflict with union decisions. Third, some parents, members of the public and teachers did not feel comfortable with the fact that *Nikkyōso* officially endorsed the Japan Socialist Party (JSP) and demanded that union members support the party and provide financial assistance for election campaigns.

Unions' Attempts to Raise Salaries

Teachers' salaries have been maintained at relatively low levels by the National Personnel Authority (*Jinjiin*, NPA), which determines wage rates for government employees. In 1946 the government established the first post-war system of teachers' wages, comprising 30 steps defined by level of academic qualification and years of service. For a short time after the 1947 labour agreement between the MOE and the teachers' unions, the Wage Commission (which consisted of representatives from the government, unions and the Central Labour Commission) determined wages through direct negotiation. However, since the government deprived its employees of the right to strike and abandoned the previous labour agreement in 1948, the NPA has determined salary schedules for teachers and provided the government with official advice on salary increases. Around this time sex-based differences in teachers' pay were abolished.

Government employees' lack of entitlement to basic labour rights has been illuminated by the verdicts of several court cases. For instance, in 1966 the Supreme Court suggested that the basic labour rights specified in Article 28 of the Constitution be granted to government employees. In 1969 the Supreme Court judged that the prohibition of bargaining among government employees could be unconstitutional, and stated that organising labour for the sake of bargaining does not constitute a criminal offence. These cases provided a sense of optimism for teachers in their struggle to raise their wages.

In view of the NPA's salary-fixing arrangement, government employees have focused on two actions in their organised movements to raise salaries. The first is to ensure that the NPA issues advice on salary increases, and the second is to have the government accept that advice. Over the period from 1950 to 1953 the government ignored advice from the NPA , and from 1954 to 1959 the NPA did not even issue any advice. In 1960 this led government employees (who were deprived of the right to strike) to negotiate directly with the government, which resulted in a 12.4 per cent pay increase. These movements continued in the 1960s, and succeeded in forcing the government to accept the NPA's advice on salary increases. *Nikkyōso* was an active participant in these movements. It organised the first nationwide strike in 1966, involving 320,000 teachers, and a series of annual nationwide strikes for four consecutive years.

Ordinary teachers did not enjoy substantial salary increases, although the MOE started providing a 'management allowance' to principals (in 1958), vice-principals (in 1961) and middle-management teachers (*shunin*) (in 1976). Teachers' demands for 'overtime allowances appropriate to their work' led to the government's 1971 decision to provide a 4 per cent increase as an 'adjustment allowance' to all teachers (instead of overtime allowances). Teachers finally gained a 10 per cent salary increase in 1974, when the government acknowledged the need to attract quality applicants into teaching by providing substantially better remuneration to teachers than that received by general government employees. This was, however, interpreted by sceptics as the govern-

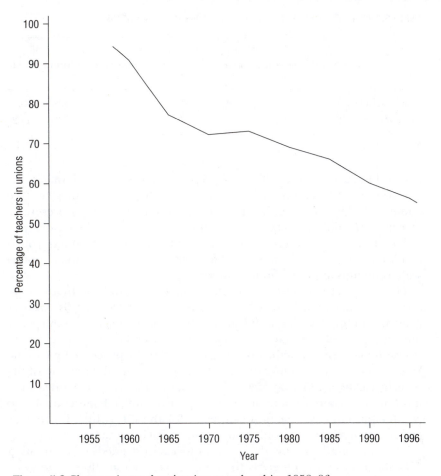

Figure 5.2 Changes in teachers' union membership, 1958–96
'Unions' here refers to the unions listed in Table 5.2 (*Nikkyōso, Zenkyō, Nikkōkyō, Zen'nichikyōren, Zenkankyō,* and others).
Sources: Japan, Monbushō, Chihō-ka (1996:55); Kawakami (1997a:10)

ment's political move to weaken government employees' labour movements by separating teachers from other government employees.

The Decline and Reorganisation of Teacher Unions

Union membership has been in decline over the last four decades (see Figure 5.2). In 1958 almost 95 per cent of teachers at primary and secondary schools were members of the major unions. By 1980 membership had declined to 70 per cent, and the latest figure (collected

Table 5.3 Union membership of new teachers, October 1996

	Nikkyōso %	Zenkyō %	Nikkōkyō-uha %	Zen'nichi-kyōren %	Zenkankyō %	Others %	Total %
New teachers	18.4	2.4	2.0	2.1	–	5.9	30.8
All teachers	33.0	9.6	1.4	2.5	0.4	8.3	55.2

Source: Kawakami (1997a:11)

in October 1996 by the MOE) was 55.3 per cent. Even fewer new teachers join unions: only 30.8 per cent of new teachers joined up in 1996 (see Table 5.3). The low membership rate among new teachers presents a threat for the union movement that union leaders now take seriously.

The decline in union membership over the years has resulted from a combination of several factors, and has been accelerated by the national-scale reorganisation of labour movements.

The first factor is the direct attacks made on *Nikkyōso* by the conservatives who feared *Nikkyōso*'s influence in the 1950s and 1960s. *Nikkyōso* actively promoted various political and civil movements, such as the peace movement, and fiercely opposed the conservatives' initiatives to strengthen the power of the police force in 1950, the peace treaty with the Western powers (excluding the Eastern nations), and the revision of the security treaty in 1960. Besides, *Nikkyōso* was considered to be one of the most powerful and influential unions supporting the left, and was able to conduct an effective election campaign for the JSP (which it officially endorsed) across the nation, including the rural backwaters.

The direct attacks by the conservatives succeeded in containing *Nikkyōso* in two ways. One was the tangible restrictions that came to be imposed on teachers' union activities. In the late 1950s teachers' political activities became restricted, as discussed in Chapter 2. In the 1960s a few prefectural education boards (e.g. Tochigi and Gifu) threateningly advised teachers to leave their unions. (This incident was later brought before the ILO. However, the action seems to have been successful: in 1996 these two prefectures maintained the lowest rate of union membership.) The other constraint on *Nikkyōso* was brought about through indirect influence on young teachers' perception of unions. The conservatives' campaign to cast *Nikkyōso* as an aggressive left ideologue (which supported the JSP and mobilised its members for civil and political movements) made the union less appealing to them. They simply did not want to be viewed by the public as left ideologue teachers.

The second factor in the fall in teachers' union membership has been the decline in the rate of unionisation across all fields of employment over the years; the current overall figure stands at approximately 23 per cent. Since the majority of workers are not union members, younger teachers are inclined to follow that option.

Third, the slow economic growth from the late 1970s and subsequent budgetary constraints have meant that wages for public employees have not been raised despite active campaigns by the unions. Until 1974 teachers had experienced considerable rises in their salaries, and had been able to feel the tangible benefits of the unions, but this has not been the case since then. New teachers take for granted the working entitlements that the past union movements fought for and won (e.g. maternity leave) and do not appreciate the benefits of supporting the union movement, very much like young women's attitude towards old feminism.

A further three factors derive from the series of events that took place in relation to the large-scale reorganisation of unions. We shall first briefly describe the changes in the national organisation of unions in the 1980s, and then examine how the process of such changes, and the changes themselves, affected (or damaged) the teacher union movement.

There was a drastic change in the Japan Socialist Party's political platform in 1980. Since the late 1960s the JSP and the Japan Communist Party (JCP) had always agreed on basic platforms (of 'protection of democracy and ordinary people's lives, and abandonment of the Japan–US security treaty'). In 1980, however, the JSP, along with the Clean Government Party (*Kōmei-tō*), agreed on a coalition government plan that supported 'the elimination of the JCP and the maintenance of the security treaty and the Japanese self-defence force'. The Clean Government Party had in 1979 agreed with the Democratic Socialist Party (*Minsha-tō*) to the coalition government plan.

At the time, there were three trade-union 'national centres': *Sōhyō* (consisting mainly of public employees), *Dōmei* (consisting mainly of employees in the private sector), and *Chūritsu Rōren* (also comprising private-sector employees). *Sōhyō* had resorted to strategies of direct confrontation, and had been a major player in the JSP, while *Dōmei* had been adopting mild strategies, hoped for cooperative management–labour relations, and supported the Democratic Socialist Party. *Chūritsu Rōren* was positioned between them and supported no particular political party. In response to the above-mentioned changing political scene, *Sōhyō*, being the main supporter of the JSP, decided to endorse the JSP's new political platform, and to consider integration with *Dōmei*. This was the beginning of the reorganisation of union national centres, and *Nikkyōso* needed to examine its stance in the new developments. Opinions were divided within *Nikkyōso* as to whether its parent union centre, *Sōhyō*, should integrate with *Dōmei* and adopt more moderate strategies, and whether *Nikkyōso* would join the newly integrated national centre.

In the end, *Dōmei* and *Sōhyō* merged to make a new union national centre called *Rengō*. *Rengō* announced that it would support the idea of management–labour cooperation and the coalition government. Divisions within *Nikkyōso* continued as to whether or not *Nikkyōso* should join *Rengō*. Finally, the 1989 annual meeting decided that it would join *Rengō*, but this was boycotted by the non-mainstream factions within *Nikkyōso* who opposed the decision. These factions, unhappy about *Nikkyōso*'s new platforms, then formed *Zenkyō* in November 1989; joined another newly formed national centre of unions, *Zenrōren*, comprising unions opposed to the directions taken by *Rengō*; and were subsequently expelled from *Nikkyōso* in December 1989. The old *Nikkyōso* was thus divided into two organisations, which in turn resulted in a similar dissolution in 24 prefectural-level teacher union organisations.

In 1990, *Nikkyōso* announced its decision to adopt more moderate strategies and its new slogan, 'participation, recommendations and reforms'. It decided to make peace with the MOE and the government. This move signified an end to the antagonistic relationship that the teachers' union movements had maintained since 1948, and an historic change in the union's political and philosophical platform. Through it *Nikkyōso* acknowledged a regret that its past stances had led to an unproductive oppositional relationship between *Nikkyōso* and the LDP and MOE; and assessed its own past activities in a critical light. In September 1995, the *Nikkyōso* general meeting resolved that it would actively participate in educational reforms as a partner of the government, the MOE and the business sector, and presented concrete changes in its platforms. They were to stop resisting the use of the Japanese national flag and anthem in schools; to stop advocating teachers' independent design of curricula and to promote teaching based on the Course of Study; to reconsider its view that the staff meeting is the supreme decision-making body; to modify its opposition to in-service education provided by the government; and to modify its proposal to abolish the middle-level management positions (*shunin*).

In the process of these changes in the 1980s, the teacher union movement suffered. First, *Nikkyōso* did not function effectively as an organisation due to internal conflict. The divided opinion over *Nikkyōso*'s affiliation with *Rengō*, combined with that over appointment of head-quarters officials, paralysed its union activities to the extent that the annual study meeting (which many teachers attend for professional development) could not be held in 1986 and 1987. In 1984, when the Ad-Hoc Council on Education started an inquiry (to be covered in the following chapter), *Nikkyōso* established a task committee to counter the Council and provide its own recommendations for reforms, but was unable to mobilise teachers nationwide as effectively as it would have liked.

Second, not only could *Nikkyōso* not function properly as a union over this period, but its members came to view the union with cynicism. They saw that the union's essential activities (e.g. the annual study meeting) stopped due to union officials' indulgence in what ordinary teachers considered low-priority matters (i.e. the disagreement over its position and its parent *Sōhyō*'s position in the reorganised labour union movement at the national level, and over the appointment of the union headquarters officials). Ordinary teachers increasingly felt that their immediate concerns at schools were not being attended to by the union.

Third, *Nikkyōso*'s change in its position, from a political watchdog union that confronted the government to a 'cooperative partner', made it difficult to maintain a strong identity. The identity of the old *Nikkyōso* and its member teachers had been created and experienced in opposition to the conservatives, by constantly challenging the conservative initiatives (which it considered 'reactionary'), both in education and in other social and political issues.

Fourth, the breakup of the old *Nikkyōso* into two unions (*Nikkyōso* and *Zenkyō*) that joined separate union national centres weakened teacher union influence in two tangible ways. The size of *Nikkyōso* became smaller due to the breakup. Joining the larger union national centre, *Rengō* (which integrated the old *Sōhyō* and *Dōmei*), meant that *Nikkyōso*'s relative power of influence within its national centre declined. Consequently it was more difficult for the new *Nikkyōso* to put educational issues on the agenda of *Rengō*, unlike the old *Nikkyōso*, which used to play a crucial role in *Sōhyō* and was able to place pressing educational concerns on the mainstream union movement agenda.

Nikkyōso's 'partnership' with the MOE has been evident in a series of events during 1996. The Minister of Education was invited to make a speech at *Nikkyōso*'s annual meeting, which promoted a cooperative relationship between the two parties. *Nikkyōso* was represented in the MOE's advisory council for the first time, when its former secretary was appointed to the Central Education Council. Some hold a pessimistic view that *Nikkyōso* will lose its independent voice to criticise the MOE's initiatives, and will play only a supplementary (and therefore less influential role) in educational policy making. Others hold that *Nikkyōso* will now be able to voice its concerns as an insider directly involved in the policy-making process, rather than as an outsider excluded from that process; and that its influence will be more direct. The fate of *Nikkyōso*'s role in the future remains open for speculation.

Also open for speculation is the role of *Zenkyō*, which advocates a philosophy more akin to that of the old *Nikkyōso*.[6] Although *Zenkyō*'s membership is smaller than *Nikkyōso*'s (as shown by the MOE's survey), *Zenkyō*'s relative influence within its national centre (*Zenrōren*) is slightly

more significant than that of *Nikkyōso* within *Rengō*. The future of the
teacher union movement is not bright.

The Culture of Teaching

The culture of an occupation is a set of shared norms, values, taken-for-
granted assumptions and a sense of mission that frame the patterns of the
members' work activities. Institutionalised teaching, across societies,
involves helping the young to acquire knowledge and learn about themselves, and prepares them for the adult society. In so doing, teachers
develop a particular culture of teaching. Below, we will examine what are
considered to be 'Japanese' features of this culture, as compared to those
that are 'American', and then discuss interschool differences in Japan.

Comparison with the US

Imagine that you have been a primary-school teacher in your society and
now have an opportunity to teach at a Japanese school, say on a teacher
exchange program. You would perhaps feel at home at your new school
to a degree, finding some familiarity in school events and activities. You
would also find differences.

Studies suggest that some aspects of the Japanese culture of teaching
differ from that in the US (N. Sato 1994; Shimahara and Sakai 1992,
1995; Itō 1994; G. Satō 1988).[7] First, the professional roles and responsibilities that Japanese teachers assume are much more extensive than
those of their American counterparts (N. Sato 1994:127; Shimahara and
Sakai 1995:187; Itō 1994:143–5; G. Satō 1988:112). While the American
teachers concentrate on children's cognitive development, Japanese
teachers consider that children's emotional, social, physical and mental
development is as important as their cognitive development. Japanese
teachers devote themselves to improving aspects of student development
that the American teachers would not consider part of their role, by
being concerned with such matters as hygiene, problem behaviours
outside school, and visits to students' homes. Japanese teachers are
preoccupied with the development of 'the whole person', which is
manifested in 'lifestyle guidance' at middle schools. Due to the inclusive
nature of their work, Japanese teachers are busier than their American
counterparts (N. Sato 1994:132). Because Japanese teachers are aware of
the public expectation of their work (which is extensive and almost
'infinite'), they assess their own work performance more negatively than
do American teachers theirs (G. Satō 1988:97).

Second, the wider roles and responsibilities that Japanese teachers see as
their work are a reflection of the central notion of traditional Japanese

pedagogy, what is often referred to as *kizuna*. It is an intimate interpersonal relationship that fosters empathy, characterised as the 'touching of the hearts' (Shimahara and Sakai 1992:156); and is a bond marked by the shared feelings of trust and inclusiveness between teacher and children (Shimahara and Sakai 1992:157). To cultivate *kizuna*, teachers share intrinsic and unpretentious interpersonal experiences that engage children (Shimahara and Sakai 1992:156). The authors (Shimahara and Sakai 1992:157) argue that *kizuna* differs from the Western emphasis on emotional involvement in teacher–student relationships in two ways. First, the authority of the Japanese teacher emerges in the context of routine interaction with students, rather than through teachers asserting it as given. While Japanese new teachers are encouraged to 'mingle with students without disguise and pretence' in order to develop *kizuna* (which will eventually confer authority to the teacher), American new teachers are often told not to make the mistake of trying to be friends with the children. The second difference is that *kizuna* is not a means to an end but a cultural attribute, although it is said to be a paramount principle promoting effective classroom management.

Third, Japanese teachers' belief in their wider roles and in *kizuna* are reflected in the ways that they conduct lessons. Compared to American teachers, Japanese teachers pay more attention to, and try to involve, slow and mediocre students. Over 60 per cent of Japanese teachers conduct their lessons at a level appropriate to their less able students, while 60 per cent of their American counterparts teach at the level of their above-average students (G. Satō 1988:90–4). Seventy per cent of Japanese teachers deliberately ask slow learners to answer in classes, while over 60 per cent of American teachers do so with above-average students (G. Satō 1988:93). Japanese teachers are more likely to disagree to ability-based tracking of groups, since they are concerned with their potentially detrimental effects on slow learners (G. Satō 1988:110).

Fourth, there is much stronger informal communication, inter-dependence and 'camaraderie' among teachers in Japan. This is in part due to the physical arrangements of the staffroom, where the desks of teachers in the same grade are grouped together, with the result that constant consultation takes place among them (N. Sato 1994:134). Regular staff transfers every several years (even at the principal and deputy-principal levels) also provide teachers with chances to widen their human networks. Japanese teachers interact more among themselves than their American counterparts in recreational activities as well (G. Satō 1988:118).

Fifth, teachers believe that the routine informal sharing of experience among themselves is the most effective way of enhancing their individual professional development and has the most significant impact on their teaching, in comparison with other forms of in-service training programs (N. Sato 1994:135–6; Shimahara and Sakai 1995:160; M. Sato 1992: 164–5). This requires a place where, and sufficient time when, teachers can regularly share their experience. (The staffroom, as noted above, provides such a venue.) This also requires all teachers to value the philosophy of working together. To quote one teacher's comment:

> ... when I have a problem I just walk over to the next classroom to ask for suggestions. The important thing is that I can talk to her (a senior colleague) at any time when I have a problem. (Shimahara and Sakai 1992:155)

Japanese teachers count on informal assistance from colleagues much more than American teachers, who consider that their professional development is helped more by those in formal positions of responsibility (e.g. principals, subject head teachers) (Itō 1994:151–2). We suspect that the relative absence of routine informal interaction among teachers in the US causes teachers to resort to formal channels for guidance. This difference could also be related to the equality ethos observed among Japanese teachers, a point we will take up later.

During her fieldwork, N. Sato (1994:136–7) was amazed at the number of regular voluntary informal study groups that teachers held outside working hours. In 1981 (the only available survey) 53 per cent of all teachers participated in such activities (M. Sato 1992:162–3), whereas such initiatives are very rare in the US. During such activities, teachers bring their students' work (e.g. drawings, essays, taped chorus, video-taped classes), hold critical discussions and receive suggestions (N. Sato 1994:136–7). Sato attended a monthly meeting of this kind which took place on the first Sunday of every month from 2 pm to 9 pm! There are many more professional journals for teachers produced by teachers than there are academic journals in education written for and by university academics. Approximately one-third of educational journal articles were written by university academics, the remaining two-thirds by practising teachers (N. Sato 1994:136).

Sixth, there is an ethos of equality in status among teachers. Once employed, all teachers are regarded as equal, regardless of their age and experience; and a tacit code exists that no teacher tells another teacher what to do to his or her face, unless of course requested by the teacher himself or herself (Shimahara and Sakai 1995:154). A beginning teacher in Shimahara and Sakai's study revealed:

> In the school there is relative equality among teachers. For example, I am seen as equal to my senior colleagues by other teachers and parents. I have a class and am responsible for my children to the same extent as my neighbour teacher is. I am independent as much as she is with respect to teaching and classroom management. (Shimahara and Sakai 1995:154)

The ethos of equality has been an obstacle to the implementation of the MOE's new initiatives at school level. We explained earlier that the introduction of *shunin* (medium-level positions of responsibility) was resisted, and in some prefectures teachers pooled *shunin* allowances for scholarships to students. More recently, the new internship program for novice teachers was implemented quite differently from the MOE's original conception. Supervising senior teachers were not prepared to discharge duties of direct and systematic instruction, as instructed by the MOE, but saw their role primarily as advisers, assisting interns who requested assistance (Shimahara and Sakai 1992:152–3).

The ethos of equality among Japanese teachers partly explains the perceived gap between Japan and the US in the power of the principal. American teachers believe that the principal's leadership strongly affects the school's educational policies. Japanese teachers, on the other hand, rate the influence of ordinary teachers much higher than the principal's leadership in forming school policies; and believe that what is expected of principals is not to exercise strong leadership but to create cooperative consensus amongst all teachers (Itō 1994:150).

These features of the culture of Japanese teachers (in comparison to their American counterparts) affect the ways in which teachers organise their activities. The features that are considered to be conducive to effective teaching can become a hindrance to it for some teachers. The all-inclusive nature of teaching can be a source of burn-out; strong interdependence among teachers can act as an unnecessary pressure for conforming to group norms; an individual teacher's failure to form a rapport with colleagues may result in not only an uncomfortable work environment but also a denial of valuable opportunities for professional development.

Interschool Differences

While Japanese schools share many of the above features of the culture of teaching, there are finer variations across schools. Two survey studies (G. Satō 1988; Yuu 1988) provide an interesting insight into differences between schools. Such differences derive from the local characteristics of the school (e.g. students, parents, community) and the internal composition of the teaching staff.

Four types of schools were identified in terms of the culture of teachers (see Figure 5.3) (Yuu 1988:182–91). The first is the 'content' type, in which teachers trust and are satisfied with the school administration (principal and vice-principal), and actively exchange opinions professionally and maintain informal interaction among themselves. Enthusiastic veteran teachers take leadership roles and, as well as being skilful specialist subject

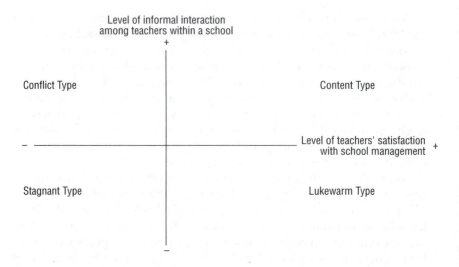

Figure 5.3 Four types of teaching culture
Source: Yuu (1988:181)

teachers, act as role models for young teachers. In the second, 'conflict' type, teachers do not trust the school administration, and while they actively interact with each other, they are divided into small groups. Although there are a few enthusiastic teachers, some in leadership roles, the lack of consensus among staff prevents the school from implementing new initiatives. A considerable number of teachers, the largest among the four types of schools, want to be transferred to other schools, due to continuous disagreement of a covert nature. In the third, 'stagnant' type, teachers neither trust the principal and vice-principal, nor maintain satisfying and active interaction among themselves. Without inspiring leadership, they neither show much enthusiasm for teaching nor are interested in socialising among themselves. The last is the 'lukewarm' type, which often characterises small schools in rural areas, where teachers are satisfied with the administration, and do not maintain an active professional interaction among themselves. These teachers feel comfortable socialising at school, but lack enthusiasm for professional improvement.

Regional environments influence the type of teaching culture that a school develops (Yuu 1988:204–5). Schools located in the old city centres tend to be of the content type. This is perhaps because a transfer to city centre schools (which typically enjoy the prestige of a long history) is generally perceived as a promotion, a view supported by Tsukada's study in another prefecture (1997). Schools located in newly developed suburbs, where tertiary-educated fathers hold metropolitan white-collar jobs, tend to show conflict-type characteristics. Not only are parents' expectations of schools and teachers high, they are concrete and diverse. In contrast, parents in the countryside neither possess high expectations of schools, nor monitor the teachers' performance as closely as their suburban counterparts. Schools there tend to be of the stagnant type.

These regional characteristics also affect the ways individual teachers perceive their workload and assess their own performance, which in turn contribute to the development of particular cultures of teaching in different schools. Teachers in big cities and large-sized schools, in comparison to those in the country and small schools, perceive that a larger portion of their professional work is devoted to guidance in non-academic issues (Yuu 1988:106); and are more likely to underrate their own teaching performance (Yuu 1988:97). In large urban schools, students become more anonymous and their behavioural problems may require more attention. In urban areas teachers are perhaps more aware of parental expectations of schools and teachers, and of their moni-toring, which affects teachers' own assessment of their work.

The composition of its teaching staff also influences the kind of teaching culture that a school develops. The strong presence of veteran teachers with leadership qualities, union teachers, female teachers and young novice teachers each makes a particular contribution to the development of the teaching culture. In return, the type of teaching culture of a school to which individual teachers are transferred has a significant impact on their professional outlook. Given that teachers are transferred every several years, one could expect that the nature of the teaching culture in a particular school would be fluid over time.

Diverse Faces of Teachers: Life Histories

Imagine, again, that you are an exchange teacher assigned to a school in Japan. After you had spent a considerable time at the school, you would probably notice that the teachers (who might have appeared uniform at the outset) are diverse in their approach to teaching and in their relationships to others, and have their own private lives. Within any school, one sees informal groups of teachers: young teachers, those who are involved in sports, those who go out drinking regularly, women, union teachers, homeroom teachers of the same grade and those keen on the promotion track (Yuu 1988:164). The ways in which they express their individual characteristics may differ, depending on the culture of teaching at the school. After examining age and gender differences, we shall illustrate a typology of teachers, drawing on available studies. Since male and female teachers follow quite distinctive trajectories, we shall examine them separately.

'Miss Fujiwara, what are you worrying about?'

'This is my last class bulletin of the academic year . . .'

'Well, well . . . various events and pupils' faces come to mind, don't they?'

'No, only unpleasant events that happened to me come to mind.'

Source: Asahi Shinbun 19 March 1996 © Hisaichi Ishii

Age and Gender

The age of teachers seems to affect teaching in several ways. Older teachers are more confident in their teaching. Only 27 per cent of teachers in their twenties believe that the majority of students understand their lessons, while the figure is 66 per cent for teachers in their fifties (Fukaya 1992:63). Older teachers are more likely to target their classes at slow-learning students (G. Satō 1988:94), and to hold a more authoritarian view of students' non-academic behaviour and manners (G. Satō 1988:99–100). The older teachers tend to go home from school earlier than their younger colleagues, and spend more days at home during the summer vacation (Fukaya 1992:62–3). This is partly because young teachers are more likely to supervise sports club activities after school and during vacations. Eighty per cent of teachers in their twenties are involved in sports clubs, while the equivalent figure for those in their fifties is 37 per cent (Fukaya 1992:62).

Task divisions are also observable across gender. First, female teachers tend to be homeroom teachers of junior grades while male teachers take senior grades at primary and middle schools. At primary schools, for instance, 22 per cent of female teachers were homeroom teachers of grade one (8 per cent of male teachers) and 10 per cent took grade six (26 per cent of male teachers) (Zenkyō 1993:47). Second, male teachers at middle and high schools tend to supervise after-school sports clubs, while female teachers are involved with non-sports clubs. Consequently male teachers spend 2 hours 41 minutes on club supervision a week, as opposed to 54 minutes on the part of female teachers. Due to their involvement with sports clubs, more male teachers (22 per cent) than female teachers go to school on Sundays; and men work more days during summer vacations. Third, male teachers also spend considerably more time on school administration and clerical work than do female teachers (Zenkyō 1993:47–8).

Indeed, female teachers spend slightly less time at school (9 hours 8 minutes a day, as opposed to 9 hours 32 minutes for male teachers) (Zenkyō 1993:24). Female teachers consequently have slightly more time outside school, but spend more than three times as much time (2 hours 25 minutes) on housework and child rearing as do male teachers (45 minutes), and consequently have less time to themselves (Zenkyō 1993:24).

Male High School Teachers

Tsukada (1997:14) suggests that male high school teachers can possess one of four orientations based on: (1) whether they hold union membership or aspire to be principals; and (2) whether their main

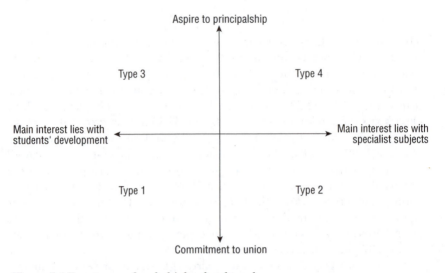

Figure 5.4 Four types of male high-school teacher
Source: Tsukada (1997:14)

interest lies with education and teaching, or with their specialist subject (see Figure 5.4). The first type is union teachers, who are interested in teaching itself, and often have a special interest in low-achieving students. Mr Takeuchi, whom we present in a case study below, is of this type. The second type comprises union teachers who are enthusiastic about their academic subject rather than teaching itself. For instance, such teachers of English may pursue conversation classes or study overseas in their own time. The third type is made up of those who pursue the promotion track to principal while maintaining an interest in education and teaching. Mr Imai, also described below, belongs to this type. The fourth type contains those who want principalship but are keen to pursue their academic subject speciality.

A teacher's orientation is not necessarily static over time but may change, when, for instance, he or she encounters significant people at different kinds of schools. Regular transfer across schools allows this to occur. A teacher with no interest in promotion at the outset may gradually find a sense of fulfilment in contributing to the running of the school. By their late thirties, however, teachers emerge with a definite orientation (Tsukada 1997:56–7). Among teachers of the same orientation, the time of entry into teaching can be a differentiating factor. Older retired principals had exercised more authoritarian leadership, and benefited more from their universities and the personal networks they had consciously cultivated, than more recently appointed principals

(Tsukada 1997:82). Time of entry into teaching is also likely to affect the prevalence of a particular orientation. For instance, the change in the union's stance as perceived by teachers (from being constantly opposed to the MOE to being a cooperative player in policy making) is likely to produce less militant teachers in the future.

A categorisation of teachers as seen by a union classroom teacher (Yagyū 1992) provides more detail. Yagyū identifies the following types: (1) 'My homist' teachers, who perform the required work proficiently between 8:30 am and 5 pm, without committing to 'extra' work or union business. Their main concerns are family and hobbies. (2) Female teachers, married with children, who are forced to become 'my homist' teachers out of necessity. (3) Teachers for whom teaching is largely or solely a means for earning a living and pursuing an active social life (e.g. gambling, entertainment and parties). (4) Charismatic veteran teachers, who are sociable (within the union as well), look after junior colleagues, and who perform efficiently. (5) Teachers who are efficient, both at teaching and at clerical and administrative tasks. Their administrative excellence could lead to a promising career. (6) Teachers in their fifties who are no longer enthusiastic about teaching and await retirement. (7) Disillusioned teachers in their fifties who feel bitter about not achieving the promotion that they had aspired to. (8) Union activist teachers with no interest in promotion. (9) Teachers who are absorbed in teaching as if it were a hobby. (10) Teachers who currently show an overt aspiration to the promotion track.

Below we present the life histories of two male high-school teachers from the same prefecture, drawing on a recent study (Tsukada 1997). They are both in their fifties but have undergone quite different professional paths. Readers may want to refer to Chapter 2, and follow how they experienced the post-war education systems as teachers at the individual school level. Their stories reveal their distinctive stances in relation to the union, their pedagogical beliefs, and the realities of promotion.

Case Study 5.4: A Male Union High-school Teacher – Mr Takeuchi

Mr Takeuchi is now 56, teaching at a prestigious academic high school as an 'ordinary teacher'. His father was a powerful figure in the region's education system. Mr Takeuchi disliked his father, and was determined not to become a teacher, or not to pursue the promotion track to principal if he did become one. His involvement in university student movements, like many others in that period, and his dislike of his father led him to maintain anti-establishment attitudes. Indeed, throughout his 30-year teaching career Mr Takeuchi has been actively involved in union activities, and has pursued the kind of teaching that accorded with his own pedagogical beliefs.

Mr Takeuchi entered high-school teaching at the age of 25, in 1964. His first school was an old, prestigious high school, where not many novice teachers could land. There he was disappointed with the realities of schooling, which were far from the democratic education that he had long idealised. Mr Takeuchi hated his colleagues' expectation that he enjoyed advantage from his father's status, and decided to avoid his father's influence. When a powerful senior teacher at the school offered to arrange his marriage, he declined the offer, which later led to the teacher's deliberate annoyance towards him. The school was so conservative that union activities were almost nonexistent. Mr Takeuchi participated in the union because he believed that working conditions should be improved. Mr Takeuchi's dislike of teachers who overtly wished to enter the promotion track, as well as his long-cherished commitment against the establishment in relation to education (including his own father), made him decide at an early stage that he would never pursue the promotion track. He even declared this to his fiancee before marrying her.

Instead of political ambition, Mr Takeuchi pursued his pedagogical belief in student-centred teaching. Once placed in charge of the volleyball club, for which he had no expertise, he studied how to coach it with enthusiasm. In classroom teaching, Mr Takeuchi valued students' participation in class discussion, and tried to upgrade the academic achievement of the class as a whole. Some teachers criticised his teaching and harassed him by lobbying to deprive him of a homeroom class. Mr Takeuchi requested a transfer.

In 1971, after six years at his first school, Mr Takeuchi was transferred. Although it would take much longer to commute to the new school, he did not lodge an official complaint since he did not think that it would be successful. His union colleagues did it for him, without success. The second school was a comprehensive high school (academic course, commerce course and machinery course) in the country, and was not as intensively geared for university entrance examinations as the previous school. To quote Mr Takeuchi, 'I felt a significant drop in the standard of academic achievement among students at the second school. But I wanted to teach and guide them in such a way that each of them could enter the university that he or she desired'.

He experienced a great sense of fulfilment when low-achieving students gradually improved their marks; this in turn urged him to pursue the kind of teaching that instilled self-confidence in low-achieving students. In opposition to the union platform, which criticised the evil of the entrance examination itself, he conducted supplementary lessons for entrance examinations, in order to gain the trust of students and their parents, but refused to receive extra fees for these lessons. He thus obtained 'good' results in improving students' academic achievement and in raising their self-esteem. Again, Mr Takeuchi suffered from harassment by some non-union teachers for these actions, but he ignored it. In his 15th year at the school, Mr Takeuchi received a sudden notice of transfer. Judging from other transferred teachers, he believes that this was a part of the principal's long-term strategy to gradually remove union-active teachers from the school.

The third school that Mr Takeuchi (then 47) joined was a 'difficult' school. He was assigned to a homeroom class in the 11th grade which had driven away most of the previous year's homeroom teachers, and was stunned to find that the level of academic achievement in the classes was even lower than at the second school. Mr Takeuchi took his mission very seriously. He demanded that students make an effort to study, while respecting them as individuals. The students simply did not know how to study. Mr Takeuchi started with the basics and guided them to develop their own ways of learning. The students' improved academic achievement as well as their heightened self-esteem gave Mr Takeuchi unparalleled professional pleasure.

He was transferred to his fourth school in 1994 at the age of 54, after he requested a transfer to care for his parents. The new school was his *alma mater*, a traditional school of the area. Many people would consider this move (from a difficult school to a traditional school) to be an honour, but Mr Takeuchi was unhappy with the workplace environment. This was because the school endorsed the existing system of entrance examinations, and focused on providing students with a pile of learning materials without, in Mr Takeuchi's view, due guidance. Mr Takeuchi conducted his lessons at a much slower pace than other teachers, but with more attention to learning processes, following his pedagogical beliefs. For this some colleagues were critical of him. Besides, the school had very few union members, the majority of teachers being interested in the promotion track. Mr Takeuchi still feels uncomfortable in such an environment.

Mr Takeuchi believes that the union has long provided 'the significant others' whom he can trust wholeheartedly throughout his professional life; a withdrawal from the union would mean to him a kind of betrayal of his beliefs, his colleagues and family members. Mr Takeuchi wishes to spend the remaining four years of his teaching career at this school (Tsukada 1997:32–40).

Case Study 5.5: A Male High-school Principal – Mr Imai

Mr Imai thought a teaching post in the country would be the best occupational option for him, since he was not physically strong, having been diagnosed with tuberculosis at 17. At university he joined a social science club, read contemporary leftist books and enjoyed discussions on social and political issues. He also participated in the university's self-governing committee.

He entered teaching at 22, in 1958. His first school was an old, traditional school, causing five novice teachers at that time to challenge its conservative nature. Mr Imai joined the union, as did everyone in those days, and participated in the demonstrations to oppose the US–Japan security treaty in 1960. From his second year, Mr Imai had homeroom classes for five years. He reflects that he was an enthusiastic teacher, conducting individual supplementary lessons for several needy students in his class early in the mornings and on Sundays.

In 1964, after six years at the first school, Mr Imai was transferred to another prestigious school. He taught high-achieving students mathematics for entrance examinations, and derived a great pleasure in winning respect for his teaching during eight years at the school. Mr Imai continued his involvement in union activities, and was selected as the school's union representative for two years. It was through this involvement, however, that his enthusiasm for the union started to wane. He discovered that a branch of the political party behind the union made important decisions that were officially assumed to be those of the committee of school representatives. This caused him to feel that the school reps were being used.

In 1971 when a new school zoning system was introduced in the region, Mr Imai (then 36) was transferred to another, less prestigious school in the same zone. The new zoning system aimed to erase school ranking through a random placing of students to schools in the same zone, regardless of the students' preferences. Mr Imai's major task at the second school was to deal with the PTA, who were upset that they could not secure places for their children at the more prestigious school, which would have been assured under the previous system. The principal of Mr Imai's new school hoped that Mr Imai, having previously taught at the prestigious school, would be the right person to reassure the PTA that their children would not be disadvantaged by attending his school.

This was the beginning of Mr Imai's move onto the promotion track to principalship. From being appointed the departmental head of general affairs to manage the PTA, he subsequently became the departmental head of guidance for life after school, and of student management. He relinquished his union membership. Mr Imai instead devoted himself to upgrading students' destination universities, and thus the school's profile. He initiated a system whereby supplementary classes were offered to all students early in the morning before normal classes started, and to the final-year students both in the early morning and after school. He felt a fulfilment from improving student achievement, and from receiving students' appreciation for his work. Mr Imai was starting to enjoy 'managing' the school. His interest in school management was furthered by a subsequent 25-day study trip to the US, which was organised by the local education board. The principal of the school later shifted to a prestigious metropolitan school, and in his final year of service recruited Mr Imai to the school as vice-principal.

At the time of his move and promotion in 1981, Mr Imai was 46. The school was an old, prestigious school located in the city centre. Most of the teachers were long-serving, and many of them were union members, consistent with other old, prestigious schools in the city. The school being a union stronghold, the teachers insisted that their overwork be addressed, and offered little organised 'intervention' in students' studies, unlike Mr Imai's previous school. Teachers insisted that students' independence be respected. Hence there was less enthusiasm for supplementary lessons. This was partly because many students attended classes at a famous private preparatory school in the city during both the term and summer vacations. Since the level of academic achievement among students was high anyway, the school could successfully send a large number of students to prestigious universities even if it did not devote itself to preparation for entrance examinations. The school's principal hoped that Mr Imai's arrival would change other teachers' attitudes.

Five years later, Mr Imai (then 53) returned to his first school as principal. The school was an old, traditional school outside the city, and accommodated a diversity of students. One-third of its graduates proceeded to four-year universities, one-third to two-year junior colleges and the remainder to employment or private specialist schools. Mr Imai's vision was of a 'department store school', which offered guidance for both university entrance examinations and for examination for vocational qualifications. He introduced an exchange student program with American schools, and emphasised the importance of club activities.

Mr Imai believes that a principal's job is 'to make adjustments among people, rather than to exercise power'. He does not have his own budget or control personnel appointments. His major task is to communicate with teachers, appraise their work and support them. (Tsukada 1997:15–22)

Mr Imai seems to have followed a path to principalship that is conventional among principals in his age group. When he entered teaching, virtually all teachers joined the union. After an active involvement in it, he found more pleasure in making a contribution to the school-level planning and management. The unprecedented expansion of high schools coincided with his rise, and he was able to try out his newly discovered skills in a series of positions of responsibility which were also expanding. Mr Imai did not project himself as the kind of authoritarian principal often pictured by some union activists, i.e. as one who overtly sought to reduce the union's influence in his school.

Mr Takeuchi's professional path, on the other hand, is characterised by his commitment to the union cause and his own pedagogical beliefs. For Mr Takeuchi, principalship was not appealing, since it represented an alliance with the 'establishment', and he consciously wanted to remain an ordinary teacher until retirement. Both teachers were committed to what they perceived to be their professional missions, and pursued them without serious impediment to their personal lives. This is where the experiences of female teachers differ.

Female Teachers

The professional life courses of female teachers are typically quite different from those of their male colleagues. They are likely to see their professional mission as lying within the walls of their own classrooms (rather than at the school level), and to be less attracted to promotion to vice-principal and principal. Indeed female principals are rare, although their numbers increased in the last decade at primary schools. In 1995, female principals accounted for only 9.6 per cent of principals at primary schools (where 61 per cent of full-time teachers were female);

Table 5.4 Ratios of female teachers at each school level

	All teachers %	Principals %
Primary school	61.0	9.6
Middle school	40.0	1.9
High school	23.2	2.4

Source: Japan, Monbushō (1995a:46, 108, 272)

corresponding figures for female principals at both middle and high schools were even lower (see Table 5.4) (Japan, Monbushō 1995a:46, 108, 272).

Hasuo (1994:152–3) devised six orientations that primary- and middle-school female teachers might identify with. The first is school-management-type teachers, who are willing to participate in school administration while performing their normal teaching duties. The second is classroom-education-focused teachers, who pursue their educational ideals in their classes, with little interest in school management. The third type, predominant among female teachers, is family–school balancing teachers, who try hard to fulfil career and family responsibilities to their satisfaction. They can be frustrated by the compromises that they often need to make. The fourth is reformist teachers, who try to effect educational improvements, democratisation of the workplace and the betterment of teachers' working conditions. The fifth is self-interested teachers who want fulfilling personal lives and hobbies while performing adequately as teachers. The sixth is those who see little attraction in teaching and consider early resignation.

These orientations often change in accordance with age. Female teachers in their first three years of service maintain either a classroom-education-focused (39.6 per cent for primary and 28.9 per cent for middle school) or self-interested orientation (47.9 and 56.7 per cent respectively). Between their fourth and twentieth year of teaching (ages typically 25 to 42), when they have families, the family–school balancing orientation becomes dominant, while the classroom-education-focused orientation remains strong. Only in their mid-forties, when their children require less care, do some female teachers start to shift their orientation to school management (20 per cent at primary, 14 per cent middle school) (Hasuo 1993:121–3). Other female teachers, in particular those at middle schools, shift instead to the self-interest orientation and pursue personal interests, such as theatre and music (Hasuo 1994:150).

In contrast, male teachers in their twenties already show a school-management orientation, and almost one-third of them possess this orientation in their thirties (Hasuo 1993:121–3).[8] This study revealed that a lower proportion of female teachers, relative to male teachers, had experienced medium-level positions of responsibility that would form a path to principal positions (Hasuo 1993:117). Male primary teachers' identification with school management starts much earlier than with middle-school teachers, which, we suspect, is due to the relatively small proportion of male teachers at primary schools (39 per cent at primary and 60 per cent at middle schools in 1995) (Japan, Monbushō 1995a:46, 108). However, there are substantially more male primary teachers in Japan than in Anglo-Western industrialised societies.

Due to the small proportion of female teachers who eventually make vice-principal, the most veteran female teachers at a school are often granted a special status by the school and by other teachers. They are often called *jōseki* (literally 'upper seat') (Akashi and Takano 1993). A survey of such female teachers (Akashi and Takano 1993) reveals some of the characteristics of their life courses.[9] The majority remained classroom teachers, with fewer than 30 per cent holding official medium-level positions of responsibility, and assumed that they would remain so until retirement (Akashi and Takano 1993:59–60). These teachers consider the most fulfilling aspect of teaching to be seeing the positive changes in the children they teach. Although they hold no official positions of responsibility, over 90 per cent of them are members of their schools' planning committees; and many play a consultative role for younger female teachers in relation to both work and private matters (Akashi and Takano 1993:61–2).

Half of the teachers surveyed had been approached by their principals about taking the promotion track to administrative positions, but 93 per cent declined (Akashi and Takano 1993:69). The most frequently cited reasons were their desire to remain classroom teachers until retirement, a concern with balancing career and family responsibilities (including giving priority to their husbands' careers), and a lack of confidence, perhaps due to limited experience with medium-level positions of responsibility (Akashi and Takano 1993:69, 73). Thus opportunities were available to half of these teachers but, as in Anglo-Western industrial societies, circumstances in the family (e.g. lack of husbands' help with family chores and in caring for the elderly) and in the society (e.g. lack of convenient daycare, and other arrangements that assume few married women with children pursue careers) do not allow many of them to aspire to, and pursue in reality, the promotion track to school principal. In comparison, female teachers who actually became principals had experienced a series of medium-level positions of responsibility (Akashi and Takano 1993:73).

Case Study 5.6: A Female Middle-school Teacher – Ms Kawa

Ms Kawa (pseudonymous name) entered middle-school teaching at the age of 22 in 1954. She was the first female teacher assigned to a homeroom class at the school. Most of the teachers were young, and the school environment was comfortable. She was impressed with the vice-principal – despite graduating from a pre-war normal school, he was progressive and encouraged female teachers' professional development. However, Ms Kawa faced two problems. First, she found it difficult to have rapport with, and understand, boys. She tried hard, but her inability to relate to boys used to lead her to tears, and she started thinking that she was unsuited to teaching and would quit. The second problem was her disagreement with her senior teacher's philosophy of teaching Japanese, which demolished her confidence in her own teaching. Feeling that she was too young to insist on a teaching style that differed from her superior's, she shifted to the English Department.

Ms Kawa married a high-school teacher in her third year of teaching, and soon fell pregnant. She recalls that her male colleagues were cooperative, but she felt that pregnancy and childbirth placed a tremendous pressure on her work. Not wanting her colleagues to see that her pregnancy adversely affected her work, she persevered, encouraged by past female teachers who had been in the same situation. This was in the era before adequate maternity leave entitlements existed. Through her struggles, Ms Kawa learned that the most important aspect of teaching is whether a teacher cherishes students as individuals.

After four years, Ms Kawa was transferred to her second school (aged 26, in 1958). The school's policy was not to let females take homeroom classes. Ms Kawa was disappointed. Excluded from homeroom duties, she set two goals for herself. First, she learned student-management skills by observing a male colleague, who was respected by so-called difficult students. Second, she improved her English language proficiency by attending an intensive language course during the summer vacation. To attend this course, Ms Kawa used to take her three-year-old and two-month-old sons to her mother's house by bus early in the morning, before catching a train. On the way back she fed the children dinner at her mother's and then took them home by bus. The experience not only gave her confidence in English but also in herself.

By the time Ms Kawa (then 31) was transferred to her third school, she was facing the most demanding time, balancing family responsibilities with her career. The pressure caused her to fall ill – she was diagnosed as having a condition which is caused by long periods of standing following childbirth. During hospitalisation, Ms Kawa regretted that she had not spent enough time with her children and for herself, and again considered resigning. Her school friend, who was a lawyer, encouraged her to remain in teaching.

In 1967, in her 14th year of teaching, Ms Kawa was transferred to her fourth school. Three years later she joined her fifth school at the age of 38. During these years she accumulated further experience, and started to hold medium-level positions of responsibility. The principal then recommended that Ms Kawa sit the qualifying examination for vice-principal and take a Saturday course to prepare for the examination. She declined to take up his recommendation. First, she thought that having more time for her children and for her personal needs was more important. Second, the 'unpleasant' ways in which some teachers sought vice-principalship during the period of conflict between the union and the school administration discouraged her. Subsequently she tried to act to make sure that colleagues knew of her lack of interest in the promotion track.

In 1975 Ms Kawa was transferred to her sixth school. The MOE's new 1977 curriculum reduced English classes from five classes a week to three. This change went against Ms Kawa's strong belief in the necessity of frequent classes for language learning. She was not confident that she could achieve her teaching goals in the new circumstances, and decided that she would be better off returning to teaching Japanese. Teaching Japanese in the ways that she believed in gave her a great sense of fulfilment. This was heightened by a wonderful colleague in the same department.

In 1978 Ms Kawa joined what was to become her last school, at the age of 46. At this time she started noticing the negative effects of the country's rapid economic growth on her students. In the cities, schools became larger, with commonly 600 students in one grade. Teachers hardly recognised students unless they taught them. Increased competition and the larger number of students wishing to pursue further education meant that parents' expectations of schools changed as well. From her fourth year there, the school started facing difficulties in managing students, like many other urban middle schools in the early 1980s. Ms Kawa had to deal with students who were involved in violence, solvent sniffing, leaving home and other delinquent activities, until late at night almost every day. In those days there were no 24-hour shops, and she found herself neglecting the simple tasks of feeding her family. When her husband finally said to her, 'If you don't quit teaching, I will', she decided to resign for the sake of her family's health. She claims that her husband held positions of responsibility, and was busier than herself; and felt that if she continued teaching, one of her family members would have fallen ill. In 1984 Ms Kawa resigned from her 30-year teaching career at 52, eight years before the retirement age.

The above three cases illustrate the complexities in individual perceptions of teaching as a career and, more specifically, in individual attitudes towards promotion. First of all, Mr Takeuchi's aversion to promotion is strongly connected to what he claims is 'his commitment against the establishment'. By 'the establishment' in education, he means those who administer, and hold power in, the region's system of education; people who, he considers, cannot be trusted and conspire to weaken union teachers like himself (as was seen in his interpretation of his sudden unwanted transfer). Mr Takeuchi seems to equate obtaining promotion with joining that establishment, and rejected promotion on that ground. His attitude seems to derive, at least partly, from his

involvement in student movements at university, and from the fact that
his father, whom he personally disliked, belonged to the establishment.
In contrast, although Mr Imai was also active in the university student
movement and in unions, he has developed a quite different interpretation of teaching as a career, and of the regional system of education.
He achieved principalship after pursuing a career orientation that he
enjoyed and excelled at. He did not mention 'the establishment', nor did
he seem to share Mr Takeuchi's view that 'seeking the promotion equals
joining the establishment'. His perception of the education administration differs quite markedly from Mr Takeuchi's. On the other hand,
Ms Kawa's rejection of the promotion track was not because she
philosophically disliked joining the establishment, like Mr Takeuchi. She
did not seem to interpret 'the establishment' as being in opposition to
ordinary teachers, although she did refer to some of her colleagues
who struggled for promotion for its own sake, which she considered
'unpleasant'. Ms Kawa simply chose to place priority on her family
responsibilities and personal needs and, therefore, to remain an
ordinary teacher.

Individual teachers thus construct their own understandings of the
establishment, and of the relationship between the educational
administration and ordinary teachers like themselves. This point needs
to be kept in mind when discussing the politicised relationship between
the MOE and unions as the establishment versus ordinary teachers at the
national level.

Summary

We have presented the institutional systems that produce teachers in
Japan (teacher education, certification and appointment), and that
provide the framework within which teachers conduct their work. The
systems of salary increment, school transfer and promotion are distinct
from the equivalent Anglo-Western systems; these seem to affect how
teachers see their own profession and how it is perceived by the society.

We have illustrated how teachers conduct their work and experience
the schooling process at the school level under such institutional systems.
Teachers are examined as professionals and workers, who have mobilised
to achieve what they believe to be just education, a decent standard of
living and basic labour rights. *Nikkyōso* had been a watchdog, constantly
opposing the government's policy initiatives in education until the 1980s,
with some success. *Nikkyōso*'s move to make peace with the MOE, and to
assume a partner role in educational policy making (similar to that
played by teacher unions in the Anglo-West) in the early 1990s radically
remapped the teacher union movement. The union's appeal to ordinary

teachers has been in decline in the last three decades. Fewer new teachers join unions. We have explored the causes for this decline and attributed it to several factors.

While changes in the national legislation regarding teachers and reorganisation in the union movement took place outside schools, the everyday classroom practice of teaching continues. Individual teachers continue to discharge what they consider to be their responsibilities in their classrooms. Ms Niwa and teachers like her have their students write essays about their immediate lives, in order to reach their true feelings. Mr Nakamoto teaches differential calculus to disinterested students in his ingenious way, so that the students come to enjoy it. Some teachers may still resort to physical punishment in order to maintain the order that they consider important.

The everyday classroom practice of teaching ensures the continuity of the culture of teaching. The culture of teaching in Japanese schools differs from that in the US, in terms of beliefs about child development, professional responsibility, professional development, and the patterns of interaction among teachers themselves. When we look closer, there are also interschool differences, which derive from the local character-istics of the school and the internal composition of the teaching staff.

While living in the shared culture of teaching, teachers are individuals who hold their own priorities both in their public and private lives. We have tried to portray this personal aspect by depicting the life histories of three teachers. Mr Takeuchi was a union high-school teacher who remained an ordinary classroom teacher throughout his career, in contrast to Mr Imai, who climbed the promotion ladder to become a high-school principal. Ms Kawa was a middle-school teacher who struggled to balance her family responsibilities with her teaching career. We have suggested that gender, age and union affiliation have been important factors differentiating the experiences of individual teachers, but that this may change in future.

Having examined teachers at the institutional system level, the school level, and the individual level, we hope to have shown that teachers actively make their own sense of a system that imposes constraints on, and governs, their professional lives. Teachers do possess a certain amount of autonomy in conducting what they believe to be their responsibility, and will continue to do so despite changes taking place at the national policy level. It remains to be seen to what extent teachers' daily practice will be affected by the reforms of the 1980s and 1990s.

Further Reading

Duke, Benjamin C. (1973). *Japan's Militant Teachers*. Honolulu: University of Hawaii Press.

Shimahara, Nobuo (1991). Teacher education in Japan. In Beauchamp, Edward R. (ed.), *Windows on Japanese Education* (pp. 259–80). Westport: Greenwood Press.

Shimahara, Nobuo and Sakai, Akira (1995). *Learning to Teach in Two Cultures*. New York: Garland.

Notes

1 This is because government school teachers are local government employees as well as educational public employees, and are subject to the Law of Special Regulations concerning Educational Public Service Personnel (LSREPSP) (*Kyōiku Kōmuin Tokurei-hō*, article 13).

2 For instance, the national body conducts centralised in-service education for student guidance and leadership, while the prefectural bodies conduct in-service education for newly appointed teachers, for teachers with five to ten years' service, for principals and vice-principals, for specific subject teachers, and for extracurricular activities, amongst others.

3 A dominant interpretation of article 20 of the LSREPSP is that a principal examines each case and determines: (1) whether or not the teacher under-takes the education as a part of his or her work during working hours; and (2) whether the proposed education directly relates to the teacher's work and, if so, should the teacher devote his or her working hours full-time to the training. Against this interpretation, others emphasise the unique nature of teaching and teachers' autonomy. They argue that a principal's authority should be limited to confirming whether or not the teacher's participation in in-service training causes inconvenience to the daily operation of the school.

4 What follows is that policy:

The school will:

(1) develop children's capacity to be considerate group members (by cultivating self-discipline and independence).

(2) make moral education lessons more attractive to students (who would learn cooperation, responsibility, affection, ethics, love of truth and justice, human rights, and the joy of labour).

(3) encourage students to learn to enjoy studying and to recognise their own development. (An emphasis was placed on the relationship between everyday life and school subjects; parental participation in the reorganisation of the school curriculum; and writing activities in all subjects.)

The family will:

(1) assist children in developing appropriate daily habits.

(2) assist children in learning to take care of themselves and to study independently.

(3) ensure that children complete homework as a daily routine.

(4) create occasions where parents have meaningful interaction with children (e.g. telling stories about their grandparents, their experience of war and natural disasters, their life histories, and their work).

The community will:

(1) organise cultural and athletic activities for children.

(2) hold a meeting where children learn from life histories of their grandparents' generation.

5 *Nikkyōso* is the common abbreviation for *Nihon Kyōshokuin Kumiai*; *Zenkyō* for *Zen'nihon Kyōshokuin Kumiai*; *Nikkōkyō-uha* for *Nihon Kōtōgakkō Kyōshokuin Kumiai*; *Zen'nichikyōren* for *Zen'nihon Kyōshokuin Renmei*; and *Zenkankyō* for *Zenkoku Kyōiku Kanrishokuin Dantai Kyōgikai*.

6 *Zenkyō* advocates the following philosophy:

(1) We shall maintain independence from interest groups in business and politics, and seek to establish the economic, social and political status of teachers.

(2) We shall defend a decent living standard and human rights for working people, in cooperation with a wide range of workers and labour unions.

(3) We shall strive, with parents and the public, to defend autonomy of education and freedom to research, and to establish education based on the principles of the Japanese Constitution and the Fundamental Education Law.

(4) We shall strive to defend freedom of speech and democracy, and to advance social progress, with the public.

(5) We shall strive to defend world peace, self-determination of ethnic groups, and human rights, and to strengthen solidarity with the international community.

(6) We shall maintain the pledge 'not to send our children to the battlefields again' and strive to provide a peaceful future for children.

7 N. Sato (1994) and Shimahara and Sakai (1992, 1995) studied primary schools, using ethnographic research methods. N. Sato and Shimahara are American-based anthropologists. N. Sato's fieldwork was conducted in 1987–89, while Shimahara and Sakai's was in 1989. Itō (1994:140–1) sent identical questionnaires to 455 high-school teachers in the US in 1989, and 548 Japanese counterparts in 1992. G. Satō (1988:88–89) surveyed 812 middle-school teachers in the US, and 880 middle-school teachers in Japan in 1984–85.

8 The study was based on a survey of 573 female teachers and 364 male teachers at primary and middle schools.

9 The survey included *jōseki* teachers at 519 primary schools, most of them past their late forties. Ninety-five per cent of those surveyed were married. About half of them have husbands who are also teachers. Over 60 per cent have more than two children (Akashi and Takano 1993:59).

CHAPTER 6

Problems and Reforms in the 1980s and 1990s

By the 1980s Japan's system of schooling had been attracting praise from foreign observers for its efficiency. Japanese schools were seen to provide a high level of education for the whole population (not just a few elites). It was claimed that the resulting well-educated and disciplined population had contributed to the well-being of the society as a whole, fostering economic prosperity and social stability. Studies on Japanese education from this perspective abound, as already discussed in Chapter 1.

Inside Japan, however, critics were becoming more vocal about the 'problems' in Japanese education. Besides the competitive nature of entrance examinations to universities, which had long been criticised as excessive, the increasing incidence of bullying (*ijime*) and school refusal emerged as topics of heated discussion in the media. These problems alarmed the public, who then grew concerned with the system of education which they believed was to blame for it. Every parent takes a personal interest in his or her children's education. Employers feared that a flawed education system might cause a deterioration in the quality of future workers. Intellectuals were concerned with the welfare of the society. In this context, the Liberal Democratic Party (LDP) was astute in taking up the system of schooling as an election campaign topic, forcefully arguing that reforms were needed to address these problems. It had another agenda as well: educational reform was to be a part of a large-scale administrative reform, in the name of 'total settlement of the post-war political accounts' (*sengo seiji no sōkessan*).

In this chapter we will first examine the problems in education that have been widely discussed in the 1980s and 1990s, namely bullying (*ijime*), school refusal and corporal punishment. We will then illustrate the government's attempts to bring in changes to the education system over the same period. We will examine the inquiry by the Ad-Hoc

194

Council on Education (a supra-cabinet advisory body), which heralded large-scale reforms, and the changes that subsequently did take place. Finally, we will discuss more recent moves to introduce changes to the education system in the 1990s.

Contemporary 'Problems'

We discuss the issues of bullying, school refusal and physical punishment, because these are most 'tangible', in that they are dealt with in the media most frequently. The media, governments and academics widely discuss these phenomena as 'problems' that require urgent remedies, perhaps because they are individual actions that 'average' people would consider 'deviant' and hence can easily be defined as problems in ways that convince many people. This does not mean that these phenomena are in reality the most significant 'problems' of schooling. Any problem is in fact an arbitrary construction. When a social practice is not perfect (i.e. it can be improved), it is, by definition, 'problematic'. Since very few social practices are in fact satisfactory to all parties concerned, any practice can be defined as a 'problem'. The structure of schooling, for example, which makes it difficult for children from poor families to benefit from state-sponsored education, could be seen as a problem. But this would not be identified as such by the government or the media so readily since it is less visible, and since many other people benefit from the system as it is.

That being said, we will first illustrate the realities as shown in nationwide survey statistics, and then bring in the voices of a few affected students. We will follow this with an examination of the government's and schools' responses, and of the surrounding controversies.

Bullying

Bullying (*ijime*) has long existed as a part of interpersonal relations among school-age youths in Japan, as in many other societies. Indeed, many (e.g. Kawakami 1995:27; Hirose 1995:43–5; Inoue 1995:41; Kasama 1995:50) assume that bullying forms a natural part of the growing-up process. It is the extensive and sensational media reports of youth suicide related to bullying (e.g. Murakami 1985; Schoolland 1990:107–37) that have made it the most publicly discussed educational 'problem', and have resulted in a moral panic (Noshige 1985; Morita 1986a; Tokuoka 1988).

The first wave was in 1986, when a school child committed suicide and left a note saying that he could no longer endure school bullying. The second wave started in 1994. Over an 18-month period, eleven suicide cases were reported (Katsumata 1995). Psychiatrists observed that the kinds of media report on bullying-related suicide encouraged other vulnerable youths to take a similar path (Inamura 1995:45). Numerous publications explored the causes of bullying and suggested preventative measures. The National Diet Library Online Information Retrieval Network (NOREN), for example, reveals that 66 monographs on bullying were published in 1995. There are a large number of articles in various journals (professional and academic) that discuss bullying.

The Realities of Bullying

Nationwide data on bullying have been collected by the MOE since 1985. In the first wave in 1985, 55,066 incidents of bullying were reported. The incidence of reports gradually decreased to 21,598 in 1993, and then jumped to 60,096 in 1995 (see Figure 6.1). In 1995, 34.1 per cent of primary schools, 58.4 per cent of middle schools and 39.6 per cent of high schools reported incidents of bullying. In the same year, the average number of bullying incidents at any one school was 1.1 at primary schools, 2.8 at middle schools and 1.0 at high schools. The most widespread forms of bullying are 'teasing', verbal threats and exclusion, followed by violence. Moving up the school grades, bullying tends to move from exclusion to violence. Teachers play a major role in identifying the cases of bullying at primary schools (31.2 per cent), while at middle and high schools, bullied students' reports to the school are the dominant channel of identification (34 per cent)[1] (see Table 6.1).

These statistics need to be treated with caution. First, the number of bullying incidents should be much larger, since the MOE's surveys covered only those incidents that individual schools identified as such and reported to local education boards (Imabashi 1995b:54–5). Second, the dramatic increase in the number of reported bullying incidents may be due to an increased awareness of bullying and to the new initiatives to combat bullying at individual schools. (If for a particular school no cases of bullying were reported, the school would look as if it was not taking bullying seriously.) The difficulty in identifying bullying arises partly because whether or not an action constitutes bullying is determined by the recipient of the action, very much like sexual harassment. An action can start as a simple joke, which may later become hurtful to the recipient. The difficulty is compounded by the sheer logistics that teachers face. They are too occupied to observe every action of 40 or more students in their charge, in and out of the classroom.

Besides the nationwide survey, the MOE organised a specialist research group on bullying (*Jidōseito no Mondaikōdō nado nikansuru Chōsa Kenkyū Kyōikusha Kaigi*). The group examined 94 primary, middle and high

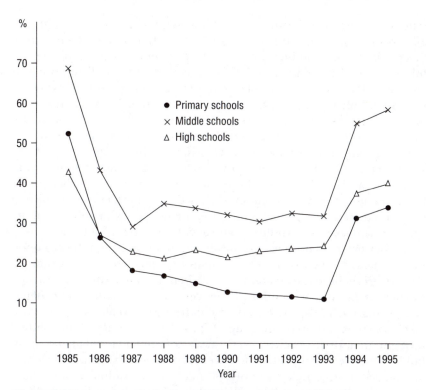

Figure 6.1 Percentage of schools experiencing bullying, 1985–95
Source: Kanekura (1996:7). Kanekura provides a summary of the report *95-nendo Seitoshidō jō no Shomondai no Genjō to Monbushō no Sesaku* (*Mondai Kōdō Hakusho*)

Table 6.1 The realities of bullying, 1995

	Primary school	Middle school	High school
Percentage of schools that reported incidents of bullying	34.1	58.4	39.6
Average number of bullying incidents at any one school	1.1	2.8	1.0
Three most widespread forms of bullying	1 Teasing 2 Exclusion 3 Verbal threat	1 Teasing 2 Verbal threat 3 Violence	1 Violence 2 Verbal threat 3 Teasing
Main method of identifying cases of bullying	Teachers (31%)	Bullied students report to school (34%)	

Source: Kanekura (1996:7–8).

schools that had previously reported bullying incidents[2] (*Asahi Shinbun* 23 and 27 May 1996). The study revealed that 12 per cent of students at these schools were bullied and that 17 per cent inflicted bullying on others. Half of the bullied students desired 'revenge'. Bullying students and the bullied often change places, rather than one person always being a target of bullying. The relationship between a bullying student and his or her victim is not that of one-way hatred: bullying occurs among 'friends' and 'ordinary classmates' (60 per cent). Any student can be a target of bullying. Forty per cent of primary-school bullies had themselves been bullied, and the equivalent figure for middle schools was 30 per cent. There are also those who are concurrently bullying and being bullied. Third-party students' reluctance to intervene in bullying committed on their classmates was prominent: approximately half of the students said that they would take no action to stop bullying.

Neither teachers nor parents may be aware of bullying inflicted upon their charges and children. Homeroom teachers, for example, incorrectly believed that their classes had no incidence of bullying (40 per cent at primary schools, 30 per cent at middle schools and 70 per cent at high schools). The bullied children were realistic about their teachers' perception of bullying. (Only 40 per cent of the bullied thought that their teachers were aware of the incidents.) Typically, bullied children are unlikely to reveal the incidents to their teachers (70 per cent at primary schools, 80 per cent at middle schools, and 90 per cent at high schools). Hiroyuki's essay, below, will provide an insider's explanation for this. But the victims who contacted their teachers thought that their teachers' responses to the incidents resolved the bullying, contrary to the popular belief that revelation to teachers attracts further bullying of the student. About 80 per cent of the parents of bullying students were unaware that their children were bullies. Thirty to fifty per cent of the bullied children believed that their parents did not know. The cause of bullying was perceived quite differently by teachers and parents. While teachers point to the decline of family-based moral guidance, parents raised children's lack of concern for other people's needs and a poor sense of justice as explanations.

Comparison with Other Societies

Bullying amongst youth has been a recent educational concern in the UK, Norway, Holland and Australia. Educational specialists who have worked on bullying in these countries joined an international symposium on bullying held by the MOE and the National Institute of Educational Research in 1996 (Takashina 1996:24–7; *Asahi Shinbun* 22 July 1996; *Monbu Kōhō* 18 July 1996). The reported frequency of school bullying in Japan is relatively low, in comparison to that in the US (Nihon Seishōnen

Kenkyūsho 1985, quoted in Morita 1986b:16), Holland, Spain and the UK
(Hirano 1995:189). In the same questionnaire to students, 15.9 per cent of
students at two primary schools and 10.4 per cent of students at two middle
schools in Saitama prefecture were victims of bullying in 1991, while the
equivalent figures were 26.1 per cent and 25.2 per cent in Yorkshire, and
27 per cent and 10 per cent respectively for Sheffield (Hirano 1995:188).
Australian studies have estimated that more than 20 per cent of students
are bullied at school (*The Age* 9 February 1998).

Some writers have attributed the bullying phenomenon to particular
features of Japanese society (e.g. Takegawa 1993:208–22; Tanaka 1995:58;
Takigawa 1995). Fukaya (1996:178–80) argues that rigidly structured
school activities, large class sizes and a limited choice of schools contribute to bullying. Bullying among Japanese children is said to have
unique characteristics. First, Japanese students (19.7 per cent) are less
likely to intervene in bullying than their American counterparts (39.1
per cent) (Morita 1986b:16; Sengoku 1995:196). Second, bullied
students in Japan often develop a hatred for school and eventually refuse
to attend, while such cases are rare in the US (Machizawa 1995:100).
Third, Japanese youth are more ambivalent about the essentially vicious
nature of bullying than are US students. While 94.4 per cent of the US
respondents insisted that one must not bully others, the equivalent
Japanese figure was 64.2 per cent (Machizawa 1995:100). Fourth, more
Japanese youths responded that they would join in bullying (10.7 per
cent for boys and 3.8 per cent for girls) than American youths (5.2 per
cent and 2.6 per cent respectively) (Machizawa 1995:100). Fifth, more
bullying occurs at middle schools than at primary schools in Japan, while
Norway and Holland show the opposite tendency (Takashina 1996:25). A
detailed comparison of bullying must await the report of an international
research team, which is expected later.

Below is an essay written by a 17-year-old boy, Hiroyuki, in which he
recounts the bullying that he received three years prior to his writing. For
reasons of space, we have abridged his essay (Tamura 1996).

Case Study 6.1: Bullying – Hiroyuki's Story

The bullying started at the end of the second term of grade eight. It was
not until the third term, though, that I was seriously suffering from it. It
started as frivolous teasing, which gradually developed into what I call
bullying. The perpetrators were my ex-friends. They often kicked and hit
me for no reason. More painful was a sense of psychological oppression
which prevented me from telling them to stop.

I used to hate the end of classes, because I feared that they might bully
me again during breaks. I felt secure during classes. When teased, I often
did not talk back because I feared that they might tease me more. That

sometimes happened. The bullying became more tormenting over the next few months. Kicking became more frequent and intense. The three major perpetrators said to me, 'Commit suicide' and 'Disappear'. Several more students often joined these three boys. I was at a loss as to what to do. It took a long time to settle down emotionally once I returned home.

Let me reflect on how my perception of bullying changed over time. In the beginning I found it simply unpleasant. As it progressed, I desperately sought ways to have them stop. Naturally at first I considered asking the perpetrators to stop it. But I didn't think that they would accept such a simple request from me; I feared that, given that they had greater numbers, it would aggravate the situation, and decided that going against them alone was not feasible. The second option was to talk to somebody, but this was difficult, partly because I feared that I might be bullied for revealing the incidents to teachers. But more significantly, I did not want to acknowledge that I was being bullied. I wanted to believe that I was not the kind of person whom others want to bully. To me, acknowledging that I was bullied was tantamount to acknowledging that I was a weak and worthless person. I would be deeply ashamed of and sad about it. That acknowledgement was humiliating. This is why many of the bullied children deny it when asked, 'Have you been bullied?'. When I realised that neither option was feasible, I thought that I would be able to escape from this misery if I were dead. In fact I gradually came to think that I was an unpleasant person, who deserved to be dead. I am positive that many bullied children follow this psychological path leading to suicide.

It required great courage on my part to open up to my mother. I recall that I pointed out the names of the major perpetrators on a class list, since I could not bring myself to verbalise them. After that, my mother contacted the school and I stayed home the following day. Up until then the school was unaware of my prolonged suffering. My homeroom teacher discussed the issue with the class, which seemed to have some influence on the perpetrators. They individually apologised to me the next day when I returned to school. The bullying finished there, superficially, but we never returned to a normal classmates relationship.

Schools' Responses to Bullying

Homeroom teachers' follow-up actions at individual schools, as in Hiroyuki's case, have been the most common ways to deal with bullying. As well, some teachers actively devise initiatives to prevent bullying from occurring in the first place. Reports of such efforts by dedicated teachers abound in professional journals like *Kyōiku* and *Jidō Shinri*.

The government's responses to bullying started in 1994, when it established a specialist research group on bullying, which has issued four reports to date. The latest report (July 1996) proposed several concrete measures. First, it encouraged teachers to gain counselling skills, and the school to maintain good working relationships with counselling institutions. Second, schools were urged to actively employ nurse-teachers (*yōgo kyōin*) in the school's sick-bay, since the bullied children found sick-bays the least threatening place in school. Some critics argued, however, that the bullied children seek help from the nurse-teacher precisely because she or he plays no official role in the school's student guidance, and that the suggested measure would deprive them of such help (Wakahoi 1995:34; Terumoto 1995:23). Third, it urged schools to be more flexible in granting legitimate school absence to bullied children, in reorganising homeroom classes mid-year, and in arranging school transfers for bullied children.

The most controversial proposal was that the school should, if necessary, impose an official suspension on a bullying student in order to protect the bullied student. If the incident involved criminal actions, such as excessive violence and blackmail, it was recommended that the school resort to the police. Some critics supported these 'strong' measures in principle (Hirose 1995:45; Wakahoi 1995:35; Kawakami 1995:29); and indeed this is an accepted practice in Australasian schools. Others (Terumoto 1995:23) consider them to be too authoritarian for educational institutions. Even the supporters predict that individual schools would find these measures difficult to implement, since schools would fear that the objectivity of the suspension might be questioned (Terumoto 1995:23; Kobayashi 1995:19); and since the suspension would interfere with the child's right to education, and may not benefit the bullying child (Kobayashi 1995:19). More important, these 'tough' measures contradict the 'culture' of Japanese schools and what schools see as their missions. For instance, such measures would 'disadvantage' the students in their post-school lives when they applied for places in higher education institutions and in the workforce, by leaving an official record of 'suspension' (Kawakami 1995:29).[3]

Official suspension, and referral to the police, of bullying students may be acceptable as 'urgent' measures when the cases involve violence. However, bullying requires both 'urgent' and long-term measures to be resolved. Some of the proposed 'urgent' measures may not be seen as pedagogically sound in the eyes of some critics. However, schools face the demanding task of having to protect the rights of the weak while simultaneously providing pedagogically sound guidance.

School Refusal

School refusal (*futōkō* or *tōkō kyohi*) normally refers to a long-term absence from school for reasons other than poverty or illness. The MOE's operational definition of school refusal for the purpose of collecting data includes those who miss 30 days or more of school for reasons other than poverty or illness (Isotani 1994:18). School refusal is a diverse phenomenon, comprising four main categories: so-called

Nonoko meets her neighbour Kikuchi.

'Kikuchi, can you let me share your umbrella?'

'Other boys may tease me – like, "Nonoko and Kikuchi are in love under the same umbrella".'

'Take the umbrella for yourself.'

'What is Kikuchi doing over there?'

Source: Asahi Shinbun 16 July 1997 © Hisaichi Ishii

'school phobia', school refusal involving mental disorder (such as schizophrenia or depression), ordinary truancy (due to laziness, and often accompanied by delinquent behaviour), and an intentional refusal of a positive kind (Makihara 1988:142).

Among these categories, school phobia has received the most media attention. School phobia (as distinct from truancy), which was first identified in the 1940s in the US, derives from a severe fear towards school, and is often accompanied by major emotional disturbances. In Japan the term 'school phobia' appeared in academic journals in the 1960s (S. Satō 1988:24). The category boundaries are often unclear, but they are important, since different types of school refusal tend to lead to different post-school lives. Those with school phobia usually adapted to later life more easily than those exhibiting a mental disorder or delinquent behaviour (Ichimaru et al. 1994).[4]

An increasing number of children have come to refuse school since 1966 when the MOE started collecting data, reaching a peak in 1994 (Nihon Kodomo o Mamoru Kai 1996:126; Kurita 1990). The percentage of such primary students jumped from 0.04 in 1985 to 0.09 in 1990 and to 0.20 in 1995. The equivalent figures for middle schools were 0.47, 0.75 and 1.42. (Japan, Monbushō 1996; Inamura 1994:65) (see Figure 6.2). School refusal tends to appear more frequently in densely populated urban areas than in rural regions; and within an urban centre, industrial areas tend to produce more school refusal and more delinquency than commercial and residential areas (Inamura 1994:196–7).

As an official response, the MOE conducted a study on the views of students with over 30 absent days and those of their parents (Japan, Monbushō, Shotō Chūtō Kyōiku-kyoku Chūgakkō-ka 1994).[5] Asked about what triggered their absence, primary- and middle-school students listed 'events at school' (44.5 and 43.8 per cent respectively), in comparison to 'individual problems' (27.8 and 36.9 per cent), and 'family problems' (14.8 and 4.0 per cent). Asked about the causes, the largest number of primary- and middle-school students stated 'individual problems' (e.g. lack of sociability), followed by relationships with friends and classmates at school. Their teachers and parents, however, saw none of the 'individual problems' that the students thought they had. Poor academic performance did not rank high in their explanations, although, naturally, middle-school students were more concerned about academic achievement than primary-school students.

The study provided a few insights into the children's perceptions of their school refusal. First, students who refuse school tend to end up blaming themselves unnecessarily for the problems they faced, as illustrated vividly by Hiroyuki's essay above. Second, relationships with classmates and friends are very important for children's school lives. This contention has

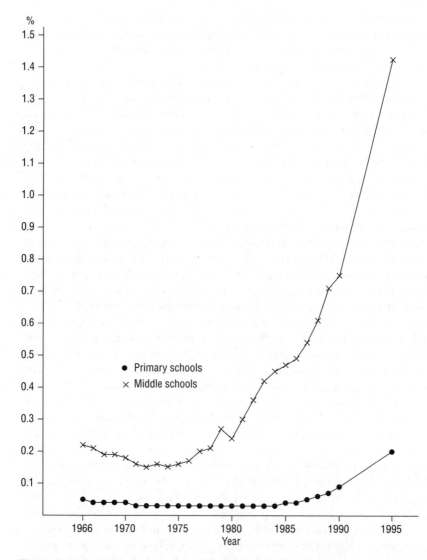

Figure 6.2 Percentages of school refusal students, 1966–95
Sources: Inamura (1994:65) (1966–90 data); Kanekura (1997:4) (1995 data)

also been supported by other studies. Shimada's psychological study showed that troubles in relationships with other children cause more compounded forms of response (e.g. anger, anxiety, apathy and withdrawal) than troubled relationships with teachers, or poor academic performance (Shimada 1995:13–14). Another study concluded that

90 per cent of grade-two (primary) students and 85 per cent of grade-eight (middle-school) students found school enjoyable; and that whether school was enjoyable or not depended on their friends at school (Nihon Kodomo o Mamoru Kai 1996:124). These findings suggest that the core of the 'problem' of school refusal lies in students' relationships with friends and classmates — not so much with teachers, academic performance or the competitive school environment – and that measures to counter school refusal need to centre on relationships between students.

What do these students do instead of attending normal classes? Frequently cited were: doing nothing (70 out of 237); pursuing their favourite activities outside the house (35); becoming sick in the morning and staying home (29); and visiting special rooms (such as the sick-bay) in the school (20) (Japan, Monbushō, Shotō Chūtō Kyōiku-kyoku Chūgakkō-ka 1994:65). These students (half of whom eventually returned to school) thought some of the school's responses were effective. For example, the school helped them to find something personally interesting and enjoyable; and allowed them to stay in the sick-bay or principal's rooms instead of forcing them to return to the classroom. The homeroom teacher and classmates telephoned and came to take them to school; and teachers developed a greater understanding of individual students (Japan, Monbushō, Shotō Chūtō Kyōiku-kyoku Chūgakkō-ka 1994:68). The following account (told pseudonymously) is typical (Yamada 1995).

Case Study 6.2: School Refusal – Wataru's Story

I quit high school six years ago, and am now 24 years old. I don't exactly know why I ended up like this, but my family environment is perhaps a factor. We have little intimate family conversation at home.

In fifth grade, children started to develop 'friendships', beyond being just 'playmates'. I was neither outgoing nor talkative, and didn't know how to talk to classmates. I stopped playing with them. They started calling me 'a dark person', and I started to think that I was indeed 'a dark person'. But I didn't notice that I was any different from other students at that time.

At middle school, I felt even more awkward and reluctant in making friends, since everybody was then expanding his or her relationships. In grade nine, several friends still invited me to join them, but I kept declining their invitations, saying that I wanted to study for entrance examinations, since I did not know how to relate to them. Gradually they stopped inviting me. When I completed middle school, I was determined to change myself at high school.

I was too optimistic about high school. How could I manage to relate with classmates there when I couldn't manage it at middle school? Although I attended classes every day, I did not talk to anybody during breaks, went home straight after school, and watched television or listened to music. I spent two years deceiving myself like that. In grade 11, school became like a hell to me. Since I did not talk much, some kids bullied me, forcing me to do things for them. I was the kind of student whom classmates either disliked, sympathised with or were indifferent to. Not motivated to study, I slept during classes. I soon started questioning why I went to school. Then my elder sister married and left home. My mother and hard rock music were the only support that I found in those days. The music made me forget everything unpleasant. In grade 12, after the first day I could not bring myself to leave for school, although my homeroom teacher came to see me at home. I did not feel like doing anything. For several months I did not go out, take a bath or have a haircut. My father ignored me. I felt like killing him.

In the end I quit high school. I entered a correspondence high school, but did not last due to my fear of attending study sessions. At 20 I was still the same. I could not go out since my appearance was terrible and I was scared of meeting neighbours. I could only trust my mother and the music. Around that time, my mother attended a lecture on a cooperative institution called 'friend space', which welcomes youth who refuse school and employment. After one of its counsellors visited me weekly for eight months, I finally found the courage to visit the 'friend space'. It took over a year before I gradually made acquaintances there. I now feel that I am making progress slowly.

We now turn to a story about a student, Takashi (pseudonym), who could not attend normal classes but spent school time in the school's sick-bay. This is called 'sick-bay schooling' (*hokenshitsu tōkō*), an option that children who refuse school often take as a transient measure. The nurse-teacher of the school tells the story, which we have shortened considerably (Yoshida 1993:41–5).

Case Study 6.3: Sick-bay Schooling – Takashi's Story

I am a school nurse-teacher at a government high school. I have had many students who refused school but could come to the school sick-bay and be in my care. Takashi is one of them.

Takashi never missed classes until the event took place in September, term two, which triggered his school refusal. When he was about to leave the classroom for home after preparation for the school's cultural festival, Ichirō, his classmate, told him not to go. Takashi ignored Ichirō, who then grabbed Takashi's shirt. Takashi shook off Ichirō and punched him in the face, injuring him and sending his glasses flying. Takashi's mother took the repaired glasses to Ichirō's home, but was told that Takashi was violent, which led to conflict between the respective parents. Takashi refused to go to school for about three weeks, until his mother persuaded him to return. But that did not last long. When Takashi's mother visited the school, I advised that Takashi receive psychiatric treatment. Takashi has been attending treatment sessions since then.

Two weeks later, the school suggested that Takashi study in the school sick-bay. We made sure that he avoided the morning commuting time and left for home before school finished. In the sick-bay I got Takashi to study notes and write essays, and arranged subject teachers to tutor him so that he could catch up with his study. He also sat the term examinations in the sick-bay.

On the first day of the third term, I told him to attend the beginning-of-the-term ceremony; but that if he couldn't he should come to the sick-bay, which he did. After school I took Takashi to his classroom, confirmed where his seat was, and said, 'Please try to come here for even five minutes from tomorrow. You need to show your efforts to the school, since we granted sick-bay school attendance and examinations in the second term on the grounds that you would make an effort'. However, the following day I received a telephone call from his mother who said, 'Takashi is hanging on to his bed, crying. He does not talk to me. He has not come out of his room to go to the toilet or for meals'. He was absent again on the following day. We suggested that Takashi should resume the sick-bay schooling, continue with this, and sit the examinations in the sick-bay. Luckily the graduation assessment meeting approved Takashi's sick-bay schooling as part of the required attendance for graduation. He thus graduated from school.

I believe in the merits of sick-bay schooling. First, it helps the student, maintaining human contact with the nurse-teacher when he or she is cut off from the rest of the school. Second, the sick-bay offers a middle-ground bridge between home and classroom. The sick-bay always accommodates a few students, which gives the sick-bay schooling student the chance to make contact with a small number of other students, and to ease a sense of fear of other people. Third, teachers come to better understand the student, since they can keep in touch with him or her. Fourth, the student can study. Fifth, they can still achieve the level of attendance required for graduation.

Sick-bay schooling has become more frequent since school refusal and bullying started to increase. The nurse-teacher above was taking care of three students at the time of reporting. As noted above, the government report on bullying praised the value of sick-bay schooling for students who no longer trust their classmates and teachers; and now proposed to attach a more official role to the nurse-teachers.

Studies on the post-school lives of children who experienced school refusal have concluded that prospects were positive. Eighty per cent recover adequate capacity to manage human relationships and obtain independence as adults (Makihara 1988:150). School refusal cases which involve younger children and accompany fewer psychiatric disorders are more likely to result in complete recovery (Makihara 1988:151).

Corporal Punishment

Corporal punishment continues to take place at school, although in 1947 the School Education Law (article 11) legally prohibited it. Since the mid-1980s, the public has become more aware and critical of the realities of corporal punishment in schools, after the media reported a few sensational cases of teacher violence against students in the name of punishment.

The number of teachers who received official reprimands for administering corporal punishment increased fivefold (from 78 to 436) between 1981 and 1995 (see Figure 6.3). In 1995, 1026 cases of corporal punishment were reported, involving 1027 teachers and 1766 students at 846 schools, slightly up in number from the previous year. On average, 2.1 per cent of government schools practised corporal punishment. The largest number occurred at middle schools: in 1995 occurrences of corporal punishment were officially reported at 4.5 per cent of middle schools, involving 0.02 per cent of students and 0.2 per cent of teachers. Corporal punishment most frequently occurred during classes (34.2 per

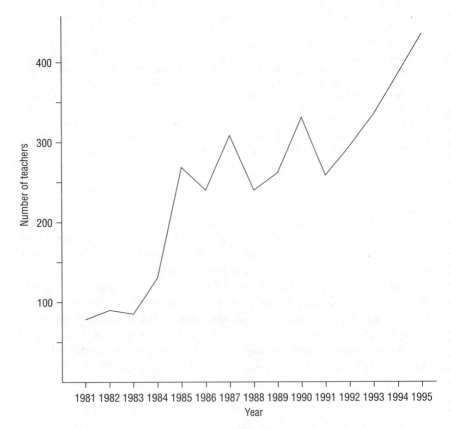

Figure 6.3 Number of teachers who received official reprimands for administering corporal punishment, 1981–95
Sources: Shimizu (1996:120–1) (1981–91 data); Kanekura (1997:9) (1992–95 data)

cent), followed by after school (14.3 per cent), breaks (13.4 per cent), club activities (13.1 per cent), school activities (8.2 per cent) and others (16.7 per cent). Most punishment involved hitting with the hand (66.7 per cent). Other forms included kicking and hitting with sticks. Sixty per cent of students did not suffer any injury, but some cases resulted in bruises, damaged eardrums and broken bones.[6]

The increase in the number of reported cases of corporal punishment and of official punishment of the teachers concerned does not necessarily reflect the real increase in corporal punishment practised at schools. It indicates, rather, that the public awareness of corporal punishment has made the authorities more attuned to the occurrence of it and that they are more likely to take action when cases are uncovered. Imabashi (1995a:41) warns that corporal punishment is in reality more prevalent, based on his survey of 209 university students in 1994. Sixty-seven per cent of the students responded that they had seen more than several cases of 'corporal punishment which inflicted pain, such as punching or kicking, and hours of standing still in silence at primary, middle and high schools'.[7]

The official reprimanding of teachers who are reported to have conducted corporal punishment has been problematic. In 1995 less than one-third of the reported cases resulted in official punishment of the teachers concerned (286 cases, among the 1026 reported cases) (Japan, Monbushō 1996), although the number of officially reprimanded teachers increased to almost five times that for 1981 (when the public outcry had not yet occurred) (Shimizu 1996:121). Critics argue that such soft responses are inconsistent with the School Education Law, which prohibits corporal punishment (e.g. Imabashi 1995a:44). The majority of these teachers (about 80 per cent) received 'instruction' (kunkoku), instead of official punishment (chōkai shobun). There are four types of official punishment: dismissal (menshoku), suspension from duty (teishoku), reduced salary (genkyū), and warnings (kaikoku). The 'warning' (kaikoku) differs from 'instruction' (kunkoku) in that the former can lead to deferred salary increases on the basis that the teacher has not performed his or her duty satisfactorily (Imabashi 1995a:44). In 1995, of 436 teachers who received official reprimands, 8 were suspended from duty, 29 received a decrease in salary, 40 received 'warnings', and 358 received 'instruction' (Japan, Monbushō 1996). The kind of official reprimand that teachers receive for inflicting corporal punishment also depends on individual prefectures (Imabashi 1995a:43–5).[8]

The students are often unaware of the illegal nature of corporal punishment, and hold an ambivalent attitude towards it. In the above-mentioned survey (Imabashi 1995a:41), 63 per cent of the students were unaware that corporal punishment was illegal. Thirty-seven per cent of them thought that a certain degree of corporal punishment can be justified, for example, when a verbal explanation does not work (Imabashi 1995a:42). Only 14 per cent of them responded that 'there is no place for corporal punishment'.

We have attempted to provide an accurate picture of bullying, school refusal and corporal punishment (albeit less sensational than the media reports), by drawing on nationwide data and individual accounts. These three problems have been widely discussed, and have given the government a convenient reason to advocate major educational reforms.

The Ad-Hoc Council on Education

Education reforms in the 1980s were conducted in the context of a large-scale administrative reform, initiated by the second Ad-Hoc Council on Administrative Reform (*Rinji Gyōsei Chōsa-kai*, or *Rinchō*) which issued five reports by July 1983. The running theme of the *Rinchō* reports was 'independence and self-help'. Its core recommendations were: that more responsibility be borne by individuals for their own welfare; a more active role for private enterprises in education; a greater contribution to the global community; and budget cuts for education, social welfare and agriculture. In the field of education, *Rinchō* recommended: a temporary halt to the plan of reducing the average class size to 40 pupils; a cut in the national government's financial contribution to compulsory education, public educational and cultural facilities and private schools; greater appreciation of individual differences among students; and the introduction of ability-based education.

Prime Minister Yasuhiro Nakasone had long held a view that various post-war institutions (including education) were 'imposed' by the Occupation authorities, and wanted 'the total settlement of the post-war political accounts' (*sengo seiji no sōkessan*) through large-scale reforms of these institutions. Besides administrative and financial reforms, Nakasone wanted educational reform based on a similar inquiry by a supra-cabinet advisory body (like the second Ad-Hoc Council on Administrative Reform), rather than relying on the MOE's permanent Central Education Council.

Nakasone was known for supporting the revision of the Japanese Constitution. His political philosophy, 'a renewal of national administration and a construction of national community', emphasised national solidarity based on a so-called unique ethnic tradition, that is, a 'Japanese-like community' based on a strong sense of belonging to the state among individuals. To achieve his project to 'reform the structure of the state', education was to form the crucial component. The LDP was swift in preparing for education reforms. Immediately after winning the election in 1983, the LDP established five subcommittees within its Education System Research Council (*Bunkyōseido Chōsa-kai*). Its mission was to conduct a thorough re-examination of the post-war education system. Schoppa (1991) provides an excellent analysis of the educational policy-making process under Nakasone.

The Ad-Hoc Council on Education's Reports

The Ad-Hoc Council on Education (*Rinji Kyōiku Shingi-kai*, or *Rinkyōshin* in short) was established in August 1984 to inquire into, and recommend on, the educational reforms that Nakasone had envisioned. The Council was a provisional supra-cabinet advisory body, the second of this kind in the post-war era. In establishing such a supra-cabinet council, Nakasone hoped that the inquiry would be more independent of the MOE and would bring about larger-scale changes than he had seen in previous attempts since the 1950s.[9] The Council was asked to inquire into 'the policies to effect changes to education that will respond to social changes'. The Council's membership was dominated by representatives of the business sector, the bureaucracy and Nakasone's own intellectuals, and did not include any educationalists. In particular two groups were influential: the Kyoto Group, headed by the president of National Panasonic, and Nakasone's personal advisory council. Introduction of competitive principles and liberalisation had been recommended by the two groups prior to the establishment of the Council.

Over three years, the Council provided four reports, which we summarise below. The first report (June 1985) recommended the following:

- appreciation of 'individuality' as the basic principle of the reform;

- valuing of a wider range of choices and moral education;

- diversification of admission procedures to national universities, and creation of a common examination in which private universities would also participate; and

- establishment of six-year secondary schools and module-based high schools.

The second report's (April 1986) recommendations were:

- pursuit of the themes 'large heart, healthy body and rich creativity', 'freedom, independence and the spirit of the public' and 'Japanese people in the global community' as the goal for 21st-century education;

- shifting of the emphasis from school-centred education to lifelong education;

- valuing of moral education;
- introduction of an Internship Program for novice teachers; and
- establishment of the University Council.

The third report (April 1987) recommended the following:

- diversification of assessment methods, and introduction of an evaluation system for vocational ability;
- introduction of 'intelligent schools';
- re-examination of the state textbook authorisation system;
- introduction of 'new international schools'; and
- encouragement of private-sector investment in education.

The fourth report's (August 1987) recommendations were:

- response to globalisation (*kokusaika*) and the information-based society (*jōhōka*);
- enhancement of the MOE's role in policy making;
- starting the academic year in September; and
- consideration of 'appropriate treatment of the national flag and anthem'.

Major Points of Criticism

The Ad-Hoc Council's reports were discussed widely.[10] The major points of discussion and criticism are listed below.

1 The proposed reorganisation was based on a narrow view that the school system functions almost exclusively for producing and differentiating human resources to meet changes in the industrial structure. Schooling's other functions were ignored.

2 The proposed 'shift to the lifelong learning system' undermines the public system of education and encourages privatisation.

3 The proposed 'internationalisation of education' is problematic. It was interpreted only in terms of the global moves of private companies, contains elements of nationalism, and does not refer to education for world peace and disarmament. The proposed 'intelligent schools' (which would respond to the information-based society) would allow information industries to take over schools.

4 The proposed internship for novice teachers and the systematic re-organisation of in-service programs increases the MOE's control over teachers.

5 The proposed 'appropriate treatment of the national flag and anthem' enhances the kind of moral education that is based on loyalty to the state.

6 The proposed system of textbook authorisation focuses on judgements of 'appropriateness', and allows the state to compile textbooks *de facto.*

7 Liberalisation (i.e. privatisation) of tertiary education aims at making tertiary education open, and directly connected, to private companies on one hand, while on the other the proposed University Council would strengthen the MOE's control over tertiary education institutions.

8 The state may try to avoid its due responsibility for bearing the cost of educating its people, by conducting an arbitrary priority-based distribution of budget, increasing the education costs borne by individuals, and encouraging private companies to play a more active role in education.

Implementation of the Ad-Hoc Council's Recommendations

Following the Ad-Hoc Council's fourth report, the cabinet passed a resolution on implementing educational reform. The government then began to revise the existing legislation. Already, in September 1987, a revision to the School Education Law had led to the establishment of the University Council. In 1988 alone the government submitted six bills to effect legislative changes in the Diet (National Parliament).[11]

The Ad-Hoc Council's recommendations resulted in the major changes implemented by the mid-1990s, often in combination with the recommendations by other permanent MOE councils which were commissioned to inquire on specific aspects raised by the Ad-Hoc Council. We will focus here on five areas: high schools, tertiary education, the curriculum at all levels of education, lifelong learning, and teacher education and certification. The last will be examined extensively, for two reasons. One is our wish to illustrate the process of policy deliberation and implementation in this area as a representative case study. The other is the general evaluation that the most significant change over the period involved teacher education and certification. Changes proposed in the latter half of the 1990s will be discussed separately in the following section.

High School Education: Diversity, Flexibility and More Choices

The changes in high-school education resulted from the Ad-Hoc Council's reports and the report of the 14th inquiry by the Central Education Council. The major features of these changes were diversity in schools, courses and subjects, and flexibility in the institutional arrangements. Both aimed to introduce a wider range of choices for students and parents.

First, the minimum period of study required for the high-school evening course and the high-school correspondence course was shortened from four to three years. Second, module-based high schools were introduced. In these schools, students accumulate modules in order to graduate, rather than by moving up academic years with the same peers. This format had been introduced to evening-course high schools in 1986, and then to day-course high schools in 1993. As of 1994 55 module-based schools existed.

Third, new types of schools were introduced in response to the Central Education Council's call for appreciation of individual differences, a wider range of choices, and diversity of the admission criteria. They were: (1) schools that offer multiple courses and allow students to take subjects across different courses towards their diploma; (2) schools that offer diverse optional subjects and courses; (3) schools that offer state-of-the-art language programs, and actively welcome returnee children and overseas students; and (4) schools that provide information-related courses (both engineering- and commerce-oriented).

Fourth, the 'integrated study course' (*sōgōgakka*) was introduced in 1994 as the third major grouping of high-school courses (in addition to academic courses and vocational courses), when seven such government schools were established. In 1993 schools started to count studies outside school towards their diplomas. They included units from other schools, studies at private specialist schools (*senshūgakkō*), and certificates of various types of proficiency.

Tertiary Education: Flexibility, Autonomy and Accountability

Following the Ad-Hoc Council's recommendations, the University Council was established in September 1987, and joint research institutions for national universities were opened up to local governmental and private universities. In December 1988, the newly established University Council issued its first report, entitled 'Making graduate studies more flexible'. Subsequent changes introduced more flexibility and diversity in undergraduate and graduate studies.

First, from 1991, universities were granted more autonomy to design their own curricula. They no longer need to satisfy the general requirement for graduation of 36 units of 'general education' subjects, 8 units of foreign languages, 4 units of physical education and 76 units of 'specialised subjects'. Almost 80 per cent of universities have re-examined their curricula, and are currently designing four-year curricula that they consider appropriate. Second, universities are now required to be more accountable to their clients, while being granted a greater degree of autonomy in curriculum design. They are required to evaluate their practices of teaching, research and management. It is estimated that over 80 per cent of universities have implemented such assessments, some introducing external evaluation (Japan, Monbushō 1988:329).

Third, graduate schools now enjoy more flexibility, which, it was hoped, would expand them and improve the quality of graduate research. Japan does not maintain many graduate students, with only 153,000 enrolled in 1995. There are fewer graduate-school students per capita in Japan than in other advanced nations: 1.1 graduate students per 1000 people (in 1994), in comparison to 7.7 in the US (1992), 2.4 in the UK (1992), and 3.6 in France (1993). The institutional arrangements for graduate studies have become diverse, including federation-type graduate schools, at which a number of universities jointly supervise graduate studies, and graduate studies that involve joint research at outside research centres. In addition, graduate schools have more dis-cretion to cater for individual differences. Able students can skip the fourth year of an undergraduate course before entering a Masters course. The minimum required lengths of study for Masters and Doctorate courses were shortened (from two years to one year, and from five to three years respectively).[12] Graduates with at least two years' postgraduate research experience elsewhere can now enter a Doctorate course without having to undertake Masters studies. Some able students have already begun to take advantage of this flexibility.

The Curriculum: Neonationalism and Elite Training

Responding to the Curriculum Council's report (December 1989), the MOE implemented the new Course of Study (*gakushū shidō yōryō*, an outline of curriculum to be covered) for kindergarten, primary, middle and high schools in April 1992. This was the fifth post-war revision of the Course of Study, and is considered to be the most far-reaching. It claimed to represent 'the total settlement of the post-war education accounts' in terms of curriculum, and to set out 'the map of human resource training for the 21st century'.

The new Course of Study addressed two major concerns that the Ad-Hoc Council maintained throughout its inquiry. One was to achieve a national integration among people, and the other was to ensure the efficient training of the elites. The former concern resulted in neo-nationalist initiatives, which would instil in people a sense of belonging to the nation-state. The latter concern derived from the desire to maintain Japan's superiority in the global economy, and explored the ways in which creative elites could be identified and nurtured at an early stage. This led to the introduction of the diverse curriculum and the enhanced principle of competition in education.

Neonationalist Moves

The new curriculum was claimed to enhance 'national integration among people' by nurturing a belief that Japan is an influential state in the global community and by cultivating an 'ethnic identity'. It involved developing 'self-awareness of being Japanese' and respect for traditional culture.

First, the new Course of Study legitimated the status of what are commonly regarded as the national flag (*Hinomaru*), and the national anthem (*Kimigayo*), by making it compulsory to use them at school. This is despite the fact that to date there is no legal foundation for *Kimigayo*'s national anthem status.[13] It also stipulated that students learn their significance and develop a respect for them (grade four social studies); and promoted reverence for the emperor (grade six social studies). The issue of *Hinomaru* and *Kimigayo* has been controversial, attracting widespread discussion in the national media, since they carry a strong legacy of wartime ultranationalism. *Kimigayo*, in particular, expresses a desire for the emperor's longevity, which the left considers inappropriate at best and offensive at worst.

Second, the new Course of Study promotes moral education across the curriculum, with a focus on 'independent Japanese' and 'reverence for life'. The new moral education was claimed to emphasise morality in practice, rather than the abstract moral virtues promoted in the previous moral education. For example, the new criteria for selecting teaching materials for primary schools include the passages 'it will be useful for pupils to develop a self-awareness of being Japanese, a love for the nation, and an attitude desirous of the nation's prosperity', and 'it will be useful to nurture an understanding of, and affection for, Japanese culture and traditions'.

Third, the new social studies curriculum threatens the kind of progressivism and the democratic ideals that the subject had promoted since the beginning of the post-war schooling. Recall that teachers experienced difficulties in understanding the newly introduced subject, social studies, since it challenged squarely what the pre-war schooling stood for (see Chapter 2). Studies of Japanese history at upper-grade primary schools concentrate on 42 specific historical heroes. Included was Admiral Heihachirō Tōgō, who was depicted as a 'military god' in the pre-war textbooks for bringing victory in the Russo-Japanese war, and who inspired militarist and nationalist feeling amongst youth. The left has been unconvinced by Tōgō's return to prominence in school textbooks in the name of 'Japan, an international state'. Middle-school ninth-graders now study fewer hours of social science. High-school social science is now divided into two subjects, geography/history and civics.

Diverse Subject Options and Training of the Elites

The new curriculum differentiates students in terms of 'ability' at an earlier stage than before, by reorganising core studies at primary schools. The required numbers of Chinese characters (*kanji*) in grades one and two were increased, and schools were granted flexibility to introduce in advance those scheduled for the next grade when considered appropriate. In arithmetic, several topics were transferred from upper grades to lower grades. While these changes may accelerate the able students' learning, critics say that they may cause negative effects for slow learners (e.g. low self-esteem and early labelling).

At middle schools, the number of periods for optional subjects was increased. Under the previous system, all students received almost identical lessons until the end of middle school (grade nine). Middle-school students took only two optional subjects: a foreign language (which was 'optional' only in a formal sense since all schools made it compulsory) and one of the four optional subjects allocated one hour a week in grade nine (music, arts, physical education, technology/home science). Under the new system, eighth-graders (instead of ninth-graders) take one of the above four optional subjects for up to three periods weekly; and ninth-graders have up to five periods a week for optional subjects. This raised two concerns among critics (e.g. Mizuuchi 1985; *Kyōiku* no. 492, 1988). First, the experience since 1977 (when optional subjects were introduced) showed that an inadequate number of teachers and facilities made it impossible for all students to study their preferred options; and students with high achievement were more likely to land the subject of their choice. Second, increased hours for optional subjects may undermine the kind of basic middle-school education that was admired by the 1970 OECD observers (OECD 1972). They reported at the time that Japan deliberately offered all students the same education, regardless of their achievement, up to the end of compulsory schooling; and praised the 'humane education' at many middle schools where high-achieving students helped slow learners.

The middle schools' new Course of Study increased ability-based classes, by emphasising 'education to suit individual characteristics'. No reference was made to slow learners, in contrast to the previous Course of Study. Rather, the changes seem to stress the kind of ability-based teaching that tries to identify talents at an early stage and then nurture them through streaming, without due attention to slow learners and learners with special needs.

The new high-school curriculum introduced an extended range of subjects. The core curriculum now comprises five subjects (instead of six). Academic subjects were increased from 43 to 60, and vocational subjects from 157 to 184. Schools are granted discretion in offering 'other subjects', which can constitute up to one-quarter of the requirements for high-school graduation. Vocational subjects are expected to reflect the changes in industrial needs, and include electronics, biotechnology, service industries, agricultural economics, automotive engineering and transport. Along with the newly introduced diversity in the types of schools and courses, upper-secondary education now provides a much wider range of choices to parents and students.

Lifelong Learning: Private Sectors

The Ad-Hoc Council's recommendations to promote lifelong learning were enacted in the Lifelong Learning Promotion Law (July 1990). It was claimed that lifelong learning would respond to the needs of the changing society and the increased demand for learning throughout an individual's life. Of particular note is an active promotion of private-sector involvement in lifelong learning. Indeed, the use of the term 'lifelong learning' (instead of 'lifelong education') was deliberate, so that the relevant administrative bodies would not be restricted to the MOE.

As for governmental bodies, prefectural governments were requested to conduct research on lifelong learning, train instructors, offer advice and assistance to educational institutions, and establish courses. The MOE Lifelong Learning Council and prefectural-level lifelong learning councils were established as permanent bodies.

Interestingly, the legislation specifically stated that the Ministry of International Trade and Industry (MITI) was to guide non-governmental and private organisations' participation in lifelong learning projects(e.g. in sports, cultural and leisure activities). The legislation also invited administrative bodies which had not traditionally been involved in 'education' to participate in 'educational' activities (e.g. vocational training at universities, training of welfare volunteers, the preparation of educational environments for children outside schools). Concrete measures in relation to these initiatives have already been subject to deliberation, and proposals have been forwarded in the Lifelong Learning Council's reports and in a report of MITI's Lifelong

Learning Promotion Subcommittee (*Shōgai Gakushū Shinkōbukai*, located within the Industrial Structure Council (*Sangyō Kōzō Shingi-kai*).

Higher education institutions have instituted changes to accommodate lifelong learning. As a result, a larger number of working adults than before are now studying for credit at universities. Graduates of junior colleges and five-year technical colleges (*kōtō senmongakkō*) can enter universities as third-year students to continue their studies towards a degree. The University of the Air (*Hōsō Daigaku*) now offers over 300 subjects and caters for 64,000 students. In 1995 over 40 per cent of universities had special admission procedures for adults in place. Graduate schools have also started to offer evening courses for working adults. These moves to involve adults in higher education are likely to continue, and we suspect that a larger number of the adult population will return to universities to further their studies.

Reforms in Teacher Education and Certification

In 1988 and 1989 major changes were made to the system of teacher education, certification and in-service training which had been in place in Japan for over 40 years. These were the most important changes in post-war teacher education and certification practice. The changes were, it was claimed, aimed at improving the quality of teachers, and raised important questions in relation to the basic principles of post-war teacher education and in-service training (Tsuchiya 1988, 1989).

The following six distinctive changes were introduced in the 1988–89 teacher education reforms:

1 A 'superior' category of teaching certificate was added to the existing first-grade and second-grade certificates. The new *senshū* teaching certificate is now granted to those who have completed a two-year MEd degree program at an approved institution, and is to be used for selecting future principals and deputy-principals.[14]

2 The requirements for teaching certificates, in particular, the number of professional subjects in education, were increased.

3 Three new routes to teaching were introduced. A one-year course for teacher education was offered (similar to the postgraduate Diploma of Education in Commonwealth countries). In order to attract experienced adults active in their fields into teaching, local education boards grant a 'special' teaching certificate to such individuals, and employ them as sessional instructors for specific fields of study.

4 The upgrading of the teaching certificate (which had been automatic after 15 years' service in teaching) is now compulsory, and requires

attendance at in-service training programs arranged by local education boards.

5 New teachers undergo the Internship Program (*Shoninsha Kenshū*). They are employed on a conditional basis for the first year, and local education boards are obliged to provide new teachers with in-service education that enhances practical teaching skills.

6 Two categories of teaching certificates for high-school social science (i.e. geography/history and civics) replaced the existing single category, each setting out different requirements.

Several trends are apparent in these changes. First, the new system diversified the ways in which people receive teacher education and certificates. It maintained the system whereby teacher certificates are granted by universities to those who have received no teacher education program (e.g. primary teachers, teachers of martial arts and engineering). It introduced a one-year course for teacher education and a system whereby prefectural education boards grant 'special teaching certificates' to experienced individuals active in their fields.

Second, the introduction of the MEd-based teaching certificate promoted stratification of teachers and of teacher education institutions. While the MEd-based teaching certificate opened ways to promote teacher education at a graduate school level, and thus to improve the professional nature of teaching, opportunities are not provided equally to those who wish to obtain such qualifications. As of August 1996 all universities that specialise in teacher education have established graduate schools of teacher education to offer such MEd programs, but there are institutions without adequate facilities.

Third, the increased requirements for obtaining teaching certificates (the kinds and volume of subjects to be taken) have caused the teacher education curriculum to reflect the school curriculum more directly, and allowed less scope for individual institutions' original input into their own curriculum. Of particular note is the introduction of various professional subjects, such as *seitoshidō* (student guidance) and *tokubetsu katsudō* (non-academic activities), which directly correspond with subjects in the new Course of Study. This has raised several concerns. New professional subjects may not be based on solid academic disciplinary studies. The condensed curriculum may be an excessive burden for teacher education students. Teaching staff in teacher education programs may be inadequate for implementing the increased requirements. The new requirements may intervene in the universities' independent curriculum design, a point that we will take up later.

Fourth, the expansion of ways to grant teaching qualifications through routes other than university teacher education programs may undermine

the basic principle of 'teacher training at university', and the professionalism of the teaching occupation. This also contradicts the policy
to improve the quality of teachers by increasing the requirements for
teacher certification.

Fifth, under the new system the teacher education curricula at
individual universities are constrained by the MOE's authorisation
process for teacher education courses. The revised Law made it difficult
for individual universities to pursue independent and creative design of
their curricula, since the MOE's authorisation has made the requirements a 'national standard' that all courses must adhere to. This is despite the fact that the requirements set out by the Law are to be used only
as the criteria for measuring individual aspirants' suitability for teaching,
rather than for restricting universities' curriculum design. The new
system has caused administrative difficulties for many universities, which
needed to apply for re-authorisation of their teacher education courses,
in response to the increased requirements under the new system.

The Internship Program and its Background

Shoninsha Kenshū (literally 'training for all new teachers', but henceforth
called the 'Internship Program') was the most controversial item, not
only among the recent teacher education reforms, but also amongst all
education reforms initiated by the Ad-Hoc Council on Education.

Under the Internship Program, all new teachers are required by their
employer (i.e. local education board) to undergo 'on-site in-service
training' for one year on a probationary basis. Its pilot implementation
commenced in 1987, and the full implementation in 1989. Although the
Internship Program was considered part of a reorganisation of in-service
training programs to improve the quality of teachers, its content and
institutional arrangements have raised several questions. These relate to
the principles of the post-war teacher education and certification system,
as well as the social status and working conditions of teachers. We will
examine its contentious introduction below, by scrutinising the process
of its development.

A probationary program (*shiho seido*) is generally understood to be a
system whereby new teacher recruits obtain conditional and probationary employment for a certain period of time. Its purposes are to provide
new recruits with practical on-site training during the year, and to select
'suitable' recruits for permanent positions.[15]

The Ad-Hoc Council on Education was interested in improving the
quality of teachers from the outset, and proposed several concrete
measures to achieve this in its first report (June 1985): (1) an
improvement of teaching practicum in pre-service education; (2) a
requirement that prospective teachers apply for positions one year prior

to entering teaching; (3) an introduction of *shiho seido* (henceforth 'probationary program'), where new teachers have probationary employment for the first year in order to receive on-site in-service training; and (4) the establishment of an 'education jury system' (*kyōiku baishin-seido*), an advisory body to prefectural education boards. At this stage, the Ad-Hoc Council did not reveal the details of the probationary program. It later sent a group from the MOE to study the probationary programs for new teachers in West Germany and England, and had the group report its findings to the Council.

The subsequent discussions held by the Third Subcommittee of the Ad-Hoc Council on Education (which worked on measures to improve the quality of teachers) revealed that it held little confidence in individual schools and teachers. In proposing the education jury system, the subcommittee deplored the state of schooling and attributed it to 'lamentable teachers' who lack 'a sense of mission and a philosophy of teaching', and referred to union activities such as strikes, and teachers' refusal of appointed principals. The proposed education jury system was to examine 'problematic teachers' and to advise employers (prefectural education boards) accordingly. The concurrent proposal for the probationary program needs to be understood in this context.

In the course of discussions from 1985 to 1987, the Ad-Hoc Council came to adopt a more moderate approach. The second tentative proposal submitted by the Third Subcommittee of the Ad-Hoc Council (October 1985), for instance, renamed the probationary program (*shiho seido*) 'training for new teachers' (i.e. the Internship Program) (*Shoninsha Kenshū*), and an educational jury system (*kyōiku baishin-seido*) an advisory committee to examine suitability for teaching (*kyōshoku tekikaku shinsa-kai*). This proposal clarified the two functions of the Internship Program. The first was to cultivate practical teaching skills and a sense of 'mission' in new teachers through on-site in-service training. The second was to assess new teachers' suitability for teaching. The major aspects of the proposed Internship Program were as follows: (1) all teachers would receive one year of in-service training in the first year of employment; (2) experienced or retired teachers would provide guidance; (3) the first year would be conditional employment; (4) if a new teacher was deemed unsuitable for teaching by the advisory committee, the employer could prevent him or her from entering teaching.

Responses to the proposed measures came from teachers' organisations and political parties. The government and the LDP supported the Internship Program. *Nikkyōso*, quite predictably, denounced it as an old probationary system which aimed at containing the union movement, and claimed that the introduction of an advisory committee to assess suitability for teaching would force teachers to conform to a uniform model. The Japan Socialist Party condemned the Internship Program as an attempt to train nationalistic teachers for the state. The Japan Communist Party remarked that the Internship Program would enhance the administration's control of teachers, making teachers obedient to the government. The All Nippon Teachers' Federation (*Zen'nihon Kyōshokuin Renmei*) supported the program as a necessary measure to improve practical teaching skills and instil a sense of mission among new teachers.

The Ad-Hoc Council publicly started using the name *Shoninsha Kenshū* (in-service training for new teachers, Internship Program) in place of *shiho seido* (probationary program) in its second report (April 1986). The Internship Program was now presented with measured expressions. The Council explained that pre-service teacher education at universities would provide the 'basics' of practical teaching skills, while the Internship Program would enhance the 'basic' teaching skills and a sense of mission, both of which were meant to assist new teachers' smooth entry into the teaching profession. It proposed that the advisory committee to assess suitability for teaching be set up *only when* relevant education boards consider it necessary. This second report of the Ad-Hoc Council was later endorsed by the Teacher Education Council in 1987.

At stake was not simply the naming of these programs (*shiho* versus *shoninsha kenshū*), but whether or not the program is able to remove 'unsuitable' new recruits. If it is, the following questions arise. Who removes 'unsuitable' recruits? What are the criteria and the process of making such an assessment? Where is the on-site training conducted during the probationary period? What are the nature and status of the new recruit during the probationary period? How does a probationary recruit gain a permanent position?

The proposed Internship Program raised concerns regarding teachers' professional status and their working conditions as public service employees. One year of probationary employment, an assessment of new teachers during that period, and the possibility, based on the assessment, of new teachers being refused entry into teaching led to vulnerability of employment status. The one-year internship period may cause new recruits extra anxiety regarding employment status; and the constant supervision and observation may encourage their obedience to the school's administration and supervisors, neither of which are likely to assist in their professional development. Besides, these conditions are inconsistent with the Local Public Service Personnel Law, which stipulates that new employees undergo only a six-month probationary period before being granted a permanent position. It is not surprising that some interpreted the Internship Program as the MOE's attempt to remove 'unsuitable' new recruits, and to increase its control over teachers.

224 EDUCATION IN CONTEMPORARY JAPAN

The Realities of the Internship Program

The Internship Program was implemented first at primary schools in 1989, and then at middle schools and high schools in the following years. At present all primary schools, middle schools, high schools, and special education schools (i.e. schools for the blind, the deaf and the handicapped) conduct the Program. In 1994, 11,317 newly employed teachers participated in the Internship Program (4811 at primary schools, 3190 at middle schools, 2429 at high schools and 887 at special education schools). Almost all schools run the Program for one or two newly employed teachers. Fifty per cent of primary schools had one such teacher, while the equivalent figures for middle, high, and special education schools were 49.9, 47.7 and 45.8 per cent respectively. At primary schools the majority (96 per cent) of intern teachers were already assigned the tasks of homeroom teachers. The corresponding figures for middle schools, high schools and special education schools were 42.2, 8.1 and 49.4 per cent (Japan, Monbushō 1995b).

Concrete activities in the Internship Program generally include on-site guidance by supervising and other teachers at school (regarding class management, academic instruction, student guidance), as well as participation in lectures and workshops outside school, and observation of other schools, welfare institutions and private companies. Approximately 10 per cent of the interns attend a 10-day training course on a ship. These programs are said to have three aims: (1) to imbue practical teaching skills, (2) to cultivate a deep sense of mission as a teacher, and (3) to widen new teachers' knowledge and thinking.

Supervising teachers are assigned to individual interns. At primary schools, over 80 per cent of the supervisors were permanent teachers, and 36.7 per cent of them held a position of responsibility for academic instruction. At middle schools, permanent teachers who do not otherwise hold positions of responsibility took this role (35.3 per cent), while the equivalent figure for high schools was 55.9 per cent. Part-time teachers, the majority of whom have over five years of teaching experience, were employed, in small proportion, as supervisors (11.7 per cent at primary schools, 9.7 per cent at middle schools, 3.9 per cent at high schools, and 5.7 per cent at special education schools) (Japan, Monbushō 1995b).

We now turn to examine how this widely debated Internship Program was implemented at the school level, drawing on Shimahara and Sakai's ethnographic study of three primary schools in Tokyo in 1989 (Shimahara and Sakai 1992; 1995). The intern teachers' interactions with supervising teachers, and their participation in out-of-school activities, were carefully documented.

The supervision of interns at these schools was deliberately non-directive (in contrast to what the MOE envisaged); supervisors rarely scheduled formal conferences to discuss teaching, and offered advice in a casual and supportive manner when requested (Shimahara and Sakai 1992:153). To quote a supervisor's comment on his role:

> I do not intend to offer advice to beginning teachers unless they ask for it . . . It is my and the principal's view that they should not be overly monitored and advised. After all they have already received training at college and are now full-fledged teachers . . . There are two important things for interns. One is the environment consisting of experienced teachers from whom they have to learn; the other is their own interest in improving themselves. (Shimahara and Sakai 1992:153)

The supervisors' reluctance to assume active supervision of interns and a tutorial relationship with them is, Shimahara and Sakai (1992: 152–3) argue, due to the culture of teaching, which maintains that interns learn best through observing and interacting with other teachers at the same grade level (rather than through formal tutoring by supervisors). Supervision of beginning teachers also conflicted with the culture of teaching that holds the ethos of status equality among teachers. In Japanese schools, teachers, once employed, are all regarded as equal in status, and there is a tacit code among them that no teacher tells another teacher what to do to his or her face (Shimahara and Sakai 1995:155). When the internship was introduced at the individual school level, classroom teachers thus interpreted and implemented it through this culture of teaching, in such a way that it was meaningful to both them and the new teachers (Shimahara and Sakai 1992:159). As a result, the study contends, the program became ineffective, as measured according to the government's aim to strengthen its control of teachers (Shimahara and Sakai 1992:160).

The interns in Shimahara and Sakai's study participated in the internship programs offered by the education centre run by the board of education in each ward in Tokyo. Groups of instructional supervisors from the Superintendent's Office organised 20 lecture sessions (two to three hours each) at the centre, two retreats (three days and four days), and workshops on computers, word-processors and film projectors covering three days. On-site supervising teachers were not fully informed of the centre's program details. Teachers at the three schools knew little about the centre's program and were indifferent to it (Shimahara and Sakai 1992:158–9). Interns did not regard the lecture sessions as useful, since they were not closely related to everyday problems (Shimahara and Sakai 1995:140), which was also how they perceived pre-service education at university (Shimahara and Sakai 1995:145).

The implementation of the Internship Program to date has revealed further issues to be addressed. First, the Program has provided few components that assist new teachers with developing the practical capacity to manage specific classroom problems, for instance, excessive competition to enter certain educational institutions, authoritarian school management and bullying at school. Second, the content of pre-service education at university is not organically related to that of the internship year. Third, the process of gaining a permanent position after a year of conditional appointment remains problematic in principle. However, despite the fears of critics, to date no intern teacher has failed to secure a permanent position after one year of conditional appointment because of poor performance. (There has been only one case in which an intern could not obtain a permanent position after six months of conditional employment at a middle school in Kyoto. The teacher took the case to court, without success.) The implementation of the Internship Program shows that schools maintain considerable operational autonomy, regardless of the politicised discussion of the Program between the MOE and left critics at the national level.

An examination of the Internship Program invites us to consider in-service education as a whole, given that the Internship Program was expected to be an important component of the whole system of in-service education. The most basic requirements for in-service education and professional development are a workplace environment and working conditions that enable individual teachers to pursue these goals continuously. We suspect that under the present working conditions, few teachers have time for in-service education within the school during working hours. As we described in Chapter 5, teachers' daily schedules are overcrowded. Diverse in-service education would be preferable. Teachers are able to participate in the government-sponsored 'official' programs, and courses offered by universities and other professional organisations. Such diversity could be introduced into the Internship Program in future.

'Reform' Directions since the Mid-1990s

'Reforms' to the education system have continued and still remain under deliberation in the second half of the 1990s. At the time of writing, the directions of the changes (both recommended and implemented) over this period have been consistent with the basic philosophy of the Ad-Hoc Council, addressing social changes such as globalisation, the information-based society, technological developments, aging and the low birth rate.

What distinguishes the reforms in the late 1990s from those in the 1980s is that slow economic growth and structural changes in industry have gained greater prominence in educational reform deliberations than the 'pedagogical concerns' that drove many of the reforms in the previous decade. The new policy promoted leading-edge technological industries, as a result of structural changes under which many multi-national companies shifted their manufacturing sectors overseas, and of the recent opening up of Japanese domestic markets, which has caused a decline in the farming and small-business sectors. These trends required new types of human resources. Demand was expected to increase for suitably qualified people to fill management positions in big corporations, and for skilled and unskilled workers to occupy temporary positions, but no longer for the high-quality, well-educated, middle-level company employees that universities had hitherto produced. The business sector thus considered that the existing education system (which offers 'equal' and uniform education) needed to be liberalised (i.e. be subject to fewer regulations) and offer more choices to individuals (i.e. be more subject to market forces).

We will explore the directions in education in the late 1990s by examining reports issued by the MOE's four permanent councils over this period: the Central Education Council (1997), the Teacher Education Council (1997), the Curriculum Council (1997), and the University Council (1996).

The Central Education Council

In April 1995 the government asked the Central Education Council to inquire into 'education for the 21st century'. The government recognised that educational renewal was needed in response to major changes affecting society, while identifying specific educational problems (e.g. excessive competition, bullying and school refusal). The Council issued two reports.[16]

The first report referred extensively to 'the realities of children's daily lives' which, it acknowledged, included a variety of practical problems. Children were described as being too busy, lacking the social skills to relate to other people, late in gaining independence, facing excessive competition for entrance examinations, and as experiencing bullying and school refusal. The Council attributed these problems to 'Japanese people's inclination to conformity', 'changes in families and communities' and 'a decline of the local community's moral guidance'. It then urged that families and local communities contribute more to children's education, so that schools can focus on the 'basics' and become 'slimmer' in their functions, and so that children can have more time to themselves. The report's attribution of the contemporary problems of education to individual players (i.e. schools, families and local communities) disguises the role of the national policies and structural causes that would have played a part. It fails to acknowledge that children live in a society in which companies require employees to work long hours, where entry into a handful of universities is the prerequisite for elite careers, and where the aging of the population causes many people to be anxious about their circumstances in their old age.

The second report's proposal for the introduction of six-year secondary schools and the approval of grade skipping heralded a move towards a multi-track school system. Six-year secondary schools will provide students with specialised subjects (e.g. arts, sports) from grade seven, and can exercise discretion in offering what they consider to be appropriate subjects in a distinctive curriculum. The multi-track system will thus provide effective education for those who excel. In fact, private schools had, to date, offered middle schools and high schools on the same campus, providing six years of continuous education. Many of them are elite schools, like Nada Middle School and Nada High School (discussed in Chapter 3), which are renowned for sending large numbers of students to a handful of elite universities. We suspect that six-year high schools are likely to be elite schools for arts and sports in the short term, and for academic elites in the long term.

The Council's proposal to diversify the selection criteria and procedures may contribute to alleviating competition, but would not be sufficient. Now that high-school education is almost akin to compulsory education (over 97 per cent of 16-year-olds proceed to high schools), the priority direction in secondary education reform should have been to enable every student who desires it to be admitted to high school without undergoing the selection process.

The Teacher Education Council

While major changes were implemented in teacher education in the late 1980s, the number of newly appointed teachers decreased sharply. This was because the low birth rate started to impact on school enrolments but class sizes did not reduce correspondingly. In 1997 the enrolment in teacher training courses was 14,500, a sharp drop from the peak enrolment of 20,100. Furthermore, in 1997 the cabinet proposed to cut 5000 places for courses in teacher training over the following three-year period, as part of the national financial reforms. In response, national universities started reorganising their courses for teacher training.

The Teacher Education Council's 1997 report outlined its views on the teaching profession in the coming era, setting out four specific capacities required of teachers: (1) to cultivate 'the ability to survive' in a changing society, (2) to act from a global perspective, (3) to manage changes as an adult member of society, and (4) to conduct their professional duties as teachers. The Council also called for greater diversity of teachers within individual schools. The Council's report (July 1997) presented the following recommendations.

1 The existing emphasis on teaching subjects in the curriculum for middle- and high-school teachers should be replaced by an emphasis on professional subjects. The proportion of professional subjects in the total curriculum should be equivalent to that for prospective primary teachers.

2 The curriculum should become more flexible. Besides the existing two categories of subjects (i.e. professional subjects and teaching subjects), universities should be allowed to offer a third category of optional subjects. This will encourage individuals to develop their specialities.

3 The minimum required length of teaching practice for middle-school teachers should be extended to five weeks (equal to that for primary teachers).

4 'Educational consultation' (*kyōiku sōdan*) (including counselling) should be consolidated, and its minimum required standard should be upgraded.

5 Universities should introduce a new subject aimed at improving the teaching of environmental issues.

The renewed emphasis on professional subjects (in comparison to teaching subjects) in the teacher education curriculum raised two concerns among critics.[17] One is the view that it undermines the comprehensive and inclusive nature of teacher education (including general cultivation of oneself) that students should receive throughout the four years of university education. The second is that resorting to professional subjects to address 'problems' (e.g. school refusal, bullying) is simplistic and short-sighted, and distracts attention from the 'real' and complex causes behind these problems.

A major change was instituted on 11 June 1997, shortly before the Council's report appeared. Prospective primary- and middle-school teachers will be required to undergo at least seven days' experience at schools for the handicapped or at a social welfare institution (excluding nursery schools) as of April 1998. Universities that offer primary- and middle-school teacher training, as well as the schools for the disabled and the welfare institutions that will receive these student teachers, are in the process of discussing the implications of this initiative for them.

The Curriculum Council

The Curriculum Council's interim report (November 1997) proposed the directions for the new curriculum under the five-days-a-week schooling that is to be instituted in 2003. Currently students attend school on every other Saturday. The Council recommended that students be allowed more time to themselves (*yutori*), that they be able to develop independent learning and thinking, as well as the basics, in a relaxed environment; and that individual schools be granted more discretion to develop their own curricula.

The report proposed a reduction of class hours by two hours weekly (70 hours yearly), and the introduction of cross-subject learning (*sōgō gakushū*) at primary, middle and high schools. It also proposed that foreign languages and a new subject, information studies, be made compulsory at middle schools. As a result, middle-school students will spend more hours in elective subjects, and high-school students will face fewer hours on required subjects. A re-examination of history subjects (e.g. the introduction of the history of science and mathematics) was also suggested. The Council's final report is due in autumn 1998.

The University Council

The University Council proposed a system of contract appointment in its 1996 report, based on the rationale that it would encourage academics to be mobile and would consequently revitalise education and research at universities. The proposed system would not be compulsory: individual universities would decide whether or not they would introduce it. The relevant legislation would provide the guiding principles, but the actual implementation was to be left to the individual universities.

Behind this move lay a combination of stakes held by various interest groups. The government and the MOE had long stated that 'the closed nature of personnel appointments at universities is a cause for the stagnation of research activities' (e.g. the third report of the Ad-Hoc Council on Education 1987). Employer organisations had for some time suggested 'introducing competitive principles in order to overcome the closed and conservative nature of universities' (e.g. Nihon Keieisha Dantai Renmei 1995a, 1995b). Contract employment for academics was seen as promoting the flow of academics between universities and government research institutes, and private companies (and their research institutions). The new system was also expected, consequently, to allow private companies to employ the researchers that they needed.

The Council's proposal faced expressions of concern and criticism from universities and academic staff members. Their main contentions are listed below.

1 Legislating for the contract appointment system will end tenure for academics, which had been and continues to be essential to university autonomy and freedom; and will pave the way to external interference in educational and research activities. It will fundamentally change the principles laid out in the relevant legislation. Neither the National Personnel Authority Rules (*Jinjiin Kisoku*) nor the Law of Special Regulations concerning Educational Public Service Personnel (*Kyōiku Kōmuin Tokurei-hō*, LSREPSP) allows contract employment, except in the case of a small number of management positions at universities.

2 Contract appointment for all academic positions (including professors) is an exception to overseas practice. In many fields of studies, finding a position in the private sector is difficult. Academic productivity may not rise as a result of contract appointments, since staff members are likely to focus on short-term projects that can demonstrate their productivity when applying for subsequent positions.

3 Given that the MOE holds the power to approve the establishment of faculties and to distribute budget to universities, universities are likely to be forced to implement this so-called 'optional' contract appointment system to ensure their survival. It is feared that universities' independence and autonomy will thus be compromised.

Despite opposition, the government passed a bill enshrining these proposals in the Diet in June 1997. The contract appointment system can apply to academic staff members at all universities (government and private) in the following cases: (1) 'positions in leading-edge science, or interdisciplinary fields' and 'in the case of education and research organisations which require diverse staff members'; (2) assistant positions (*joshu*); and (3) 'teaching and research positions for a specified project'.

The president of the Japan Society of the Sciences announced informally that the contract appointment system may result in 'undesirable outcomes, such as restrictions of the universities' freedom to conduct research, and lowered social status for academic staff members'. He requested the MOE to honour and respect any decisions made by any of the universities not to implement contract appointments. A nationwide body formed to oppose the bill also announced a formal protest at the way in which the bill was pushed through the Diet without due discussion.

The MOE ordinance regarding the bill's implementation was issued in August 1997. While many universities resisted such changes, a few institutions (both national and private) have decided to introduce contract appointments. Tertiary education and research have thus been gradually integrated into a set of comprehensive national policies covering education, science, and labour and employment for the 21st century.

Summary

This chapter began with an examination of the so-called 'pathological phenomena' in contemporary Japanese schooling, namely, bullying, school refusal and corporal punishment. We tried to picture these phenomena both in terms of nationwide trends and of individual experiences. They not only alarmed the public, who saw that something needed to be done about the current education system, but also provided a convenient justification for the government to advocate 'educational reforms'.

In the 1980s and 1990s the institutions of education underwent significant changes. These changes constituted an important part of large-scale administrative reform, and were explicitly related to the national policies on labour and employment, and science and technology. Reforms were initiated by the supra-cabinet advisory body (the Ad-Hoc Council on Education) that Prime Minister Nakasone himself appointed, in order to conduct what he called 'the total settlement of the post-war political accounts'.

While Nakasone's visions for 'educational reforms' were reflected in the reports, the changes that subsequently took place were less than what he had hoped to achieve. Despite numerous recommendations made by the MOE's advisory councils over this period, the series of effected changes were not 'reforms' (*kaikaku*) so much as 'modifications within the existing frameworks'. Nor did the changes address the contradictions and pathological phenomena to the extent that the public hoped for. This is in part because some of the recommendations were the kind of general and abstract statements that anybody would accept, but which were difficult to translate into concrete actions (e.g. 'nurture the ability to pursue a quality lifestyle', 'appreciation of individuality'). In these cases, the content of recommendations was not as important as the fact that recommendations resulted from deliberations, and demonstrated that the government was attempting to improve the state of education.

There are four major trends in these changes. They are: a wider range of choice for parents and students, a call for a renewed emphasis on the inculcation of the traditions and 'Japanese ethnic identity', the privatisation of education, and the promotion of the needs of business and industry. Other trends of note included greater accountability at the tertiary education level, and the simultaneous devolution and centralisation of the educational administration. Many of these trends have been observed in educational 'reforms' in English-speaking societies over the same period (e.g. the UK, USA and Canada).

First, a series of changes introduced a wider range of choices for parents and students. Indeed, making the system of education more flexible and diverse was the overtly advocated philosophy of the 'reforms' in the 1980s and 1990s. Flexibility and diversification were seen in various implementations. For example, the range of choices was expanded for types of schools (e.g. module-based schools, six-year secondary schools, new international schools), for courses (e.g. a hybrid of vocational and academic courses called *sōgōgakka*, and new vocational courses), and for subjects at high-school level. A larger range of options were also introduced to the curricula at the middle-school level, and undergraduate and postgraduate levels, as well as to high-school and university admission procedures. Furthermore, able students now have options to skip some grades, and to complete evening and correspondence high-school courses in a shorter length of time than before. In expanding the range of available options in this way, the system was expected to address individual differences more effectively, and to better meet the rapidly changing needs of the society in response to 'globalisation' and the 'information-economy'.

The move towards a multi-track system of schooling can be interpreted as a challenge to existing education, which had been underpinned by 'formal equality' and children's rights (in relation to human development). This is in part because the addressing of individual differences was directed principally to high achievers or students with 'special talents', with little reference made to children with other special needs (e.g. disability, minority status). The provision of education 'appropriate' to individual needs, therefore, was seen to serve, almost exclusively, those who excel in what is arbitrarily defined as 'useful talent', and consequently the business and industrial circles, a point that we take up below.

Second, Nakasone's initial pledge to restore traditional morality and what he calls 'Japanese ethnic culture and identity' was evident in a series of changes. Moral education was to be conducted across the curriculum in addition to existing as a specific subject. The use of what are commonly regarded as the national flag and anthem at schools is now official. Some contents in the curriculum display neonationalist inclinations. The emphasis on the Japanese national identity and traditional culture was raised because the global movement of people has brought the Japanese into more frequent contact with the outside world. The assumed construct of the Japanese national identity and traditional culture, which was presented as comprising primordial features of the ethnic Japanese, remains problematic. Such a construct is neither easily accepted by those who do not share that view, nor by those reminded of the ethnocentric ideology about Japanese ethnicity that was propagated during the Second World War.

Third, the needs and values of business and industry were promoted. The proposed 'intelligent schools' were to respond to the priorities of the information industries. The new curriculum promoted an efficient training of elites by transferring some of the curriculum to lower grades and thus providing accelerated learning for able students. Ability-based teaching and grade skipping will allow those who excel to extend themselves more effectively. The reorganisation of tertiary education also encourages a stronger link between universities and industries.

Fourth, the private sector's participation in the running of education was promoted. The private sector already plays an important role in tertiary education and lifelong learning. It was considered that schools had been taking up too many roles, some of which are better left in the hands of families, local communities and private organisations, so that schools can concentrate on fundamental educational goals (i.e. the basics).

The covert running theme of these changes was to enhance the central government's stake in education. This was done while simultaneously devolving more responsibility and discretion to individual institutions in the name of flexibility and diversity. For example, individual schools and local education boards were granted more discretion regarding the organisation of curricula (e.g. the early introduction of required Chinese characters, grade skipping, individual schools' creation of curricula to suit their particular missions), while neonationalist content was emphasised (including displaying the national flag and singing of the national anthem). In teacher education, universities were, again, granted more independence in organising the curriculum, and alternative paths to teaching were introduced; but the Internship Program monitors first-year teachers. The new requirements for teacher certification are likely to restrict the scope of individual institutions to design their own curricula. Many of the changes introduced in the 1980s and 1990s were thus double-edged in their effects.

Further Reading

Amano, Ikuo (1989). The dilemma of Japanese education today. In Shields, James (ed.), *Japanese Schooling* (pp. 111–23). University Park: Pennsylvania State University Press.

Lincicome, Mark (1993). Focus on internationalization of Japanese education: Nationalism, internationalization and the dilemma of educational reform in Japan. *Comparative Education Review*, 37(2), 123–52.

Schoolland, Ken (1990). *Shogun's Ghost: The dark side of Japanese education*. New York: Bergin & Garvey.

Schoppa, Leonard J. (1991). *Education Reform in Japan: A case of immobilist politics*. London: Routledge.

Notes

1 The data quoted here derive from the MOE's survey to prefectural education boards. Its results were made available in the report *95-nendo Seitoshidō jō no Shomondai no Genjō to Monbushō no Sesaku* (*Mondai Kōdō Hakusho*) (Japan, Monbushō 1996). Kanekura (1996) provides a summary of the section on bullying in the report.

2 The study was based on questionnaires sent to 9400 students, their homeroom teachers (557) and their parents (9420) (*Asahi Shinbun* 23 and 27 May 1996).

3 Okano's ethnography revealed that one school changed the official records of individual students' absent days and academic marks in order to give them better employment opportunities; and that at another school, staff members held a heated debate as to whether or not the school would follow that practice (Okano 1993).

4 Ichimaru et al. (1994) studied the post-school lives of 86 students who received counselling for school refusal over the period 1983–90.

5 The study covered 68 primary students and 225 middle-school students, 46 per cent of whom had by then returned to school, 15 per cent of whom attended other institutions and 35 per cent of whom still remained at home at the time of the research. Among the studied cases were: so-called school phobia accompanied by anxiety and emotional disorder (26.2 per cent), the 'apathy' type (21.4 per cent), simple dislike of school (9.3 per cent), the delinquent type (6.2 per cent), purposeful refusal (2.4 per cent), various combinations of the above categories (25.2 per cent), and others (9.3 per cent) (Japan, Monbushō, Shotō Chūtō Kyōiku-kyoku Chūgakkō-ka 1994:64).

6 The source of the data is the report cited in note 1. Kanekura (1997) provides a summary of the section on corporal punishment in the report. Data for the number of middle-school students and teachers derive from an MOE survey (Japan, Monbushō 1995a:93, 108).

7 Making a student stand still in silence at the back of the classroom or outside the classroom is a form of punishment frequently used in Japanese primary, middle and high schools. Students subjected to this form of punishment are expected to calm down, reflect on what they did to receive the punishment, and discuss their reflections with their teachers or with the class later on.

8 Imabashi (1995a:43–5) illustrated the case of what he considers to be a 'soft' prefecture in dealing with corporal punishment. The prefecture had 26 cases of reported incidents of corporal punishment, all of which resulted in 'instruction' to the teachers concerned. Fifteen cases (58 per cent) involved striking students in the face, six cases striking the head. Others featured manhandling, striking with a paper guillotine and kicking. The injuries to the

students included damaged eardrums, hearing disorders, broken teeth and a broken nose. Most cases occurred when other students were present (Imabashi 1995a:44–5). One wonders if such punishment was conducted as a lesson to other students. 'Tougher' local governments take quite a different stance. For example, the Tokyo metropolitan government gave official punishment to 12 teachers (decreased salary to three teachers, 'warning' to nine) and 'instruction' to four others; and 11 principals whose teachers received 'official punishment' themselves received 'instruction' (Imabashi 1995a:46).

9 There are 15 permanent advisory councils in the MOE as of July 1997. They are: the Central Education Council, the Council on Establishment of Higher Education Institutions, the Council on Science and Industrial Education, the Curriculum Council, the University Council, the Textbook Authorisation Council, the Teacher Education Council, the Science Council, the Survey Council, the Lifelong Learning Council, the Physical Education Council, the Council on Religious Organisations, the Council on Preservation of Cultural Heritage, the Council on the National Language, and the Council on Copyright. The MOE requests councils to submit reports of inquiries to the Minister of Education. Members of councils are appointed by the Minister of Education, normally for each inquiry. The Ad-Hoc Council on Education (of 1984), appointed by the Prime Minister as a supra-cabinet body, was located within the Prime Minister's Office. Besides the 1984 Ad-Hoc Council, there has been only one other education-related council of this kind in the post-war era, namely the Education Reform Council, which was set up immediately after the Second World War.

10 Many journals produced special issues featuring articles on these reports, for example, *Jurisuto* no. 825 1984; *Asahi Journal* 28(19) 1986; *Kyōiku Hyōron* November 1986; *Rōdōhōritsu Junpō* no. 1189 1988; and *Minade Kyōikukaikaku O* 4 1986. Monographs on the topics were numerous (e.g. Ōta and Horio 1985; Ōtsuki and Hamabayashi 1984; Fukayama et al (eds), 1985; Amano 1985; Mikami 1986; Tsuchiya 1989). Major daily newspapers (*Asahi Shinbun*, *Yomiuri Shinbun* and *Mainichi Shinbun*) gave wide coverage to these reports as well.

11 The six bills were:
   (1) A revision to the Law of Special Regulations concerning Educational Public Service Personnel, which would introduce the Internship Program for novice teachers (became effective on 31 May 1988).
   (2) A revision to the Law Establishing National Educational Institutions, which would establish a new type of graduate school, and reorganise the University Admission Centre (became effective on 25 May 1988).
   (3) A revision to the Educational Personnel Certification Law, which would introduce finer categories of teaching certificates and increase the requirements for these certificates (became effective on 28 December 1988).
   (4) A revision to the School Education Law, which would shorten the minimum required length for high-school evening and correspondence courses (became effective on 15 November 1988).
   (5) A revision to the Local Education Administration Law, which would allocate a permanent superintendent of education (*kyōiku-chō*) to cities, towns and villages (abandoned in the Diet).
   (6) A proposal to establish a body to implement the Ad-Hoc Council's recommendations (abandoned in the Diet).

12 Over the period 1989–96, 757 students entered a Masters course after skipping the fourth year of an undergraduate course. In 1993–94, 84 students took one year to complete an MA course; and 274 students took less than five years to complete a Doctoral course (*Asahi Shinbun* 24 May 1997).

13 Immediately after the war, the singing of *Kimigayo* in unison was discontinued. The 1958 revision of the Course of Study reintroduced it. In 1974 the then Prime Minister, Kakuei Tanaka, failed in his attempt to legalise the status of the flag and the song in the Diet. It was in 1977 that the MOE officially accorded the status of the national flag and anthem to them in the revised Course of Study.

14 A first-grade certificate is granted to four-year university graduates, while a second-grade certificate applies to two-year junior college graduates. The latter teachers are required to upgrade their qualifications within the first 15 years of their service.

15 To date, probationary programs have been proposed several times in varying forms. For example, after the Second World War the *shiho* was first proposed by the Education Reform Council (*Kyōiku Sasshin Iinkai*) in 1947. It differentiated those who had completed a teacher education course from those who had not, and required the latter to teach on a probationary basis for six months after completing relevant course work. The next proposal came from the Central Education Council in 1958. It proposed that graduates from non-teacher education universities or faculties be provided with a conditional teacher certificate and receive in-service training while employed on a probationary basis for a certain period of time. The 1962 Teacher Education Council proposed that all those who have completed the requirements for teaching certificates be provided with conditional teaching certificates. The conditional teaching certificate was to be valid for three years, during which time the new recruits were to receive on-site training. The assessment of the new recruits was to be reflected in their subsequent salaries and qualifications following the probationary period. The 1971 Central Education Council report supported the above program, while the subsequent 1972 Teacher Education Council report emphasised the 'training' aspect of the probationary program without specific reference to the new recruits' probationary status and working conditions. Since then, probationary programs have been discussed as one of the major initiatives to improve the quality of teachers. The most recent Teacher Education Council proposal to introduce the Internship Program (1987) was a combination of the 1972 proposal mentioned above, and the Ad-Hoc Council's second report (1986).

16 Below are the Central Education Council's major recommendations.
First Report (July 1996)
   (1) Education should aim at nurturing the problem-solving and independent learning abilities required to live in an unpredictable and changing society.
   (2) Schools should provide a flexible curriculum (including a carefully selected core curriculum), and personal development through moral education. They should also promote international understanding, integrated study and projects, and experience-based learning.
   (3) Community-based education should encourage learning through daily experience; by, for example, promoting voluntary services and youth-group activities. Parents and people in the local community should participate in the running of the school.

(4) Schools should concentrate on a more restricted range of tasks (i.e. developing the foundations for scientific learning and national identity) and leave other tasks of education to families and the local community. The full implementation of five-days-a-week schooling should be achieved in order to provide children with more time to themselves.

(5) As a response to globalisation and the information-based society, schools need to be promoting international understanding, improving foreign language teaching (with more emphasis on communicative competence), introducing foreign language teaching at primary schools, using the Internet, providing diverse opportunities to study science, and consolidating environmental education.

Second Report (May 1997)

(1) Education should aim at nurturing the ability to pursue a quality lifestyle. The prior emphasis on uniformity and formal equality should be replaced by the appreciation of individual differences.

(2) Admission procedures to universities, and the assessment criteria for admission, should be diversified. Admission procedures to high schools should follow suit, by allowing more than one chance for examinations, and by resorting to non-examination methods such as essays, interviews and prior volunteer activities for the assessment.

(3) Six-year secondary schools should be introduced. Such schooling will focus on one of the following: experience-based learning, community-based learning, learning for globalisation and the information-based society, environmental learning, and traditional culture.

(4) Those who excel in mathematics and physics should be allowed to enter universities one year early by skipping the last year of high schooling. (In 1998 one national university is to adopt this method.)

(5) Schools at all levels should foster participation in caring for the elderly, and in other welfare and voluntary activities.

17 See, for example, Tsuchiya (1997) and Okamoto (1997). Discussion on the report was also found in special issues of two professional journals: *Kyōshoku Kenshū* October 1997 ('Tokushū: Korekarano kyōin ni motomerareru shishitsu nōryoku – Kyōyōshin dai-ichiji tōshin no pointo'); and *Kyōiku* May 1998 ('Tokushū: Kyōin yōsei no kiki').

CHAPTER 7

Conclusion

Our focus in this book has been the diversity in the major players' (students and teachers) experiences of schooling in Japan, and in the roles that schooling plays for the society and for individuals in various social locations. We have discussed such diversities in relation to both social inequality and the level of autonomy that players maintain in contemporary Japanese society. In this process we have illuminated some of the downsides of Japanese schooling, and how and why Japanese people are critical of their own educational practices.

We began this book with a set of questions. How do major players (students and teachers) experience, and make sense of, schooling? What roles has modern schooling played for Japanese society at large, and for individuals in diverse social locations? Do they all equally receive the fruits of an education system highly praised by outsiders? If not, are there any patterns in the variations of experiences and benefits gained from schooling? To what extent have students, teachers and social groups maintained autonomy to influence the shaping of schooling practice? Where has the state stood in these dynamic processes? In what ways have teachers, parents and institutions struggled to exert influence in shaping school practice, both at the policy-making level and at the level of the school?

As we discussed in Chapter 2, the system of post-war schooling has brought, and continues to bring, fruits aplenty to the collective welfare of the society as a whole. Schools have contributed to industrial pro-ductivity, economic prosperity and relative social stability, although exactly to what extent remains open to debate. Many people have been able to experience at first hand the collective improvement of the society since the 1960s. Many received a more extensive education than their parents, and were able to capitalise on this in the workforce, enabled by rapidly expanding employment opportunities. People could feel an improvement in their lifestyles, and, for example, have access to material possessions that they never had thought possible thirty years ago. The fact that many people could 'feel' an improvement in the kind of education that they received, and enjoyed the subsequent benefit to their lives, assisted in promoting the myth that the system of education was functioning as effectively as planned.

But this is not the whole story. The education system has brought other outcomes as well. Below we shall delineate 'other outcomes' in reference to the four roles of modern schooling, and in the light of an alternative interpretation, which we set out in Chapter 1. First, schools have transmitted knowledge and skills required for membership of the Japanese adult society and of the workforce (e.g. basic literacy and numeracy). Japanese schools are said to have been successful in equipping the vast majority of children with such skills, although not as successful in producing top scientists. The knowledge transmission typical of Japanese schools, however, has resulted in an emphasis on particular learning patterns, which some observers see as a discouragement to creative, critical and spontaneous thinking. There have also been claims that the amount of knowledge to be covered is excessive. In addition some of the knowledge selected for transmission remains controversial. The school curriculum is determined by the MOE, which issues the Course of Study guidelines and authorises school textbooks. That the MOE can designate selected knowledge as 'official' is problematic, and the debate on textbook authorisation continued in court cases until recently.

Second, schools have socialised and acculturated children so that they can effectively function in the adult society. Schools are said to have instilled 'appropriate' social values, and helped in developing 'appropriate' identities in children, through overt lesson content and daily school routines. The daily routines of Japanese schools include small-group activities, delegation of adult responsibilities to students, and informal interaction among students and teachers, all of which encourage a certain set of behaviours and orientations (e.g. cooperation, empathy, deferred gratification, perseverance) and discourage others (e.g. overt independence). Nonetheless, some claim, the process of socialisation has been overtly conformist, in that those who do not conform are penalised, to the detriment of the healthy development of young people. Others suggest that bullying and school refusal derive, at least partly, from the conformist nature of the schooling processes. Besides, what constitute 'appropriate' social values and 'appropriate' identities remain arbitrary constructions. The MOE's attempts to officially articulate them through moral education were not only greeted coldly by the public, but were also interpreted by sceptics as a conspiracy to control the people.

Third, schools have sorted out children as they move up the school ladder, based on assessment of their performance in what schools deem relevant areas; and have allocated youth for 'suitable' positions in the society. Students' final destinations in the adult society, in particular those in the upper echelon of the social hierarchy, are strongly influenced by the reputations of the universities they attend. However, concerns are now expressed with two aspects of the selection process. One is the assumed merit-based selection (which is narrowly defined as a selection based purely on one's academic performance) and its fairness. There is growing evidence to suggest that those who achieve the top academic results come from families with resources, and that they need to actively utilise the family resources in order to reach such positions. The principle of equal opportunities for all is thus considered to be threatened. The other area of concern is the assumed neutral nature of 'merit', in that what constitutes 'merit' in the selection process is arbitrarily defined by the system of education.

Fourth, the practices of education have, to a large degree, legitimated what schools teach and do. The curriculum, screened by the MOE, was presented as being neutral and 'true'. The system of schooling has projected itself as providing equal opportunities and conducting a merit-based selection of students, and has claimed that the selection was therefore fair. In this way, not only have schools transmitted useful knowledge and skills to students, socialised them to fit adult Japanese society, identified their talents for 'appropriate' roles in the workforce; they have also made the students learn to accept their places in the social hierarchy.

The myth that the present system of schooling functions properly for all children faces challenges from two directions. One comes from the recent changes in the society, which were in part brought about by the expansion of education. In the early 1990s, when retention rates to tertiary educational institutions have reached record levels, young people no longer expect their offspring to receive more education than themselves, nor to experience the kind of inter-generational rise in the quality of education that exists between themselves and their parents. Improvement in material lifestyles is unlikely to be as dramatic in the future as in the past 40 years. Negative effects of affluence started to gain prominence in schools and demand firm policy responses; these included bullying, school refusal and other forms of maladjustment to school. A section of minority youth, in particular those who had received higher education, began to assert their rights, called for social justice and challenged the society that had restricted their opportunities, by utilising the education that they had received. Some women who were graduates of four-year universities followed suit, voicing their concerns and demands. Teachers have long challenged the myth of a successful system of education for all, based on their first-hand experiences of schooling, while intellectuals from the left did so from humanitarian concerns.

The other challenge comes from the revelation that schooling is not consumed and utilised equally by everyone for his or her benefit. The benefits that people obtain from schooling vary. In fact there are patterns of variation in the ways in which people in different social locations capitalise on the given schooling, just as there are patterns in the ways that the collective good (which the education system has presumably contributed to) has been enjoyed by people in divergent social locations. We have demonstrated this through an examination of case studies of microlevel schooling processes in Chapters 3 and 4.

This is despite the fact that equality has been one of the major concerns in post-war education, both at the policy level (at least initially) and at the school level. The schooling provided by government primary schools and middle schools throughout the nation has insisted on formal equality, providing the same curriculum across the nation and resisting any form of ability-based classes. Within a school, activities of small groups (consisting of heterogeneous students) are encouraged, while overt competition is discouraged. Teachers in general uphold as their ideals an egalitarian pedagogical view, a humanitarian belief in social justice in education, and an inclusive approach to teaching. Recall Ms Niwa's attempts to involve all students in writing about their immediate lives, and Mr Nakamoto's inclusive methods of teaching mathematics to low-achieving high-school girls, both of which have been praised by teachers as demonstrating the excellent practical capacities of teachers.

The ways in which children react to the schooling they receive differs as early as when they enter primary school. In observing teachers' actions and interactions with students (him or herself included), a child soon learns what qualities and actions are recognised and rewarded by the school; and some children feel more comfortable than others with the culture of school and what the school expects of them. How and why does this happen in the seemingly uniform process of schooling in Japan?

To start with, children are not equally predisposed to 'learn' the school culture and knowledge, in terms of material, social and cultural resources. Children from certain family and regional backgrounds (often the urban middle class) possess resources that are desirable or even necessary for taking advantage of what the school offers. They are willing and able to learn, and to make effective use of educational opportunities. Children without such resources find themselves disadvantaged. As we illustrated in Chapter 3, children of the poor were unable to take up what the school offered them (the knowledge, qualifications and cultural mores) in the same way as other children, because family circumstances did not provide material (e.g. stable accommodation and food), social (e.g. regular interaction with relatives and neighbours who encourage the attainment of education) and cultural resources (e.g. parents offering sufficient time and attention to children, books in the home) that were helpful for appropriating them. This was often the case despite the efforts of conscientious teachers and social workers, the result being fewer children of the poor proceeding to post-compulsory education. Since these children have few immediate adult role models who have built a career on formal schooling, and since parents are typically uninformed, they did not see the personal benefits of schooling in advancing their social positions, and dropped out of school without due consideration of the consequences. The odds are stacked against these children, although this does not mean that none of them can succeed in the system. In contrast, students at Nada High School were endowed with all they need to compete for entry to the handful of elite universities.

More significant are the divergent meaning and value that people in different social groups attach to schooling. Such differences lead members of some social groups to make decisions regarding their schooling (levels and kinds) by considering factors other than their academic achievement (which is believed to be the determinant for educational decision making).

These differences are, first, due to the fact that the assumed link between schooling and employment or social status in the adult society is not the same for everyone. As we showed in Chapters 3 and 4, girls, third-generation Koreans, the disabled and *buraku* people, for instance, face a real 'job ceiling' and a real 'promotion ceiling'; and are fully aware that they cannot convert their educational qualifications into employment relevant to their qualifications in the same ways that others can. Such interpretations affect a series of decisions that they and their families consciously make in relation to education. Rural youth from farming families are aware that good performance at agricultural high school will not enhance the prosperity of the family farms that they may take over, due to the declining nature of the industry. Second, students' direct experience of schooling influences how they perceive the value and meaning of schooling. Teenage correspondence school students, for instance, found that mainstream schooling did not cater for their distinctive needs (e.g. disability, chronic illness). For third-generation Korean students, mainstream schooling not only undervalued their ethnic culture, but also instilled the dominant (negative) view of Koreans in general. Newcomer children and parents were eager to benefit from mainstream schooling, which they subsequently found does not fully accommodate non-Japanese students' needs. Girls face two contradictory messages from school. They are told to excel academically, and then are informed of the limited employment opportunities to which they can convert their academic excellence, as well as the sex-specific roles expected in families. Third, different meanings and values of schooling also derive from distinctive subcultures that different social groups have developed through their members' shared material experiences (e.g. the poor) and traditional values (e.g. girls and ethnic groups). The Hana *buraku* community, for instance, maintained a male macho subculture based on the physical nature of work. The school did not value what Hana children brought from their community to the school (such as non-standard language usage and glorification of physical strength). The culture of 'indifference' to mainstream schooling was observable among high-school dropouts, youths at agricultural high schools, children from chronically poor families, and some *buraku* children.

We suggested that these children understood the dominant view of education and its instrumental value in adult life *at an abstract level* ('I know that education is important for a job'), rather than fiercely rejecting it. They were not, however, prepared or able to act on the dominant view *at a personal level*. They maintain an indifference to it, by being out of the game (of pursuing education for the betterment of their adult lives), or they are unaware of *concrete* measures they might employ to act on the dominant view. Perhaps they are excluded from the game, or opt out of it, due to their lack of necessary resources; and exclusion from the game forces them to develop kinds of relationships with the school that are different from those of students actively participating in the game. What these cases do suggest is that the dominant view of schooling and its benefits has not been universally accepted. The presence of such indifference amongst some youths is not likely to challenge the dominant achievement ideology, however, as long as the dominant group maintains the power to define winners and losers by its own criteria.

Covert differentiation, which has been occurring throughout primary- and middle-school years, emerges in a concrete form at the high-school entry point. In Chapter 3 we presented a typology of high schools (a handful of elite academic high schools, non-elite academic high schools, vocational high schools, evening high schools, correspondence high schools, and special education institutions). The first four types are ranked in descending order in the school hierarchy; different types of schools hold distinctive missions and school cultures, and prepare their students for different post-school destinations. We suggested that 'non-elite academic high schools' accommodate the largest proportion of the age group and vary considerably from school to school. A few students choose to terminate their education at this point and enter the workforce, which, Japanese educationalists insist, must be prevented through active intervention, since it often results in inter-generational reproduction of poverty via insecure employment.

The diverse experiences of schooling by children in varying social locations thus often results in unequal benefits to them. This is not something that teachers wish for. Neither the state nor the schools as institutions have actively conspired to produce such outcomes. Rather, these outcomes are some of the consequences of their attempts to pursue the kind of education that they believe to be desirable for the society and for individuals. The emphasis of the national policies has often been on the societal level, while teachers' concerns have tended to rest with individual students' development.

Throughout the book, and particularly in Chapter 5, we have emphasised the relatively large degree of autonomy that teachers have maintained. Japanese teachers are not agents of the MOE, although they undergo relatively uniform teacher training (approved by the MOE) and are screened through the examinations held by the education boards that employ them. Teachers also face various restrictions (e.g. on political activities and labour rights) imposed by the legislation regarding public education employees. The relative autonomy that teachers have maintained is manifested in the ways in which teachers subverted the implementation of the National Achievement Test, the medium-level management positions (*shunin-sei*) and the Internship Program, at the school level. It was concerned teachers who initiated *Dōwa* Education to address the problems faced by minority students and, more recently, devised ways to accommodate newcomer children at school.

Teachers' relative autonomy despite the centralised educational administration and various restrictions is, we suspect, partly due to the fact that they gain the most significant professional development from informal interaction with school colleagues, and because the culture of the teaching profession acts as a buffer to external interventions. The influence of strong teachers' unions had been significant until recently, in providing a unified direction (in particular, in challenging the MOE's initiatives to effect more central control in education) and a sense of identity.

Teachers create their own career trajectories, by choosing to involve themselves in the areas where they gain the most fulfilment (e.g. an academic speciality, students' personal development, promotion, sport clubs). The career histories of Mr Imai and Mr Takeuchi demonstrate this. The ways in which teachers discharge what they consider to be their professional responsibilities are diverse, as in the cases of Ms Niwa and Mr Nakamoto. Teachers' actions in influencing their career trajectories are not free standing, however, but are shaped by various constraints imposed upon them, over which they often have little control. Regular transfers move teachers from one school to another, and through them they are exposed to various types of school cultures and teachers. For some, the union has a great significance in their professional lives. For many female teachers, family-related gender-specific expectations and their desire to perform well in their professional tasks often pose a dilemma. As we saw, Ms Kawa's solution to this dilemma was sheer hard work, abandonment of promotion ambitions, and an early retirement.

Teachers' contributions to school-level policy making have always been direct, since they discuss school policies extensively in staff meetings and since the influence of the principal's leadership is not as significant as in, for example, the US. In contrast, teachers' contributions to national policies have been indirect, but no less significant. Teachers' unions had not been represented in the MOE's advisory councils until recently, and teachers communicated their views on policies through union action, often in the form of challenging the MOE's policy proposals, as we examined in the events of the 1960s and 1970s. This is bound to change, partly because the past antagonistic relationship between the MOE and *Nikkyōso* has now been replaced by a cooperative one, and partly because the influence of unions has declined, due to a combination of social and organisational changes.

National-level education policies were brought to the centre stage of public debate in the 1980s. The Prime Minister established a supra-cabinet advisory council, the Ad-Hoc Council on Education, to initiate reforms to the existing system of education, in the name of 'the total settlement of the post-war educational accounts'. In Chapter 6 we identified four major trends in the changes to the education system in the 1980s and 1990s: a wider range of choices for parents and students, privatisation of education, the promotion of the needs of business and industry (e.g. training of elites, ability-based teaching, a closer link between universities and industries, relevant vocational subjects), and a call for a renewed emphasis on the inculcation of Japanese traditions and the 'Japanese ethnic identity'.

The overt theme running through these changes was that of making the educational system 'more flexible and diverse'. This was expected to more effectively address individual differences and to better meet the needs of business and industry, and of the society in response to 'global-isation' and the needs of the 'information-based society'. Flexibility and diversity were expected to be enhanced by the private sector's involvement in education. The measures to introduce diversity and flexibility are, however, likely to lead to a multi-track system, which critics see as a challenge to existing education, which had been underpinned by 'formal equality'. That the system of education will become multi-track is, in itself, not an issue, but the nature of the multi-track system that the new policies adopt is problematic. The new measures to address individual differences have been directed principally towards high achievers or students with 'special talents', with little reference made to children with other special needs (e.g. disability, minority status). These measures seem to serve, almost exclusively, those who excel in what is arbitrarily defined as 'useful talent', and, therefore, principally the business and industrial sectors. The introduced diversity and flexibility do not deliver Rawls's social justice (1972), in that they do not bring the most advantage to the least advantaged.

Behind 'flexibility and diversity' lies the covert running theme of these changes. It is to enhance the central government's stake in education, while devolving more responsibility and discretion to individual insti-tutions in the name of flexibility and diversity. Changes introduced in the 1980s and 1990s were thus double-edged.

The reforms, which were claimed to be the most significant in the post-war period, are unlikely to effect radical change in the operation of schooling on a daily basis. Teachers, armed with a certain autonomy and egalitarian solidarity, and insulated by the culture of teaching, continue to discharge what they believe to be their professional responsibilities. In the face of new circumstances (e.g. newcomer children, new schools and colleagues, and the new Course of Study), they will continue to develop professionally and chart their own distinctive career trajectories. The reforms are even less likely to affect the nature of the present system of education, whereby children from varying social locations obtain dif-ferent benefits from schooling, often to the advantage of those children who are already advantaged.

References

Akashi, Yōichi and Takano, Yoshiko (1993). Jōseki jokyōin no raifu sutairu no kenkyū. *Chiba Daigaku Kyōiku Gakubu Kiyō*, 41(1), 57–76.

Althusser, Louis (1971). *Lenin, Philosophy and Other Essays*. London: Newleft Books.

Amano, Ikuo (1985). *Kyōikukaikau o Kangaeru*. Tokyo: Tokyo Daigaku Shuppankai.

Amano, Ikuo (1989). The dilemma of Japanese education today. In *Japanese Schooling*, ed. James Shields, pp. 111–23. University Park: Pennsylvania State University Press.

Amano, Ikuo (1990). *Education and Examination in Modern Japan*. Tokyo: Tokyo University Press.

Amano, Masako (1988). 'Jendā to kyōiku' kenkyū no gendaiteki kadai: Kakusareta 'ryōiki' no tokuchō. *Shakaigaku Hyōron*, 155, 266–83.

Arai, Masato (1987). Dentōteki seinen shūdan no saihen. *Kyōiku Shakaigaku Kenkyū*, 42, 200–14.

Arikura, Ryōkichi and Amagi, Isao (1958). *Kyōiku Kankeihō II*. Tokyo: Nihon Hyōron Shinsha.

Aso, Makoto and Amano, Ikuo (1983). *Education and Japan's Modernization*. Tokyo: Japan Times.

Azuma, Hiroshi (1986). Why study child development in Japan? In *Child Development and Education in Japan*, ed. Harold Stevenson, Hiroshi Azuma and Kenji Hakuta, pp. 3–12. New York: W.H. Freeman.

Azuma, Kiyokazu and Suzuki, Atsuko (1991). Seiyakuwari taido kenkyū no tenbō. *Kyōiku Shinrigaku Kenkyū*, 62(4), 270–6.

Ballantine, Jeanne H. (1989). *The Sociology of Education* (2nd edn). Englewood Cliffs, NJ: Prentice Hall.

Beauchamp, Edward R. (ed.) (1978). *Learning to be Japanese: Selected readings on Japanese society and education*. Hamden, CT: Linnet Books.

Beauchamp, Edward R. (ed.) (1991). *Windows on Japanese Education*. Westport, CT: Greenwood Press.

Beauchamp, Edward R. and Vardaman, James M. Jr (1994). *Japanese Education Since 1945: A documentary study*. New York: M.E. Sharp.

Blackledge, David and Hunt, Barry (1985). *Sociological Interpretations of Education*. London: Routledge.

Brinton, Mary (1993). *Women and the Economic Miracle*. Los Angeles: University of California Press.

Buraku Kaihō Kenkyūsho (ed.) (1983). *The Road to a Discrimination-free Future*. Osaka: Buraku Liberation Research Institute.

Chen, Sing-jen and Miyake, Kazuo (1986). Japanese studies of infant development. In *Child Development and Education in Japan*, ed. Harold Stevenson, Hiroshi Azuma and Kenji Hakuta, pp. 135–46. New York: W.H. Freeman.

Connell, Robert W., Ashenden, D.J., Kessler, S., and Dowsett, G.W. (1982). *Making the Difference*. Sydney: Allen & Unwin.

Cornell, John (1966). Buraku relations and attitudes in a progressive farming community. In *Japan's Invisible Race: Caste in culture and personality*, ed. George De Vos and Hiroshi Wagatsuma, pp. 154–83. Berkeley, CA: University of California Press.

Cummings, Williams K. (1980). *Education and Equality in Japan*. Princeton, NJ: Princeton University Press.

Cummings, Williams K. (1982). The egalitarian transformation of postwar Japanese education. *Comparative Education*, 26(1), 16–35.

Cutts, Robert L. (1997). *An Empire of Schools*. Armonk, NY: M.E. Sharp.

De Vos, George and Wagatsuma, Hiroshi (eds) (1966). *Japan's Invisible Race: Caste in culture and personality*. Berkeley, CA: University of California Press.

Donoghue, John (1966). The social persistence of outcaste group. In *Japan's Invisible Race: Caste in culture and personality*, ed. George De Vos and Hiroshi Wagatsuma, pp. 138–153. Berkeley, CA: University of California Press.

Dore, Ronald P. (1965). *Education in Tokugawa Japan*. London: Routledge & Kegan Paul.

Duke, Benjamin C. (1973). *Japan's Militant Teachers*. Honolulu, HI: University of Hawaii Press.

Duke, Benjamin C. (1986). *The Japanese School: Lessons for Industrialized America*. New York: Praeger.

Duke, Benjamin C. (ed.) (1989). *The Great Educators of Modern Japan*. Tokyo: Tokyo University Press.

Enokii, Midori (1993). Nihon shakai no tabunka taminzokuka to gakkō genba. *Kyōiku Hyōron*, December 1993, 24–8.

Fujimura-Fanselow, Kumiko (1995). College women today: Options and dilemmas. In *Japanese Women: New feminist perspectives on the past, present and future*, ed. Kumiko Fujimura-Fanselow and Atsuko Kameda, pp. 125–54. New York: The Feminist Press.

Fukaya, Kazuko (1996). *Ijime Sekai no Kodomotachi: Kyōshitsu no Shin'en*. Tokyo: Kaneko Shobō.

Fukaya, Masashi (1992). Kyōshoku ni okeru raifu-stēji no kōsatsu. *Shizuoka Daigaku Kyōiku Gakubu Fuzoku Kyōiku Jissen Kenkyū Shidōsentā Kenkyū Kiyō*, 1, 61–71.

Fukayama, Masamitsu, Yamashina, Saburō and Sanuki, Hiroshi (eds) (1985). *Rinkyōshin Tōshin o Dōyomuka*. Tokyo: Rōdōjunpōsha.

Fukuzawa, Rebecca E. (1994). The path to adulthood according to Japanese middle schools. *Journal of Japanese Studies*, 20(1), 61–86.

Goodman, Roger (1990). *Japan's 'International Youth': The emergence of a new class of school-children*. Oxford: Clarendon Press.

Hall, Ivan (1973). *Mori Arinori*. Cambridge, MA: Harvard University Press.

Hara, Kimi (1995). Challenges to education for girls and women in Modern Japan: Past and Present. In *Japanese Women: New feminist perspectives on the past*, *present and future*, ed. Kumiko Fujimura-Fanselow and Atsuko Kameda, pp. 93–106. New York: The Feminist Press.

Hasuo, Naomi (1993). Joseikyōin no kyaria keisei ni kansuru chōsa kenkyū. *Mie Daigaku Kyōiku Jissen Kenkyū Shidō Sentā Kiyō*, 13, 115–27.

Hasuo, Naomi (1994). Shō chūgakkō josei kyōin no kyaria keisei ni kansuru jirei kenkyū. *Mie Daigaku Kyōikugakubu Kenkyū Kiyō*, 45, 141–53.

Hawkins, John N. (1983). Educational demands and institutional response: Dowa education in Japan. *Comparative Education Review*, 27(2), 204–26.

Hendry, Joy (1986). *Becoming Japanese: The world of the pre-school child*. Honolulu, HI: University of Hawaii Press.

Henshū-bu, Gekkan Fukushi (1995). Tōkei kara mita zainichi gaikokujin no genjyō. *Gekkan Fukushi*, January 1995, 32–5.

Hess, Robert, Holloway, Susan and McDevitt, Teresa (1986). Family influences on school readiness and achievement in Japan and the United States: An overview of a longitudinal study. In *Child Development and Education in Japan*, ed. Harold Stevenson, Hiroshi Azuma and Kenji Hakuta, pp. 147–66. New York: W.H. Freeman.

Hirano, Keiko (1995). Yōroppa ni okeru ijime. In *Ijime Jisatsu: Gendai no esupuri bessatsu*, ed. Hiroshi Inamura and Yukiko Saitō, pp. 181–94. Tokyo: Shibundō.

Hirasawa, Yasumasa (1983). The burakumin: Japan's minority population. *Integrated Education*, 20(6), 3–8.

Hirose, Toshikatsu (1995). Ijime no yobō ni chikara o. *Gendai Kyōiku Kagaku*, 38(9), 43–5.

Hirota, Masaki (1990). *Sabetsu no Shosō*. Tokyo: Iwanami Shoten.

Hoffman, Diane M. (1992). Changing faces, changing places: The new Koreans in Japan. *Japan Quarterly*, October–December, 479–89.

Hokkaidō-chō (1988). *Hokkaidō Utari Fukushi Taisaku dai San-ji*. Sapporo: Hokkaidō-chō.

Horio, Teruhisa (1988). *Educational Thought and Ideology in Modern Japan*. Tokyo: Tokyo University Press.

Hunter, Janet (1989). *The Emergence of Modern Japan*. London: Longman.

Hyōgo-ken Kyōiku Sentā (ed.) (1984). *Hyōgo no Kyōiku Undō*, no. 9.

Ichimaru, Fujitarō, Shioyama, Jirō, Kodama, Ken'ichi, Fujisawa, Yoshiyuki, Kazuen, Teiki and Morita, Yūji (1994). Tōkō kyohiji no shakaiteki jiritsu ni kansuru kenkyū. *Matsuda Zaidan Kenkyū Hōkokusho*, 7, 51–66.

Ikeda, Hiroshi (1985). Hisabetsuburaku ni okeru kyōiku to bunka: Gyoson buraku ni okeru seinen no raifu stairu nikansuru esunogurafī. *Ōsaka Daigaku Ningen Kagakubu Kiyō*, 11, 247–71.

Ikeda, Hiroshi (1987). Nihonshakai no mainoritī to kyōiku no fubyōdō. *Kyōiku Shakaigaku Kenkyū*, 42, 51–69.

Imabashi, Morikatsu (1995a). Taibatsu: Kyōikujōhō to kodomo no jinken. *Kikan Kyōikuhō*, 101, 41–52.

Imabashi, Morikatsu (1995b). Ijime mondai to kyōiku hō. *Kikan Kyōikuhō*, 101, 53–8.

Inamura, Hiroshi (1994). *Futōkō no Kenkyū*. Tokyo: Shin'yōsha.

Inamura, Hiroshi (1995). Jisatsu hōdō no arikata. In *Ijime Jisatsu: Gendai no esupuri bessatsu*, ed. Hiroshi Inamura and Yukiko Saitō, pp. 45–62. Tokyo: Shibundō.

Inoue, Toshiaki (1995). Gakkō gawa wa dō uketomeru bekika. *Gendai Kyōiku Kagaku*, 38(9), 40–2.

Ishida, Hiroshi (1993). *Social Mobility in Contemporary Japan: Educational credentials, class and the labour market in a cross-cultural perspective.* London: Macmillan.

Isotani, Keisuke (1994). Tōkō kyohi jidōseito nikansuru chōsa kekka nitsuite. *Gekkan Seitoshidō,* 24(3), 18–22.

Itō, Yasuhiro (1994). Kyōshi bunka gakkō bunka no nichibei hikaku. In *Nihon no Kyōshi Bunka,* ed.Tadahiko Inagaki and Yoshiyuki Kudomi, pp. 140–56. Tokyo: Tokyo Daigaku Suppankai.

Iwai, Hachirō (1990). Josei no raifukōsu to gakureki. In *Gendai Nihon no Kaisō Kōzō Dai-3-kan: Kyōiku to shakai idō,* ed. Jōji Kikuchi, pp. 155–84. Tokyo: Tokyo Daigaku Shuppankai.

Japan, Hōmushō, Jinken Yōgo-kyoku (1985) *Taibatsu o Nakusō.* Tokyo: Hōmushō.

Japan, Keizai Kikaku Chō (1990). *Kokumin Seikatsu Chōsa 1990.* Tokyo: Keizai Kikaku Chō.

Japan, Kōseishō, Daijinkanbō tōkei jōhōbu (1995). *Jidō o Torimaku Setai no Jōkyō.* Tokyo: Kōseishō.

Japan, Monbushō (Ministry of Education) (1988). *Wagakuni no Bunkyōsesaku (Heisei 9 nendo).* Tokyo: Monbushō.

Japan, Monbushō (Ministry of Education) (1994). *Gakkō Kihon Chōsa Hōkokusho: Kōtō kyōiku kikan.* Tokyo: Monbushō.

Japan, Monbushō (Ministry of Education) (1995a). *Gakkō Kihon Chōsa Hōkokusho: Shotō chūtō kyōiku kikan, senshūgakkō, kakushugakkō.* Tokyo: Monbushō.

Japan, Monbushō (Ministry of Education) (1995b). *Heisei 7 Nendo Shoninsha Kenshū no Jisshitaisei ni Kansuru Chōsa Kekka.* Tokyo: Monbushō.

Japan, Monbushō (Ministry of Education) (1996). *Seitoshidō jō no Shomondai no Genjō to Monbushō no Sesaku Nitsuite.* Tokyo: Monbushō.

Japan, Monbushō (Ministry of Education) (1997). *Gakkō Kyōin Tōkei Chōsa Hōkokusho Heisei 7 Nendo.* Tokyo: Monbushō.

Japan, Monbushō, Chihō-ka (1996). Kyōshokuin dantai no soshiki jittai nitsuite. *Kyōiku Iinkai Geppō,* no. 553, May 1996, 43–68.

Japan, Monbushō, Kyōiku Hōrei Kenkyūkai (1947). *Kyōiku Kihonhō no Kaisetsu.* Tokyo: Kokuritsu Shoin.

Japan, Monbushō, Kyōiku Hōrei Kenkyūkai (ed.) (1949). *Kyōiku Kōmuin Tokurei-hō.* Tokyo: Jijitsūshinsha.

Japan, Monbushō, Shotō Chūtō Kyōiku-kyoku Chūgakkō-ka (1986). *Ijime no Jittaitō Nikansuru Chōsa Kekka Nitsuite.* Tokyo: Monbushō.

Japan, Monbushō, Shotō Chūtō Kyōiku-kyoku Chūgakkō-ka (1994). Tōkō kyohi jidōseito ni kansuru chōsa kekka 1993 (gaiyō). *Gekkan Seitoshidō,* 24(3), 48–70.

Japan, Sōmuchō Tōkeikyoku (1991). *Japan Statistical Yearbook 1991.* Tokyo: Sōmuchō.

Japan, Sōmuchō Tōkeikyoku (1994). *Japan Statistical Yearbook 1993/94.* Tokyo: Sōmuchō.

Japan, Sōrifu (1982). *Fujin Mondai ni Kansuru Kokusai Hikaku Chōsa.* Tokyo: Sōrifu.

Japan, Sōrifu, Seishōnen Taisakuhonbu (1982). *Seishōnen to Katei.* Tokyo: Sōrifu.

Kaizawa, Tadashi (1993). *Ainu Waga Jinsei.* Tokyo: Iwanami Shoten.

Kameda, Atsuko (1977). Joshiseito no shokugyō ishiki keisei nitsuite no ichi kōsatsu. *Ningen Hattatsu Kenkyū,* 2, 9–15.

Kanda, Michiko (1985). Seiyakuwari to kodomo. In *Nihon no Kyōiku o Kangaeru 1: Kodomo wa dō sodatsuka,* ed. Makoto Asō and Takahiro Kihara, pp. 111–31. Tokyo: Yūshindō.

Kanehara, Emon (1986). *Nihon no Naka no Kankoku Chōsenjin Chūgokujin Kanagawa-ken nai Eijū Gaikokujin Jittai Chōsa Yori.* Tokyo: Akashi Shoten.

Kanekura, Taku (1996). Monbushō no 95 nendo mondai kōdō hakusho (jō): Ijime jisatsu. *Naigai Kyōiku,* 27 December, 6–9. Kanekura provides a summary of the report *95-nendo Seitoshidō jō no Shomondai no Genjō to Monbushō no Sesaku (Mondai Kōdō Hakusho).*

Kanekura, Taku (1997). Monbushō no 95 nendo mondai kōdō hakusho (ge): Tōkō kyohi, kōnai bōryoku taibatsu nado. *Naigai Kyōiku,* 10 January, 4–9.

Karthaus-Tanaka, Nobuko (1990). *The Problems of Foreign Workers in Japan.* Leiden: Center for Japanese and Korean Studies, Rijks Universiteit Leiden.

Kasama, Tasuo (1995). Kōjōteki shien niwa kyōkan suruga. *Gendai Kyōiku Kagaku,* 38(9), 49–50.

Katsumata, Hidefumi (1995). Ijime to jisatsu. *Kyōiku to Igaku,* 43(11), 11–17.

Kawakami, Sachiko (1997a). Soshikiritsu kako saitei no 55.3%: Monbushō no 'Kyōshokuin dantai no soshiki jittai chōsa'. *Naigai Kyōiku,* 20 June, 10–12.

Kawakami, Sachiko (1997b). Menkyojō shutokusha no kyōin shūshoku 16% daini: Monbushō no 'Kyōinmenkyojō kyōin shūshoku jōkyō no chōsa'. *Naigai Kyōiku,* 21 February, 2–5.

Kawakami, Yōichi (1995). Kihonteki nin'shiki ni konran wa naika. *Gendai Kyōiku Kagaku,* 38(9), 27–9.

Kawamura, Asako (1993). Zanryūkoji ya gaikoku-seki no ōi gakkō to chiiki no genjō. *Kyōiku,* 43(2), 34–41.

Kim, Suja (1994). Ibunka ni furete mananda koto. In *Zainichi no ima Kyōto-hatsu* Part II, ed. ZZCKKK (see below), pp. 25–35. Kyoto: ZZCKKK.

Kimura, Ryōko (1990). Jendā to gakkō bunka. In *Gakkō Bunka,* ed. Akio Nagao and Hiroshi Ikeda, pp. 147–70. Tokyo: Tōshindō.

Kishizawa, Hatsumi (1993). Jendā to danjo byōdō kyōiku. *Kyōiku,* 43(8), 58–67.

Kobayashi, Tetsuya (1976). *Society, Schools, and Progress in Japan.* Oxford: Pergamon Press.

Kobayashi, Tetsuya (1989). Educational problems of 'returning children'. In *Japanese Schooling,* ed. James Shields, pp. 176–84. University Park, PA: Pennsylvania State University Press.

Kobayashi, Tsuyoshi (1995). Ijime mondai no bapponteki kaiketsu ni kotaete iruka. *Gendai Kyōiku Kagaku,* 38(9), 18–20.

Kokubun, Ichitarō (1951). *Atarashii Tsuzurikata Kyōshitsu.* Tokyo: Nihon Hyōronsha.

Komiya, Osamu (1993). Gaikoku no kodomotachi no hoiku no genjō. *Kyōiku,* 43(2), 28–33.

Kudomi, Yoshiyuki (1990). Kēsu sutadē 'Yutakasa' no teihen o ikiru. *Kyōiku,* 40(1), 6–18.

Kudomi, Yoshiyuki (ed.) (1993). *Yutakasa no Teihen ni Ikiru: Gakkō shisutemu to jakusha no saiseisan.* Tokyo: Aoki Shoten.

Kudomi, Yoshiyuki (1995). Kyōshi no bān'auto to jiko gisei teki kyōshizō no konnichiteki tenkan. *Hitotsubashi Daigaku Kenkyū Nenpō Shakaigaku Kenkyū,* 34, 3–42.

Kurita, Mataru (1990). School phobia. *Japan Quarterly,* 37(3), 298–303.

Kuroda, Kunio and Takenaka, Mutsumi (1990). Nukumori no aru seikatsu to kibō o kodomotachi ni. *Kyōiku,* 40(1), 58–71.

Kuroyanagi, Tetsuko (1982). *Totto-chan: The little girl at the window.* Tokyo: Kodansha International.

Lee, Changsoo (1981). The legal status of Koreans in Japan. In *Koreans in Japan: Ethnic conflict and accommodation*, ed. Changsoo Lee and George De Vos, pp. 133–58. Berkeley, CA: University of California Press.

Lee, Changsoo, and De Vos, George (eds) (1981). *Koreans in Japan: Ethnic conflict and accommodation.* Berkeley, CA: University of California Press.

Lee, Yōhuan (1980). *Nihon no Naka no 38 Dosen: Mindan Chōsōren no rekishi to genjitsu.* Tokyo: Yōyōsha.

Leestma, Robert, Bennett, William J., George, B. and Peak, Lois (1987). *Japanese Education Today.* Washington, DC: US Department of Education.

LeTendre, Gerald (1994). Guiding them on: Teaching, hierarchy, and social organization in Japanese middle schools. *Journal of Japanese Studies*, 20(1), 37–59.

Lewis, Catherine (1988). Japanese first grade classrooms: Implications for US theory and research. *Comparative Education Review*, 32(2), 159–72

Lewis, Catherine (1995). *Educating Hearts and Minds: Reflections on Japanese preschool and elementary education.* Cambridge: Cambridge University Press.

Lim, Yongchel (1993). *Zainichi Zaibei Kankokujin Oyobi Kankokujin no Gengo Seikatsu no Jittai.* Tokyo: Kuroshio Shuppan.

Lincicome, Mark (1993). Focus on internationalization of Japanese education: Nationalism, internationalization and the dilemma of educational reform in Japan. *Comparative Education Review*, 37(2), 123–52.

Lincicome, Mark (1995). *Principles, Praxis, and the Politics of Educational Reform in Meiji Japan.* Honolulu, HI: Hawai University Press.

Lynn, Richard (1988). *Educational Achievement in Japan: Lessons for the West.* Basingstoke: Macmillan Press.

Machizawa, Shizuo (1995). Ijimerare taiken no kokufuku. *Jidō Shinri*, 49(9), 99–106.

Mainichi Shinbun Kōbe Shikyoku (MSKS) (1991). *Erīto Kyōiku no Hikari to Kage: Shiritsu Nada chū kōkō.* Tokyo: Mainichi Shinbunsha.

Makihara, Hiroyuki (1988). Tōkō kyohi no seiin to yōgo. In *Gakkō ni Ikenai Kodomotachi: Gendai no Esupuri 1988/5*, ed. Shinichi Jinbo and Kumiko Yamazaki, pp. 142–52. Tokyo: Shibundō.

Matsuzawa, Yuzuru (1994). Sanson shakai no dōkō to miseinensō no kyōiku kankyō. *Ringyō Keizai*, 47(10), 6–11.

McRobbie, Angela (1978). Working class girls and the culture of femininity. In *Women Take Issue*, ed. Women's Studies Group, Centre of Contemporary Cultural Studies, pp. 96–108. London: Hutchinson.

Mikami, Kazuo (1986). *Kyōikukaikaku no Shiya.* Tokyo: Dōjidaisha.

Miliband, R. (1969). *The State in Capitalist Society.* New York: Basic Books.

Mino, Yasuhiro (1993). Watashi no sokoku chūgoku. *Kyōiku Hyōron*, no. 559, December, 52–5.

Mitchell, Richard H. (1967). *The Korean Minority in Japan.* Berkeley, CA: University of California Press.

Miyagi, Etsujiro (1992). Okinawa's 20th Reversion Anniversary. *Japan Quarterly*, April–June, 146–58.

Miyahara, Seiichi (1963). *Kyōikushi.* Tokyo: Tōyō Keizai.

Miyajima, Takashi (1993). Ima hajimatta gaikokujin no kodomo no kyōiku no kadai. *Kyōiku Hyōron*, no. 559, December, 18–23.

Miyatake, Masaaki (1988). Kuzureyuku katei chiiki to kodomotachi. *Kyōiku*, 38(12), 19–33.

Miyatake, Masaaki (1990). Hinkon o kokufukusuru kyōiku. *Kyōiku*, 40(1), 19–32.

Miyawaki, Hiroyuki (1985). *The Ethnic Identity, Bilingualism and Biculturalism of Korean Residents in Japan.* Working Papers of the Japanese Studies Centre. No. 5. Melbourne: Japanese Studies Centre.

Miyazaki, Ayumi (1991). Gakkō niokeru 'seiyakuwari no shakaika' saikō: Kyōshi niyoru seibetsu kategorī shiyō o tegakaritoshite. *Kyōiku Shakaigaku Kenkyū*, 48, 105–23.

Miyazaki, Ayumi (1993). Jendā sabukaruchā no dainamikusu. *Kyōiku Shakaigaku Kenkyū*, 52, 157–77.

Mizuuchi, Hiroshi (1985). *Sengo Kyōikukaikaku to Kyōikunaiyō.* Tokyo: Shin'nihon Shuppansha.

Mizuuchi, Hiroshi (1989). Sawayanagi Masataro. In *The Great Educators of Modern Japan*, ed. Benjamin Duke, pp. 149–65. Tokyo: Tokyo University Press.

Morigaki, Osamu (1979). *Chiiki ni Nezasu Gakkō Zukuri.* Tokyo: Kokudosha.

Morigaki, Osamu (1982). Kyōshokuin shūdan to tomoni fubo ga sankashi sasaeru gakkō zukuri: Fuchū shō no kyōiku jissen. In *Kyōiku Jissen Jiten Volume 5*, ed. Tetsuo Okubo, Shigekatsu Nishi and Masatoshi Yamada, pp. 160–90. Tokyo: Rōdōjunpōsha.

Morita, Yōji (1986a). Ijime rongi no nokoshita mono. *Shōnen Hodō*, 31(6), 12–20.

Morita, Yōji (1986b). Ijime genjō to sono kokufuku no tameni. *Jidō Shinri*, October special issue, 8–17.

Morris-Suzuki, Tessa (1984). *Showa: An inside history of Hirohito's Japan.* London: Athlone Press.

Mouer, Ross and Sugimoto, Yoshio (1995). *Nihonjinron at the End of the Twentieth Century: A multicultural perspective.* La Trobe University Asian Studies Papers, Research Series 4. Melbourne: La Trobe University.

Muchaku, Seikyō (ed.) (1951). *Yamabiko Gakkō.* Tokyo: Seidōsha.

Murakami, Yoshio (1985). Bullies in the classroom. *Japan Quarterly*, 32, 407–11.

Nabeshima, Sachirō (1993). Buraku mainoriti to kyōiku tassei: J.U. Ogbu no jinruigakuteki apurōchi o tegakarini. *Kyōiku Shakaigaku Kenkyū*, 52, 208–31.

Nagano Nishi Kōtōgakkō Tsūshinsei (NNKT) (eds) (1991). *Tsūshinsei Kōkōsei no Seishun.* Tokyo: Ayumi Shuppan.

Nagasu, Toshiyuki (1984). *Nōgyō Kōkō: Kindaika nōsei no shukuzu.* Tokyo: San'ichi Shobō.

Nakajima, Kuni (1989). Naruse Jinzo. In *The Great Educators of Modern Japan*, ed. Benjamin Duke, pp. 67–85. Tokyo: Tokyo University Press.

Nakajima, Tomoko (1994). Zainichi kankoku chōsenjin no esunishiti to kyōiku. *Kyōikugaku Kenkyū*, 61(3), 29–37.

Nakamoto, Masao (1979). *Gakuryoku eno Chōsen.* Tokyo: Rōdōjunpōsha.

Nakanishi, Yūko (1993). Jendā Torakku: Seiyakuwarikan ni motozuku shinro bunka mekanizumu ni kansuru kōsatsu. *Kyōiku Shakaigaku Kenkyū*, 53, 131–54.

Nakano, Akira (1989). Shimonaka Yasaburo. In *The Great Educators of Modern Japan*, ed. Benjamin Duke, pp. 167–89. Tokyo: Tokyo University Press.

Nakata, Yoshifumi and Mosk, Carol (1987). The demand for college education in postwar Japan. *Journal of Human Resources*, 22(3), 377–404.

Nakayama, Keiko (1985). Atarashii joseizō to kyōiku. In *Nihon no Kyōiku o Kangaeru 3: Kyōiku kaikaku wa kanōka*, ed. Yoshihiro Shimizu, pp. 67–87. Tokyo: Yūshindō.

Nihon Bengoshi Rengōkai (1985). *Gakkō Seikatsu to Kodomo no Jinken.*

Nihon Keieisha Dantai Renmei (Nikkeiren) (1995a). *Shinjidai no 'Nihonteki Keiei': Chōsensubeki hōkō to sono gutaisaku.* Tokyo: Nihon Keieisha Dantai Renmei.

Nihon Keieisha Dantai Renmei (Nikkeiren) Kyôiku Tokubetsu Iinkai (1995b). *Shinjidai ni Chōsensuru Daigakukyōiku to Kigyō no Taiō.* Tokyo: Nihon Keieisha Dantai Renmei.

Nihon Kodomo o Mamoru Kai (ed.) (1996). *Kodomo Hakusho 1996.* Tokyo: Kusatsuchi Bunka Shuppan.

Nishida, Yoshimasa (1990). Chiiki bunka to gakkō: Aru gyoson buraku no fīrudonōto kara. In *Gakkō Bunka,* ed. Akio Nagao and Hiroshi Ikeda, pp. 123–46. Tokyo: Tōshindō.

Nomoto, Hiroyuki (1994). Gaikokujin rōdōsha oyobi sono kodomotachi no gakushūken hoshō. *Kyōikugaku Kenkyū,* 61(3), 38–45.

Noshige, Shinsaku (1985). *Ijime wa Nakuseru.* Tokyo: Akebi Shobō.

Ochi, Yasushi, Kikuchi, Eiji, Katō, Takao and Yoshihara, Keiko (1992). Joshi gakusei bunka no gendaiteki isō. *Tokyo Daigaku Kyōiku Gakubu Kiyō,* 32, 119–46.

OECD (1972). *Reviews of National Policies for Education: Japan.* Paris: OECD.

Okamoto, Hiroshi (1997). Kikini aru kyōin yōsei: Kyōyōshin tōshin no nerau mono. *Daigakushingaku Kenkyū* 19(3), 8–11.

Okano, Kaori (1993). *School to Work Transition in Japan: An ethnographic study.* Clevedon, Avon and Philadelphia, PA: Multilingual Matters.

Okano, Kaori (1995a). Habitus and intraclass differentiation: Nonuniversity-bound students in Japan. *International Journal of Qualitative Studies in Education,* 8(4), 357–69.

Okano, Kaori (1995b). Rational decision making and school-based job referrals for high school students in Japan. *Sociology of Education,* 68(1), 31–47.

Okano, Kaori (1997). Third-generation Koreans' entry into the workforce in Japan. *Anthropology and Education Quarterly,* 28(4), 524–49.

Osada, Arata (1961). *Nihon Kyōikushi.* Tokyo: Ochanomizu Shobō.

Ota, H. (1989). Political teacher unionism in Japan. In *Japanese Schooling,* ed. James Shields, pp. 243–59. University Park, PA: Pennsylvania State University Press.

Ōta, Takashi and Horio, Teruhisa (eds) (1985). *Kyōiku o Kaikakusuru toha Dōiukotoka.* Tokyo: Iwanami Shoten.

Ōtani, Takeo (1990). Gakkō kara mita futōkō mondai. *Kyōiku,* 40(1), 49–57.

Ōtsuki, Takeshi and Hamabayashi, Masao (eds) (1984). *Kyōikukaikaku o tou.* Tokyo: Ōtsuki Shoten.

Ozawa, Yūsaku and Sanuki, Hiroshi (1993). Minzoku kyōsei no kyōiku o mezashite: Gaikokujin shitei no kyōiku to aidentiti no keisei. *Kyōiku,* 43(2), 6–15.

Passin, Herbert (1982). *Society and Education in Japan.* Tokyo: Kodansha International.

Peak, Lois (1991). *Learning to Go to School in Japan.* Berkeley, CA: University of California Press.

Prais, S.J. (1987). Educating for productivity: comparisons of Japanese and English schooling and vocational preparation. *National Institute Economic Review,* no. 119, February, 40–56.

Price, Michelle (1996). Femininity: An ethnography of subcultures in a women's university in Japan. Unpublished Honours thesis, School of Asian Studies, La Trobe University, Melbourne.

Rawls, John (1972). *A Theory of Justice.* Oxford: Oxford University Press.

Roden, Donald (1980). *Schooldays in Imperial Japan.* Berkeley, CA: University of California Press.

Rohlen, Thomas (1981). Education: Policies and prospects. In *Koreans in Japan: Ethnic conflict and accommodation,* ed. Changsoo Lee and George De Vos, pp. 182–222. Berkeley, CA: University of California Press.

Rohlen, Thomas (1983). *Japan's High Schools*. Berkeley, CA: University of California Press.

Rohlen, Thomas and LeTendre, Gerald (eds) (1996). *Teaching and Learning in Japan*. New York: Cambridge University Press.

Rose, Barbara (1992). *Tsuda Umeko and Women's Education in Japan*. New Haven, CT: Yale University Press.

Rosenbaum, James E. and Kariya, Takehiko (1989). From high school to work: Market and institutional mechanisms in Japan. *American Journal of Sociology*, 94, 1334–65.

Rubinger, Richard (1982). *Private Academies of Tokugawa Japan*. Princeton, NJ: Princeton University Press.

Sakai, Yuzuru and De Vos, George (1966). A traditional urban outcaste community. In *Japan's Invisible Race: Caste in culture and personality*, ed. George De Vos and Hiroshi Wagatsuma, pp. 129–37. Berkeley, CA: University of California Press.

Sasagawa, Kōichi (1993). Gaikokujin no gakushūken mondai to 'posuto-kokuminkyōiku-jidai' no kyōiku-gaku. *Kyōiku*, 43(2), 16–27.

Satō, Gun'ei (1988). Kyōin no shidōkan no jisshō bunseki: Nichibei chūgakkō kyōin hikaku chōsa o tooshite. In *Kyōin Bunka no Shakaigakuteki Kenkyū*, ed. Yoshiyuki Kudomi, pp. 85–146. Tokyo: Taga Shuppan.

Sato, Manabu (1992). Japan. In *Issues and Problems of Teacher Education: An international handbook*, ed. H. Leavitt, pp. 155–68. Westport, CT: Greenwood Press.

Sato, Nancy (1993). Teaching and learning in Japanese elementary schools: A context for understanding. *Peabody Journal of Education* (Japanese Teacher Education Part II), 68(4), 111–47.

Sato, Nancy (1994). Nihon no kyōshi bunka no esunografī. In *Nihon no Kyōshi Bunka*, ed. Tadahiko Inagaki and Yoshiyuki Kudomi, pp. 125–39. Tokyo: Tokyo Daigaku Suppankai.

Satō, Shūsaku (1988). Gendai no gakkō to tōkō kyohi. In *Gakkō ni Ikenai Kodomotachi: Gendai no esupuri 1988/5*, ed. Shinichi Jinbo and Kumiko Yamazaki, pp. 24–35. Tokyo: Shibundō.

Satō, Zen, et al. (1991). Kyōin no jinji gyōsei ni kansuru kenkyū. *Nihon Kyōiku Gyōsei Gakkai Nenpō*, 17, 149–62.

Schoolland, Ken (1990). *Shogun's Ghost: The dark side of Japanese education*. New York: Bergin & Garvey.

Schoppa, Leonard J. (1991). *Education Reform in Japan: A case of immobilist politics*. London: Routledge.

Seikatsu Tsuzurikata Ena no Ko Henshū Iinkai (ed.) (1982). *Ashita ni Mukatte*. Tokyo: Kusatsuchi Bunka.

Seishōnen Fukushi Sentā (ed.) (1989). *Shiirareta 'Jiritsu'*. Tokyo: Mineruva Shobō.

Sekine, Masami (1990). *Guest Workers in Japan*. Centre for Multicultural Studies, University of Wollongong, Occasional Paper Series No. 21, August.

Sengoku, Tamotsu (1995). Ijime no kōzō: Amerika to nihon. In *Ijime Jisatsu: Gendai no esupuri bessatsu*, ed. Hiroshi Inamura and Yukiko Saitō, pp. 195–203. Tokyo: Shibundō.

Shields, James (ed.) (1989). *Japanese Schooling*. University Park, PA: Pennsylvania State University Press.

Shimada, Haruo (1994). *Japan's 'Guest Workers': Issues and public policies*. Tokyo: Tokyo University Press.

Shimada, Yōtoku (1995). Shōgakusei no sutoresu. *Shidō to Hyōka*, 41(11); 12–16.

Shimahara, Nobuo (1971). *Burakumin: A Japanese minority and education*. The Hague: Marinus Nijhoff.

Shimahara, Nobuo (1979). *Adaptation and Education in Japan*. New York: Preager.

Shimahara, Nobuo (1984). Toward the equality of a Japanese minority: The case of Burakumin. *Comparative Education*, 20(3), 339–53.

Shimahara, Nobuo (1991a). Social mobility and education: Burakumin in Japan. In *Minority Status and Schooling*, ed. Margaret A. Gibson and John Ogbu, pp. 327–53. New York: Garland Publishing.

Shimahara, Nobuo (1991b). Teacher education in Japan. In *Windows on Japanese Education*, ed. Edward R. Beauchamp, pp. 259–80. Westport, CT: Greenwood Press.

Shimahara, Nobuo and Sakai, Akira (1992). Teacher internship and the culture of teaching in Japan. *British Journal of Sociology of Education*, 13(2), 147–62.

Shimahara, Nobuo and Sakai, Akira (1995). *Learning to Teach in Two Cultures*. New York: Garland.

Shimizu, Chinami (1994). OL kara mita kaisha. In *Shūshoku Shūsha no Kōzō*, ed. Katsuto Uchihashi, Hiroshi Okumura and Makoto Sakata, pp. 115–34, Tokyo: Iwanami Shoten.

Shimizu, Kazuhiko (1996). *Kyōiku Data Land*. Tokyo: Jijitsūshinsha.

Shimizu, Kōkichi (1992). Shido: Education and selection in a Japanese middle school. *Comparative Education*, 28(2), 109–29.

Simmons, Cyril (1990). *Growing Up and Going to School in Japan: Tradition and trends*. Milton Keynes: Open University Press.

Simmons, Cyril and Wade, Winnie (1988). Contrasting attitudes to education in England and Japan. *Educational Research*, 30(2), 146–52.

Singleton, John (1967). *Nichū: A Japanese school*. New York: Holt, Rinehart and Winston.

Sugimura, Hiroshi (1988). Hinkon to kyōiku o megutte. *Kyōiku*, 38(12), 6–18.

Taga, Takako (1988a). *Haisukūru Rakugaki*. Tokyo: Asahi Shinbunsha.

Taga, Takako (1988b). *Gakkō wa Hibi Dorama*. Tokyo: Asahi Shinbunsha.

Takagi, Masayuki (1991). A living legacy of discrimination. *Japan Quarterly*, 38(3), 283–90.

Takashina, Reiji (1996). Nihon no ijime sekai no ijime. *Kyōiku Jānaru*, 35(8), 24–7.

Takegawa, Ikuo (1993). *Ijime to Futōkō no Shakaigaku*. Tokyo: Hōritsu Bunkasha.

Takeuchi, Kiyoshi (1985). Joshi no seitobunka no tokushitsu. *Kyōiku Shakaigaku Kenkyū*, 40, 23–34.

Takeuchi, Yō (1995). *Nihon no Meritokurashī*. Tokyo: Tokyo Daigaku Shuppankai.

Takeuchi, Yōko (1994). Imakoso joseiga kyaria o nobasutoki. In *Shūshoku Shūsha no Kōzō*, ed. Katsuto Uchihashi, Hiroshi Okumura and Makoto Sakata, pp. 135–50, Tokyo: Iwanami Shoten.

Takigawa, Kazuhiro (1995). Ijime no haikei to nihonteki tokusei. *Kyōiku to Igaku*, 43(11), 70–7.

Tamura, Hiroyuki (1996). Ijime ni okeru shinri: jitsutaikenkara kataru. *Kōkō Seikatsu Shidō*, no. 127, Winter, 58–65.

Tanaka, Hiroshi (1991). *Zainichi Gaikokujin*. Tokyo: Iwanami Shoten.

Tanaka, Hiroshi (1993). Gaikokujin no kenri to nihon shakai no yukue. *Kyōiku*, 43(2), 66–80.

Tanaka, Katsuhiro (1995). Naze miteminuhuri o surunoka: Bōkansuru kodomotachi no shinri. *Jidō Shinri*, 49(9), 51–9.

Tanaka, Kunio (1964). *Minzoku to Gengo no Mondai*. Tokyo: Kinseisha.

Terumoto, Yoshichika (1995). Ijime no honshitsu haaku ni se o muketa kinkyū kaigi hōkoku. *Gendai Kyōiku Kagaku*, 38(9), 21–3.

Thurston, Donald (1973). *Teachers and Politics in Japan*. Princeton, NJ: Princeton University Press.

Tobin, Joseph J., Wu, David Y.H. and Davidson, Dana H. (1987). Class size and student/teacher ratios in the Japanese preschool. *Comparative Education Review*, 31(4), 533–49.

Tokuoka, Hideo (1988). Jiko jōjuteki yogen toshiteno ijime mondai. *Kansai Daigaku Shakaigakubu Kiyō*, 20(1), 159–80.

Tsuchiya, Motonori (1984). *Sengo Kyōiku to Kyōin Yōsei*. Tokyo: Shin Nihon Shuppan.

Tsuchiya, Motonori (1988). *Kyōshi no Menkyo to Kenshū wa Dō Kawaru*. Tokyo: Rōdōjunpōsha.

Tsuchiya, Motonori (1989). *Nihon no Kyōshi: Yōsei, menkyo, kenshū*. Tokyo: Shin Nihon Shuppan.

Tsuchiya, Motonori (1990). *Kodomo no Kenri*. Kobe: Hyōgo Buraku Mondai Kenkyūsho.

Tsuchiya, Motonori (1995). *Kindai Nihon Kyōiku Rōdō Undōshi Kenkyū*. Tokyo: Rōdōjunpōsha.

Tsuchiya, Motonori (1997). Kyōin yōsei no tōmen suru kadai. *Daigakushingaku Kenkyū*, 19(3), 12–15.

Tsukada, Mamoru (1991). *Yobiko Life: A study of the legitimation process of social stratification in Japan*. Berkeley, CA: Center for Japanese Studies, University of California.

Tsukada, Mamoru (1997). Kyōshibunka kara mita jukentaisei no shakaigakuteki kenkyū (Kenkyū kadai bangō 07451054). Nagoya: Sugiyama Jogakuen Daigaku.

Tsuneyoshi, Ryoko (1994). Small groups in Japanese elementary school classrooms: Comparisons with the US. *Comparative Education*, 30(2),115–29.

Tsurumi, Patricia E. (1977). *Japanese Colonial Education in Taiwan 1895–1945*. Cambridge, MA: Harvard University Press.

Ujihara, Yōko (1994). Kakusareta karikyuramu niokeru jendā. *Nagoya Daigaku Kyōikugakubu Kiyō*, 41(1), 53–66.

Umeda, Osamu (1990). Oyano shūrō gakureki to kodomo no shinro. *Kyōiku*, 40(1), 33–48.

Usui, Chizuko (1994). *Joshi Kyōiku no Kindai to Gendai*. Tokyo: Kindai Bungeisha.

Wagatsuma, Hiroshi (1981). Problems of self identity among Korean youth in Japan. In *Koreans in Japan: Ethnic conflict and accommodation*, ed. Changsoo Lee and George De Vos, pp. 304–33. Berkeley, CA: University of California Press.

Wakahoi, Tooru (1995). Rinenteki chūshōteki na kadai no rekkyo ni suginai. *Gendai Kyōiku Kagaku*, 38(9), 33–6.

Walker, James (1988). *Louts and Legends: Male youth culture in an inner-city school*. Sydney: Allen & Unwin.

White, Merry I. (1987). *The Japanese Educational Challenge: A commitment to children*. New York: The Free Press.

Willis, Paul (1977). *Learning to Labour*. Hampshire: Gower.

Woods, Peter (1983). *Sociology and the School: An interactionist viewpoint*. London: Routledge & Kegan Paul.

Yagyū, Hiroshi (1992). Kyōshi to shusse. *Kyōiku*, 42(5), 63–71.

Yamada, Wataru (1995). 24 sai no kiseki. *Gekkan Shōnen Ikusei*, 40(9), 16–24.

Yamashita, Sachiko (1994). Jibun o kaihō shiteiku tameni. In *Zainichi no ima Kyōto-hatsu Part II*, ed. ZZCKKK (see below), pp. 14–18. Kyoto: ZZCKKK.

Yamazaki, Junji (1995). Kyōshi no raifu kōsu kenkyū: Monografu josei kyōshi no baai. *Shizuoka Daigaku Kyōiku Gakubu Kenkyū Hōkoku (Jinbun Shakaikagaku)*, 45, 143–60.

Yamazaki, Takako (1989). Tsuda Ume. In *The Great Educators of Modern Japan*, ed. Benjamin Duke, pp. 125–47. Tokyo: Tokyo University Press.

Yamazumi, Masami (1987). *Nihon Kyōiku Shōshi*. Tokyo: Iwanami Shoten.

Yanagi, Yoshiko (1982). *Ikiikito Ikinuku Tameni: Jiritsu o mezasu joshi kyōiku.* Tokyo: Gendaishokan.

Yoshida, Kyūichi (1995). *Nihon no Hinkon*. Tokyo: Kensō Shobō.

Yoshida, Shūji (1993). *Futōkō: Sono shinri to gakkō no byōri*. Tokyo: Kōbunkan.

Yoshihara, Keiko (1995). Joshidaigakusei niokeru shokugyō sentaku no mekanizumu: Joseinai bunka no yōin toshiteno joseisei. *Kyōiku Shakaigaku Kenkyū*, 57, 107–24.

Youn, Kangchel (1992). *Zainichi o Ikirutowa.* Tokyo: Iwanami Shoten.

Yuu, Sawako (1988). Kyōin shūdan no jisshōteki kenkyū. In *Kyōin Bunka no Shakaigakuteki Kenkyū*, ed. Yoshiyuki Kudomi, pp. 147–208. Tokyo: Taga Shuppan.

Zenkoku Zainichi Chōsenjin Kyōiku Kenkyūkai Kyōto (ZZCKKK) (1993). *Zainichi no ima Kyōto-hatsu*. Kyoto: ZZCKKK.

Zenkoku Zainichi Chōsenjin Kyōiku Kenkyūkai Kyōto (ZZCKKK) (1994). *Zainichi no ima Kyōto-hatsu Part II*. Kyoto: ZZCKKK.

Zenkoku Zainichi Chōsenjin Kyōiku Kenkyūkai Kyōto (ZZCKKK) (1995). *Zainichi no kōkōsei wa ima*. Kyoto: ZZCKKK.

Zenkyō (1993). Sūji wa kataru: 'Kyōin no seikatsu to kinmu nikansuru chōsa' chōsa kekka no shōkai. *Educasu*, no. 1, July, 20–51.

Index

ultranationalism in education 24–6
unemployed middle-school graduates
85
union high-school teacher, male
(case study) 181–3
union teachers, criticisms of 165
United States culture of teaching,
comparison with 172–5
United States Education Mission
30–1, 32
universities 17, 56–7
contract employment for
academics 230–1
expansion in early 1900s 19–20
for women 21
Korean women's experiences of
117–18, 119
see also specific universities
University Council 214, 230–2
university entrance examination 5,
71, 95, 114, 134, 194
university management, government
intervention in 40
University of the Air 219
university students, military service
for 28
upper-secondary education, MOE
selection mechanisms 42
urban vocational high schools 72–4

veteran female teachers 187
vice-principals
appointment 148
female 187
salary structure 166
vice-principals' examination 148
vice-principals' union group 164
vocational high schools 65–6, 72–4

vocational preparation 4
vocational schooling 19–20, 56
Vocational Schools Ordinance
(1899) 19
vocational subjects, compulsory 22

wartime education 28
Wataru's story (school refusal) 205–6
welfare agencies, and families in
poverty 86–8
women
difficulties of career and family
responsibilities 76, 81
diversity of views on gender roles
and career plans 78–82
employer discrimination against
77, 80
employment prospects 75–6
workloads of teachers 151–4
workforce, teenagers entering 85,
89–90
World War Two, schooling during 28

Yama municipal commerce high
school 72
yōgoshisetsu, children in 84, 88–90
youth suicide, related to bullying
195–6
youth training institute 22
youths, lacking protective care 89

zainichi Koreans 117, 118, 119, 120
Zenkankyō 164
Zenkoku Hahaoya Renrakukai 42
Zenkyō 35, 163, 170, 171
Zen'nichikyōren 164
Zenrōren 170, 171